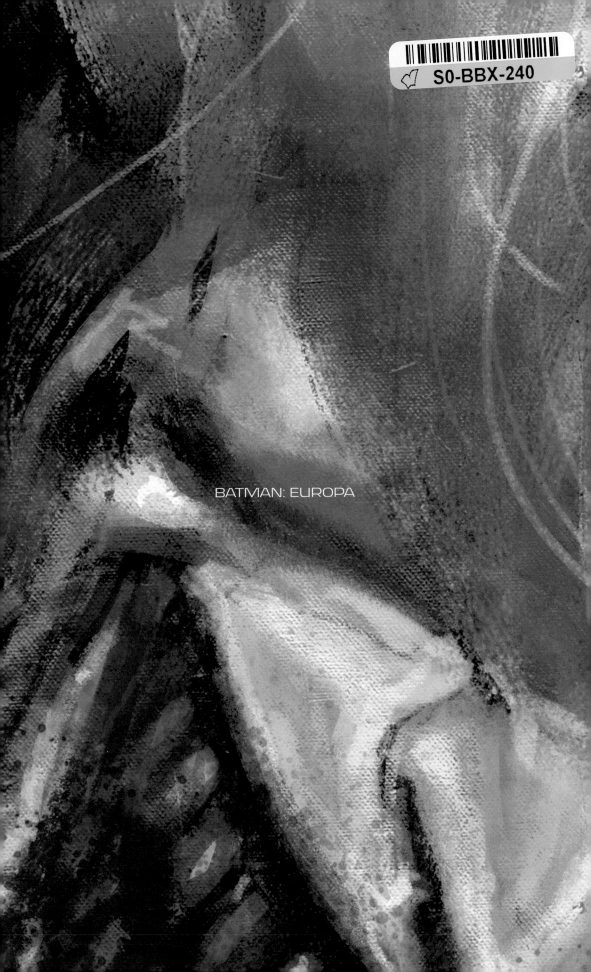

BATMAN: EUROPA

BATM

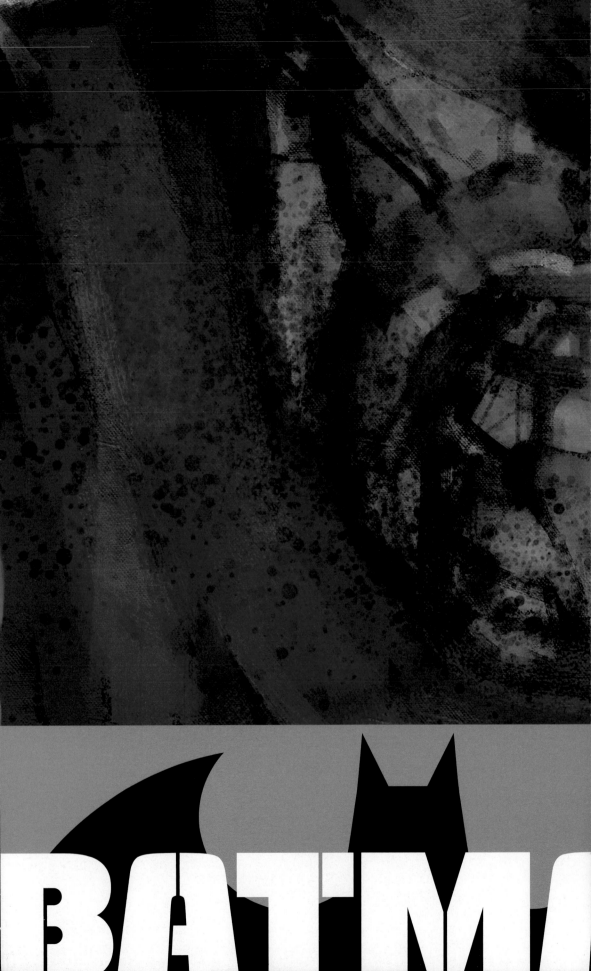

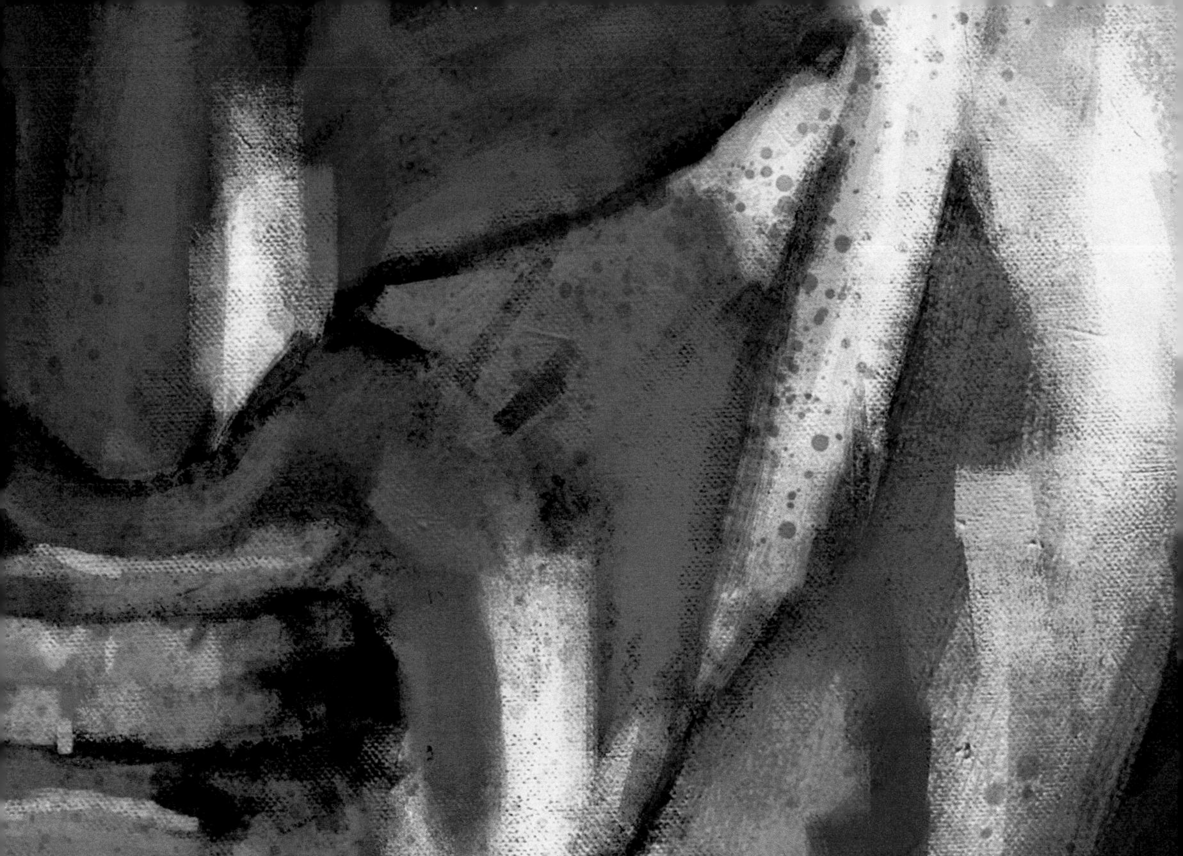

Story by Matteo Casali and Brian Azzarello
Art by Giuseppe Camuncoli Jim Lee Diego Latorre Gerald Parel
Color by Alex Sinclair Giuseppe Camuncoli Diego Latorre Gerald Parel
Letters by Pat Brosseau Collection cover by Jim Lee
Batman created by Bob Kane with Bill Finger

EUROPA

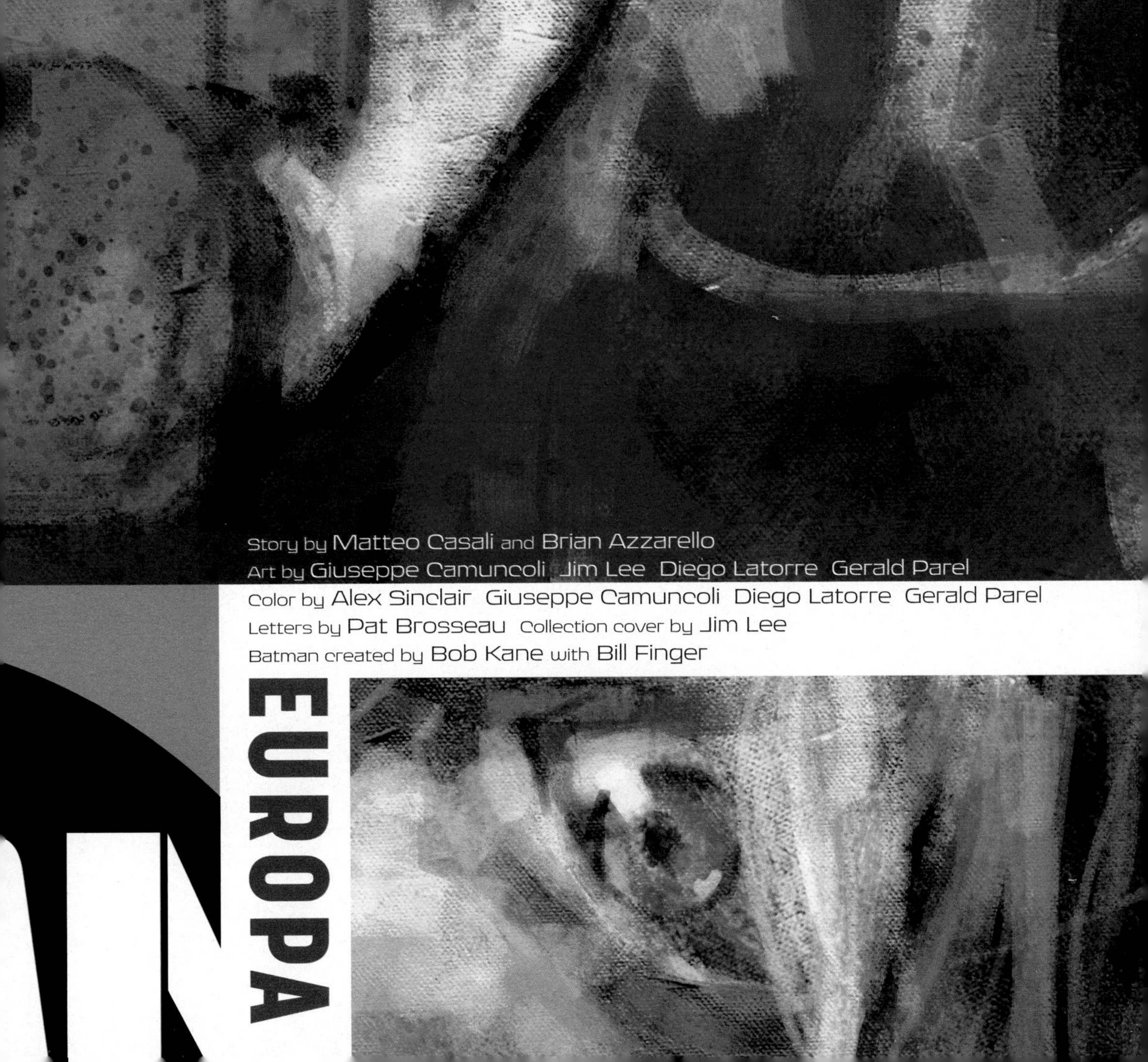

Jim Chadwick Editor – Original Series **David Piña** Assistant Editor – Original Series
Jeb Woodard Group Editor – Collected Editions **Robin Wildman** Editor – Collected Edition
Steve Cook Design Director – Books **Louis Prandi** Publication Design

Bob Harras Senior VP – Editor-in-Chief, DC Comics **Pat McCallum** Executive Editor, DC Comics

Dan DiDio Publisher **Jim Lee** Publisher & Chief Creative Officer
Amit Desai Executive VP – Business & Marketing Strategy, Direct to Consumer & Global Franchise Management
Bobbie Chase VP & Executive Editor, Young Reader & Talent Development
Mark Chiarello Senior VP – Art, Design & Collected Editions **John Cunningham** Senior VP – Sales & Trade Marketing
Briar Darden VP – Business Affairs **Anne DePies** Senior VP – Business Strategy, Finance & Administration
Don Falletti VP – Manufacturing Operations **Lawrence Ganem** VP – Editorial Administration & Talent Relations
Alison Gill Senior VP – Manufacturing & Operations **Jason Greenberg** VP – Business Strategy & Finance
Hank Kanalz Senior VP – Editorial Strategy & Administration **Jay Kogan** Senior VP – Legal Affairs
Nick J. Napolitano VP – Manufacturing Administration **Lisette Osterloh** VP – Digital Marketing & Events
Eddie Scannell VP – Consumer Marketing **Courtney Simmons** Senior VP – Publicity & Communications
Jim (Ski) Sokolowski VP – Comic Book Specialty Sales & Trade Marketing
Nancy Spears VP – Mass, Book, Digital Sales & Trade Marketing **Michele R. Wells** VP – Content Strategy

BATMAN: EUROPA

DC Comics does not read or accept unsolicited submissions of
ideas, stories or artwork.

DC Comics, 2900 West Alameda Ave., Burbank, CA 91505
Printed by LSC Communications, Kendallville, IN, USA. 11/16/18.
First Printing.
ISBN: 978-1-4012-8555-5.

Library of Congress Cataloging-in-Publication Data is available.

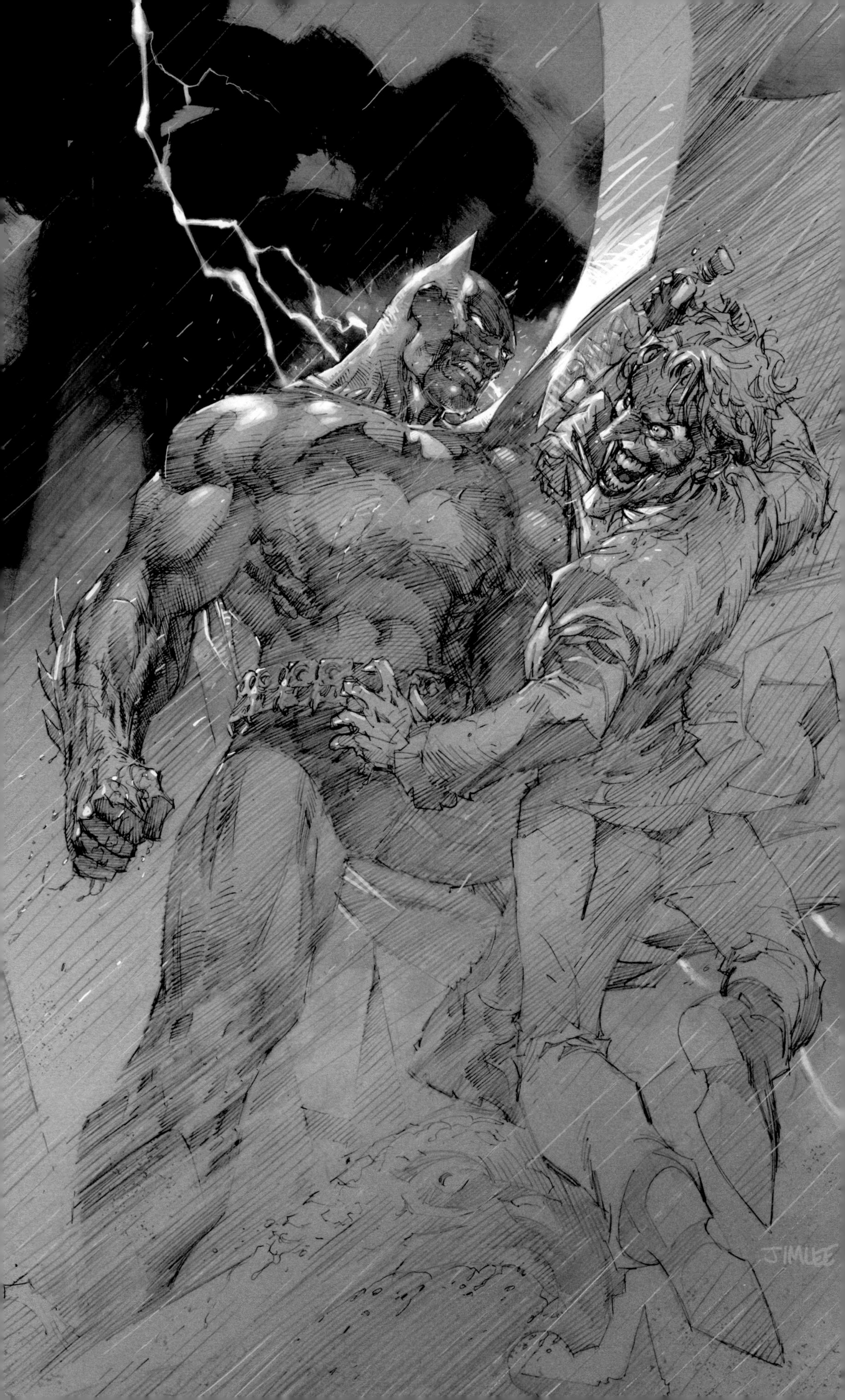
JIMLEE

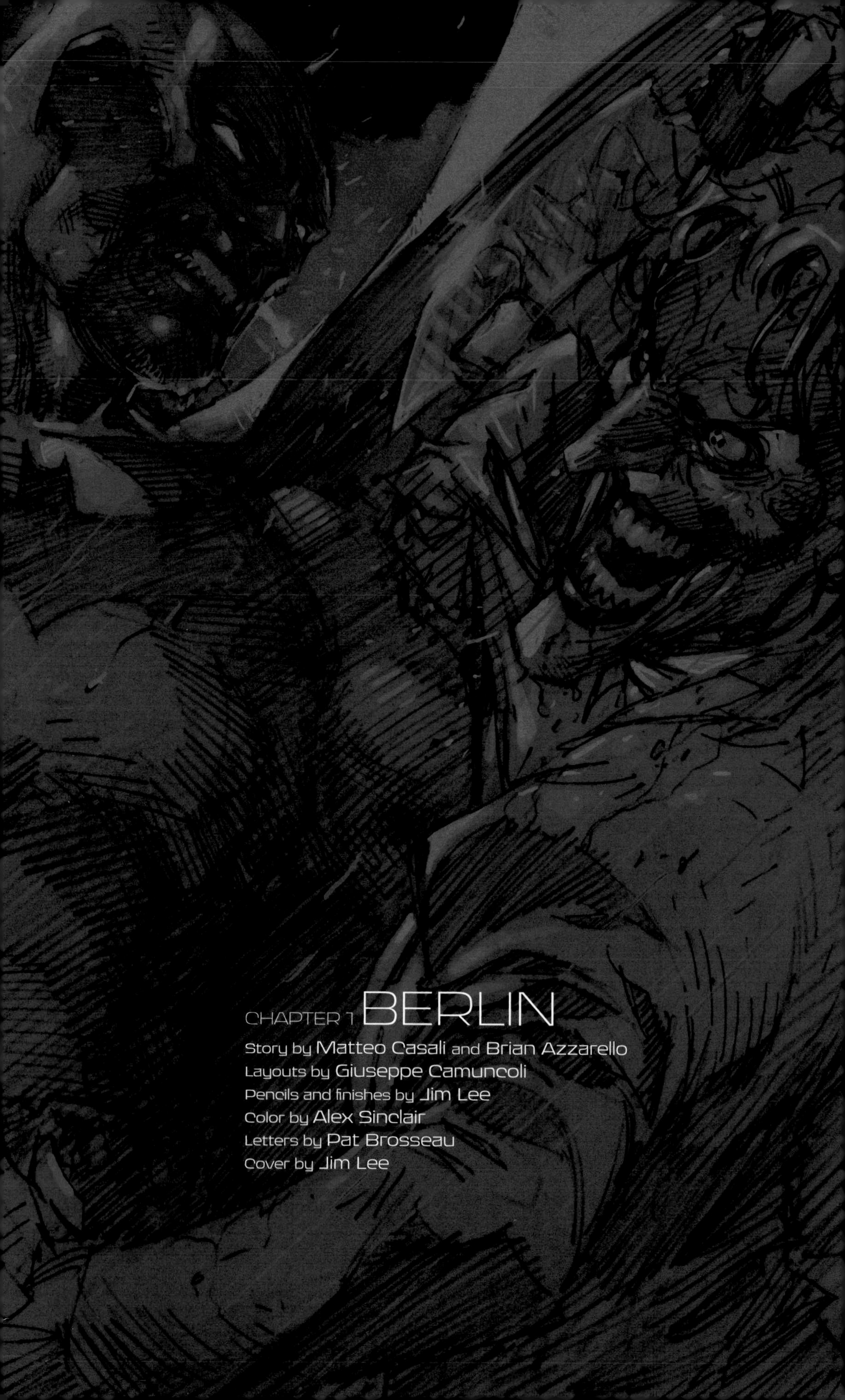

CHAPTER 1 BERLIN

Story by Matteo Casali and Brian Azzarello
Layouts by Giuseppe Camuncoli
Pencils and finishes by Jim Lee
Color by Alex Sinclair
Letters by Pat Brosseau
Cover by Jim Lee

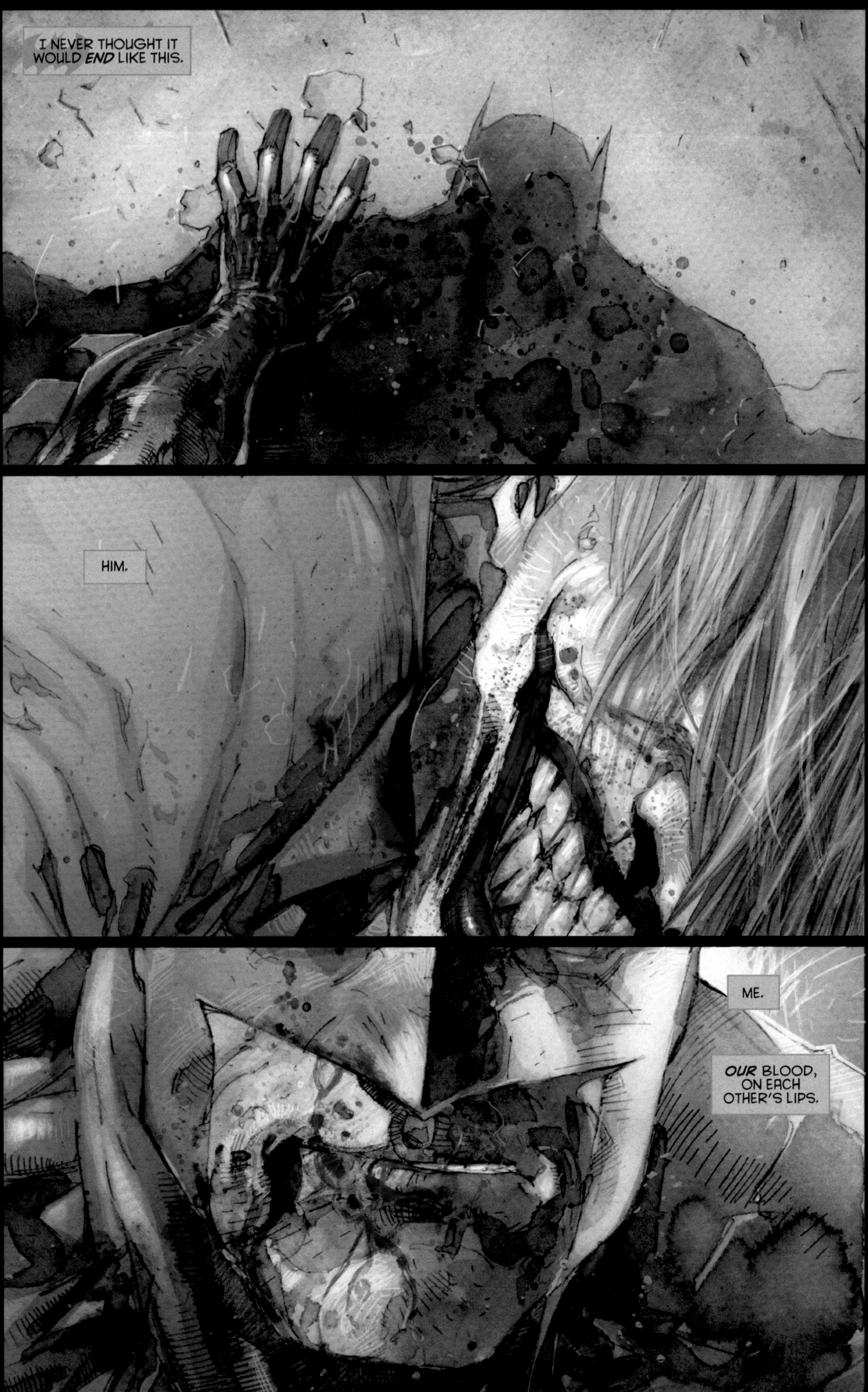
I NEVER THOUGHT IT WOULD END LIKE THIS.
HIM.
ME.
OUR BLOOD, ON EACH OTHER'S LIPS.

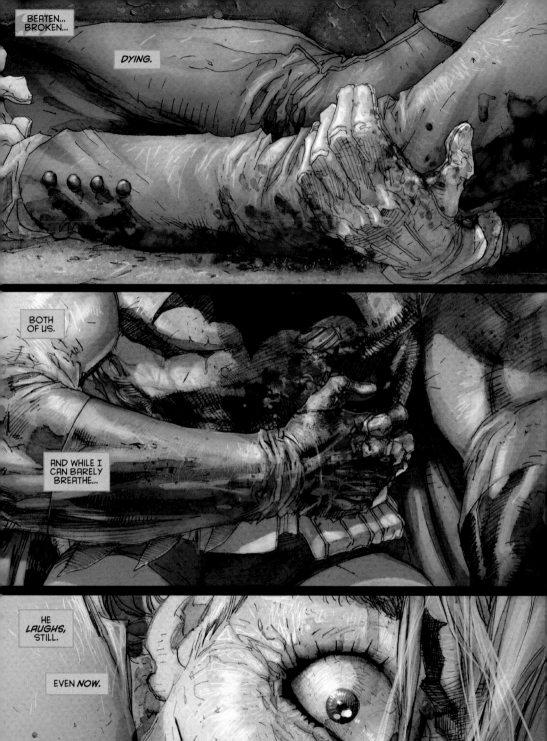

BEATEN...
BROKEN...

DYING.

BOTH
OF US.

AND WHILE I
CAN BARELY
BREATHE...

HE
LAUGHS,
STILL.

EVEN *NOW.*

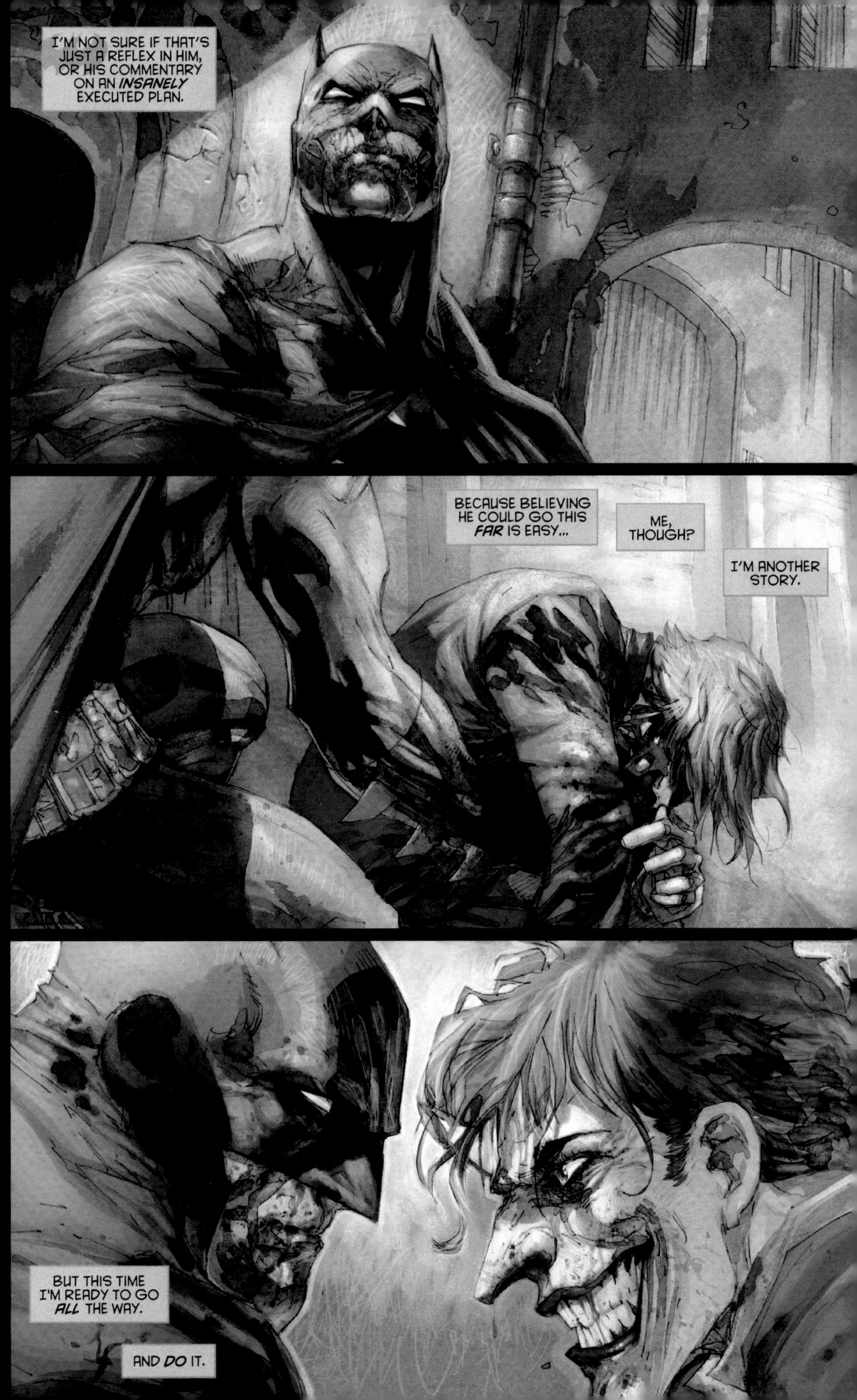
I'M NOT SURE IF THAT'S JUST A REFLEX IN HIM, OR HIS COMMENTARY ON AN *INSANELY* EXECUTED PLAN.
BECAUSE BELIEVING HE COULD GO THIS *FAR* IS EASY...
ME, THOUGH?
I'M ANOTHER STORY.
BUT THIS TIME I'M READY TO GO *ALL* THE WAY.
AND *DO* IT.

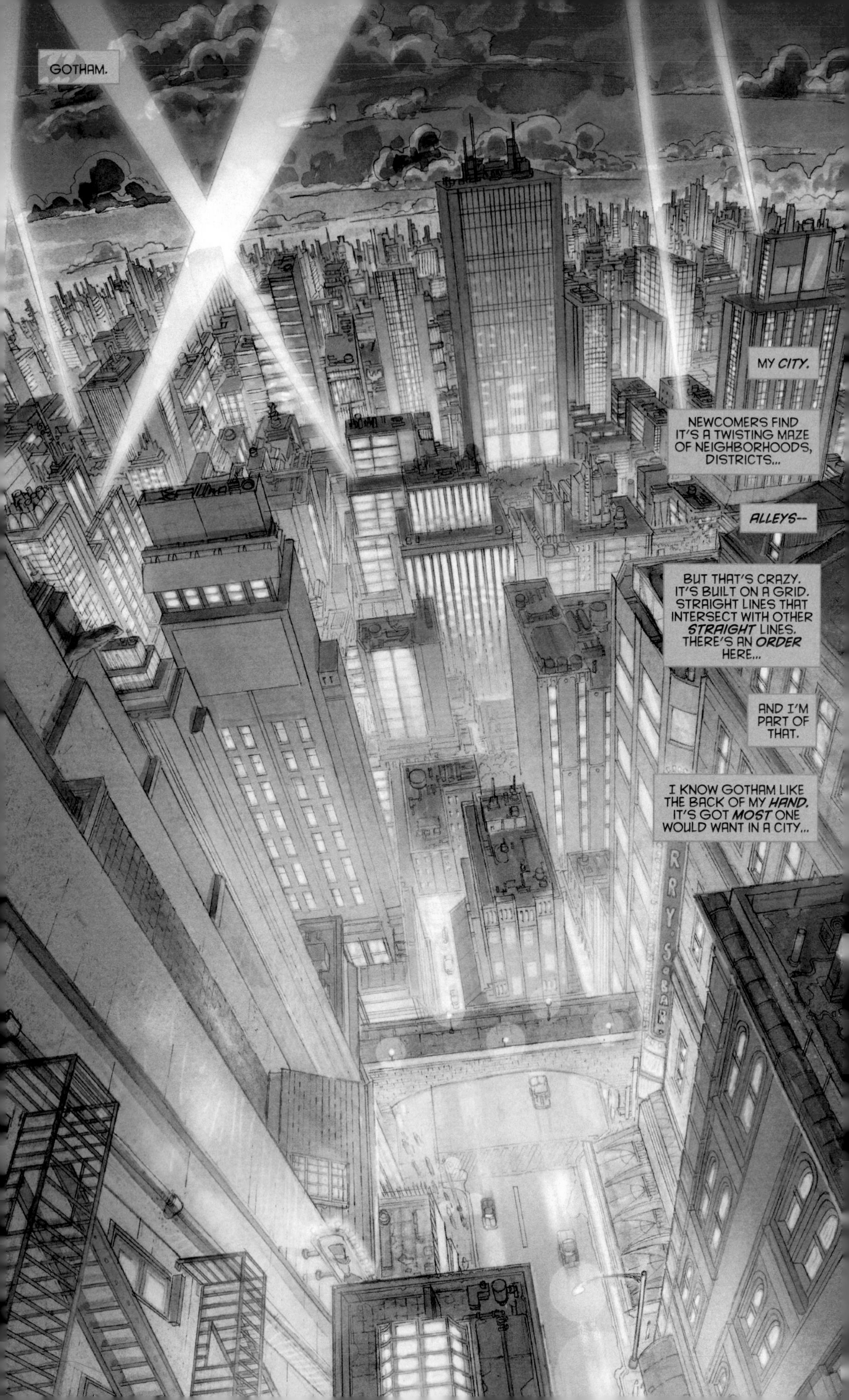
GOTHAM.
MY CITY.
NEWCOMERS FIND IT'S A TWISTING MAZE OF NEIGHBORHOODS, DISTRICTS...
ALLEYS--
BUT THAT'S CRAZY. IT'S BUILT ON A GRID. STRAIGHT LINES THAT INTERSECT WITH OTHER STRAIGHT LINES. THERE'S AN ORDER HERE...
AND I'M PART OF THAT.
I KNOW GOTHAM LIKE THE BACK OF MY HAND. IT'S GOT MOST ONE WOULD WANT IN A CITY...

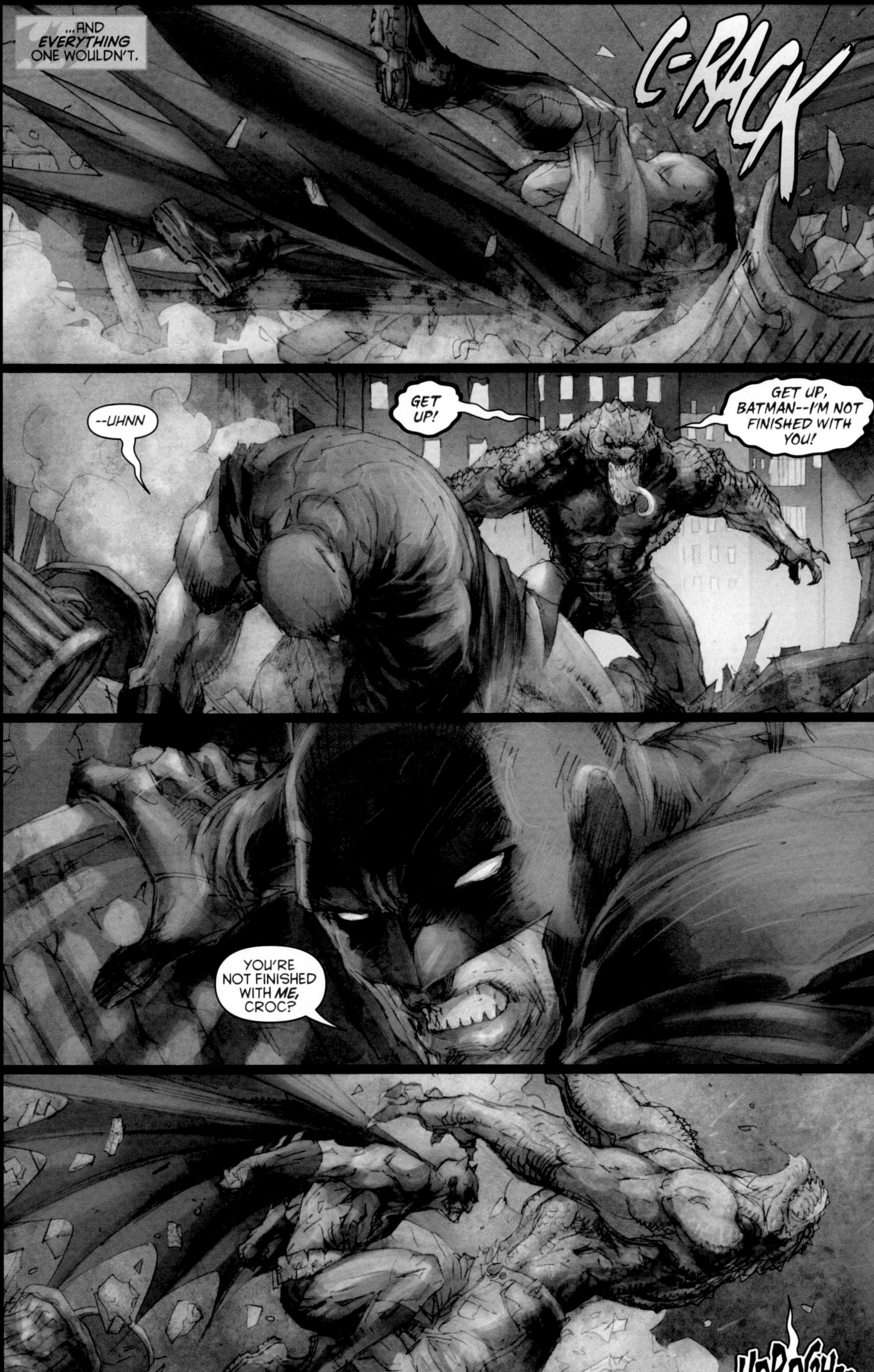
...AND EVERYTHING ONE WOULDN'T.
C-RACK
--UHNN
GET UP!
GET UP, BATMAN--I'M NOT FINISHED WITH YOU!
YOU'RE NOT FINISHED WITH ME, CROC?
URRRGH..

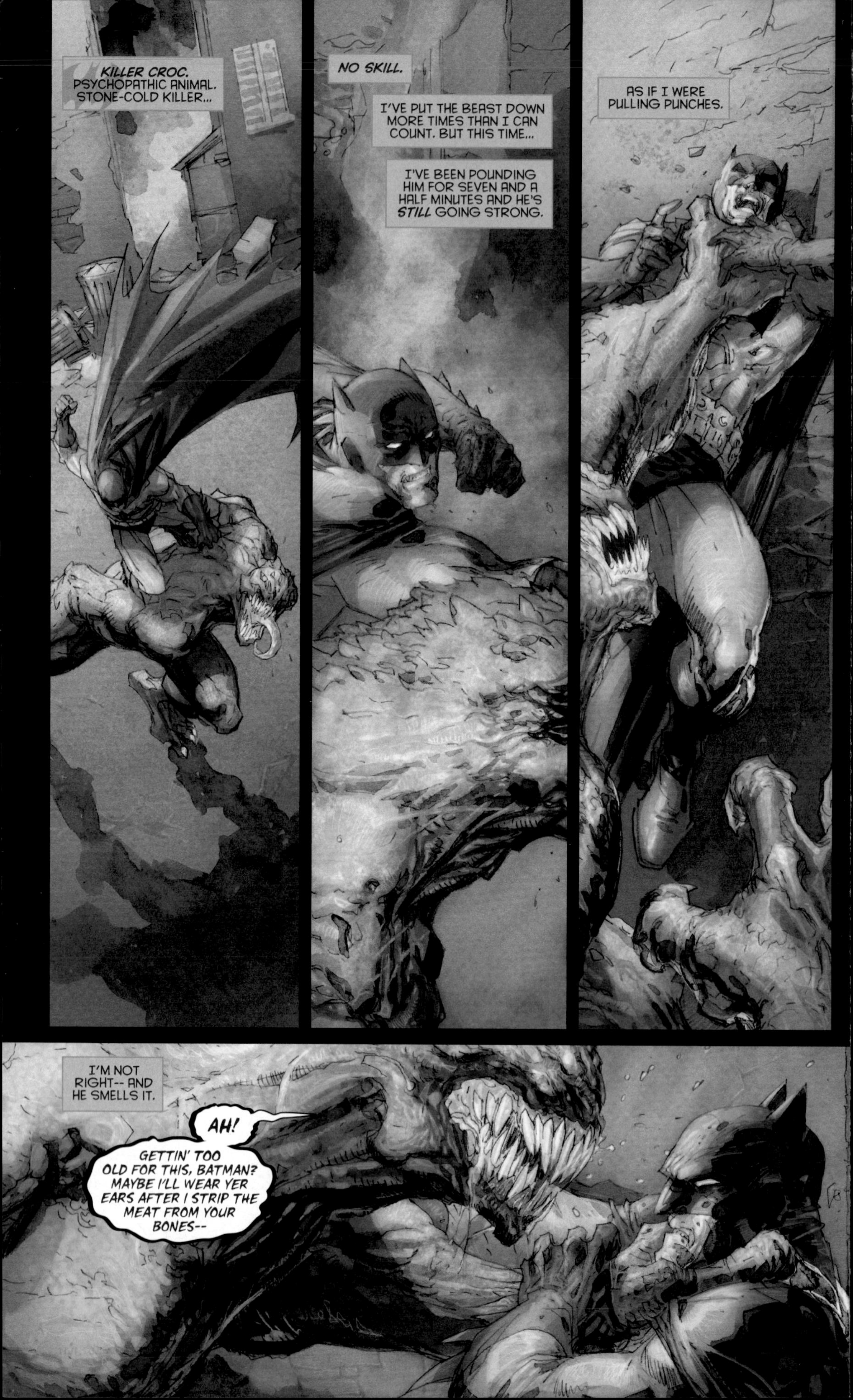

KILLER CROC. PSYCHOPATHIC ANIMAL. STONE-COLD KILLER...
NO SKILL.
I'VE PUT THE BEAST DOWN MORE TIMES THAN I CAN COUNT. BUT THIS TIME...
I'VE BEEN POUNDING HIM FOR SEVEN AND A HALF MINUTES AND HE'S STILL GOING STRONG.
AS IF I WERE PULLING PUNCHES.
I'M NOT RIGHT-- AND HE SMELLS IT.
AH!
GETTIN' TOO OLD FOR THIS, BATMAN? MAYBE I'LL WEAR YER EARS AFTER I STRIP THE MEAT FROM YOUR BONES--

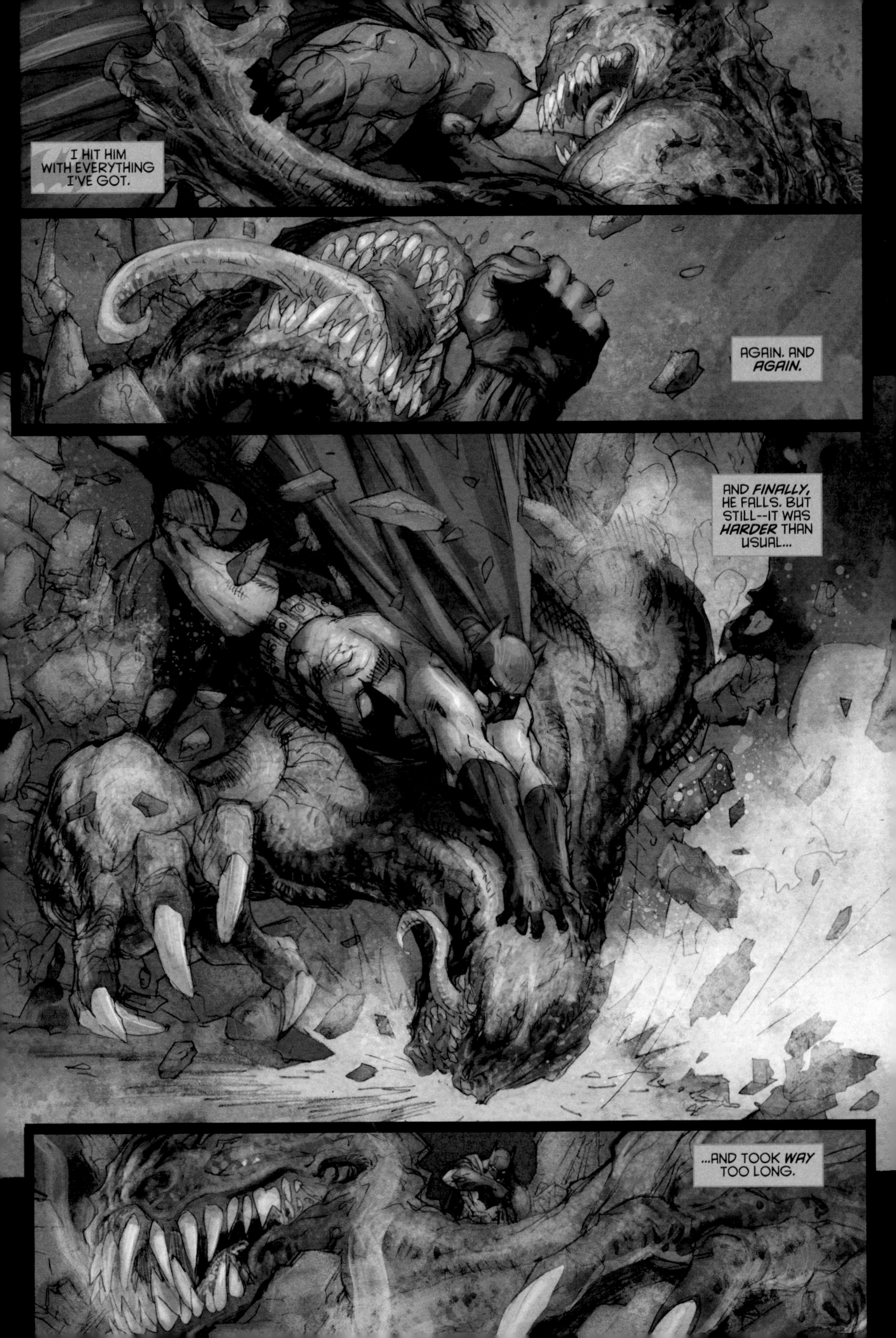
I HIT HIM WITH EVERYTHING I'VE GOT.
AGAIN. AND *AGAIN.*
AND *FINALLY,* HE FALLS. BUT STILL--IT WAS *HARDER* THAN USUAL...
...AND TOOK *WAY* TOO LONG.

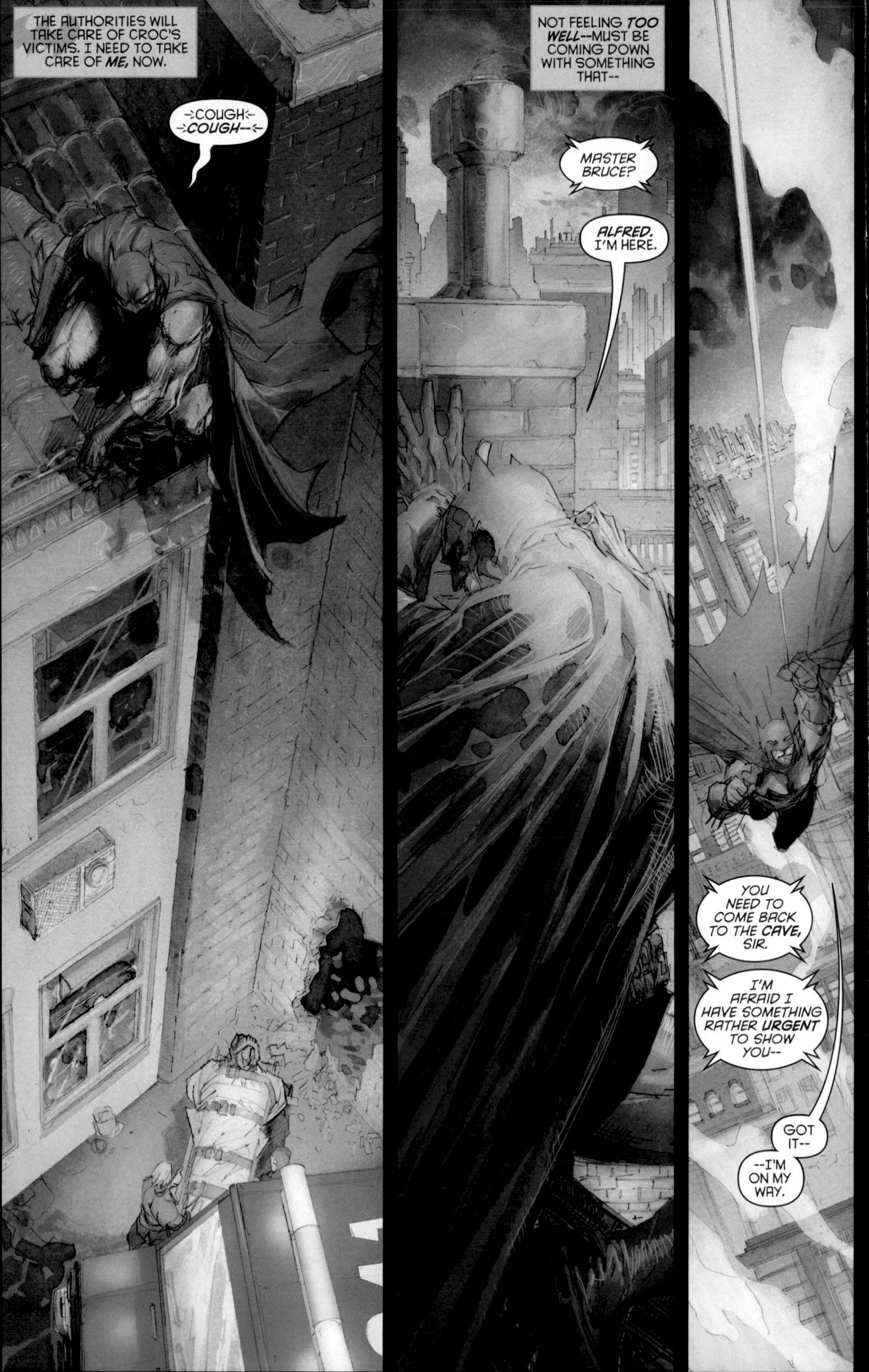
THE AUTHORITIES WILL TAKE CARE OF CROC'S VICTIMS. I NEED TO TAKE CARE OF ME, NOW.
-COUGH- -COUGH--
NOT FEELING TOO WELL--MUST BE COMING DOWN WITH SOMETHING THAT--
MASTER BRUCE?
ALFRED. I'M HERE.
YOU NEED TO COME BACK TO THE CAVE, SIR.
I'M AFRAID I HAVE SOMETHING RATHER URGENT TO SHOW YOU--
GOT IT--
--I'M ON MY WAY.

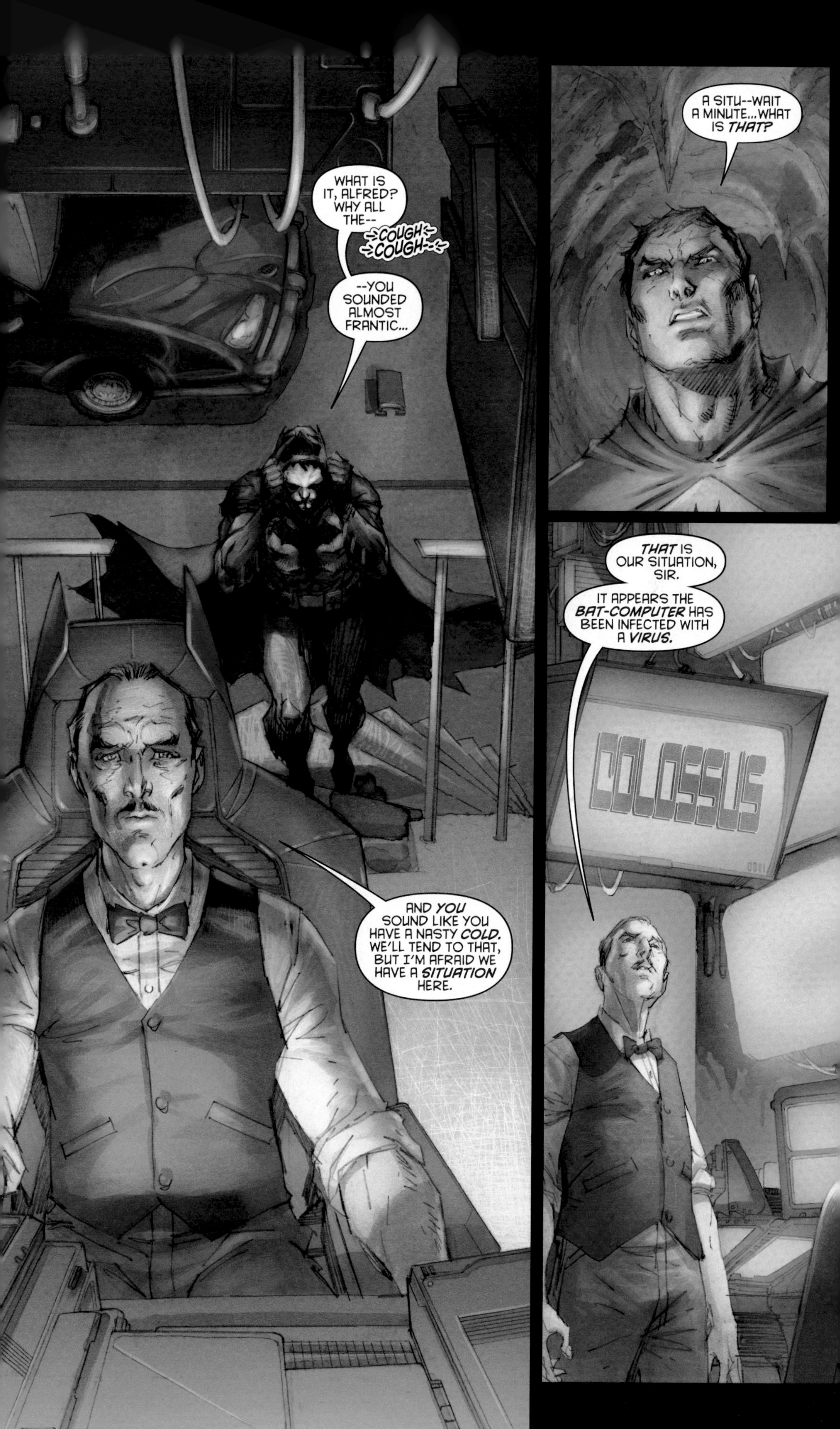

WHAT IS IT, ALFRED? WHY ALL THE--
COUGH COUGH
--YOU SOUNDED ALMOST FRANTIC...
AND YOU SOUND LIKE YOU HAVE A NASTY COLD. WE'LL TEND TO THAT, BUT I'M AFRAID WE HAVE A SITUATION HERE.
A SITU--WAIT A MINUTE...WHAT IS THAT?
THAT IS OUR SITUATION, SIR.
IT APPEARS THE BAT-COMPUTER HAS BEEN INFECTED WITH A VIRUS.
COLOSSUS

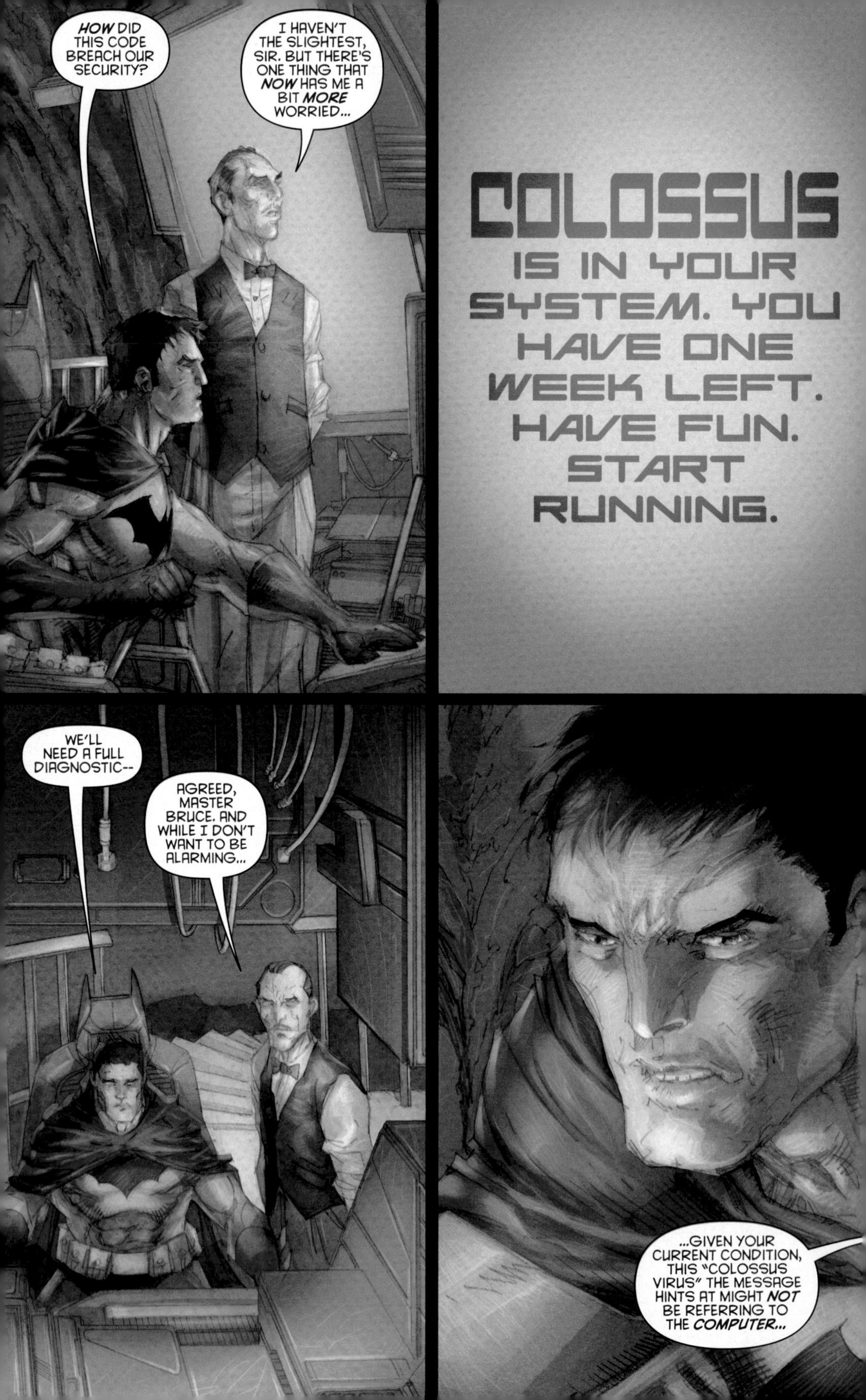

HOW DID THIS CODE BREACH OUR SECURITY?
I HAVEN'T THE SLIGHTEST, SIR. BUT THERE'S ONE THING THAT NOW HAS ME A BIT MORE WORRIED...
COLOSSUS IS IN YOUR SYSTEM. YOU HAVE ONE WEEK LEFT. HAVE FUN. START RUNNING.
WE'LL NEED A FULL DIAGNOSTIC--
AGREED, MASTER BRUCE. AND WHILE I DON'T WANT TO BE ALARMING...
...GIVEN YOUR CURRENT CONDITION, THIS "COLOSSUS VIRUS" THE MESSAGE HINTS AT MIGHT NOT BE REFERRING TO THE COMPUTER...

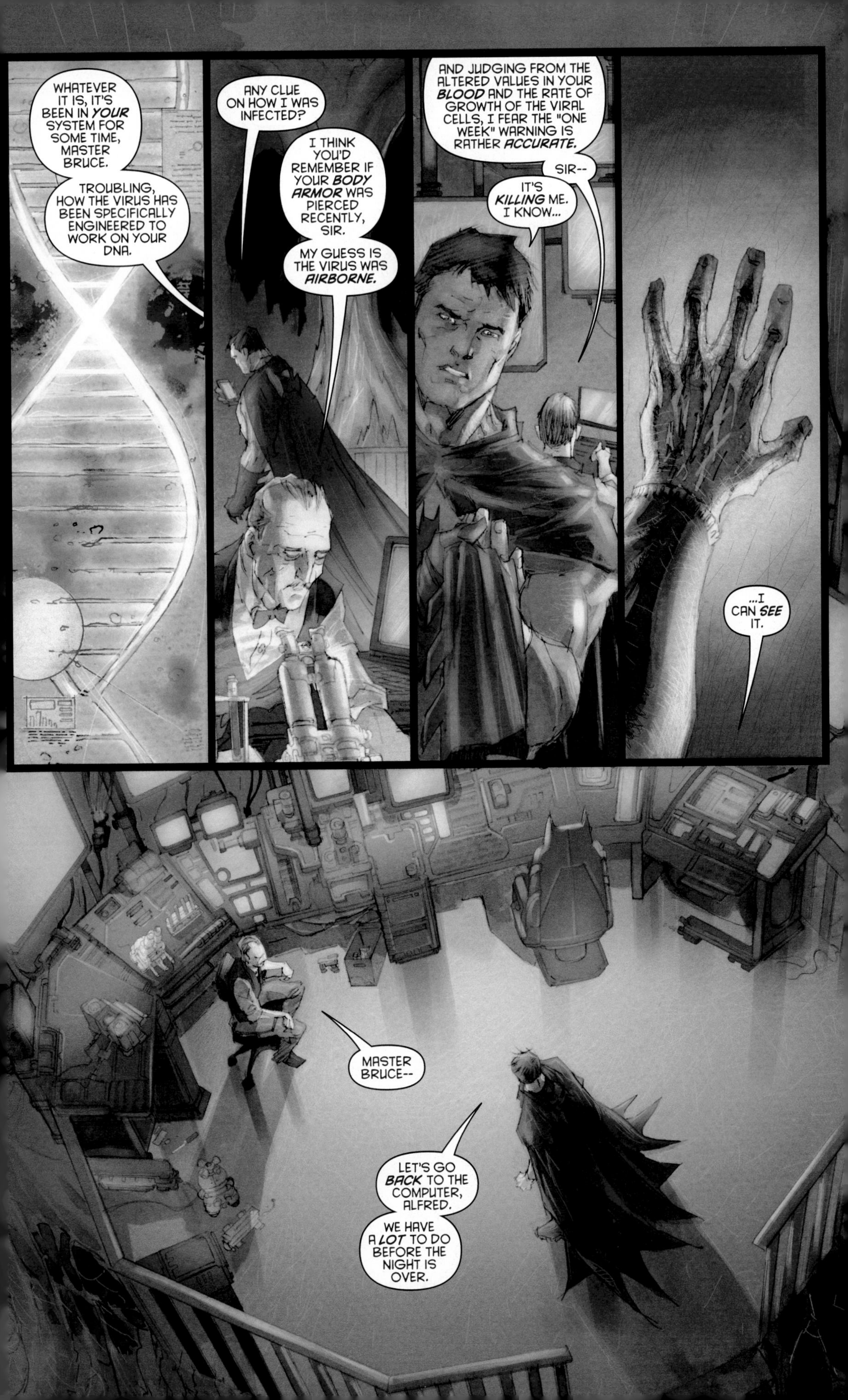
WHATEVER IT IS, IT'S BEEN IN *YOUR* SYSTEM FOR SOME TIME, MASTER BRUCE.
TROUBLING, HOW THE VIRUS HAS BEEN SPECIFICALLY ENGINEERED TO WORK ON YOUR DNA.
ANY CLUE ON HOW I WAS INFECTED?
I THINK YOU'D REMEMBER IF YOUR *BODY ARMOR* WAS PIERCED RECENTLY, SIR.
MY GUESS IS THE VIRUS WAS *AIRBORNE.*
AND JUDGING FROM THE ALTERED VALUES IN YOUR *BLOOD* AND THE RATE OF GROWTH OF THE VIRAL CELLS, I FEAR THE "ONE WEEK" WARNING IS RATHER *ACCURATE.*
SIR--
IT'S *KILLING* ME. I KNOW...
...I CAN *SEE* IT.
MASTER BRUCE--
LET'S GO *BACK* TO THE COMPUTER, ALFRED.
WE HAVE A *LOT* TO DO BEFORE THE NIGHT IS OVER.

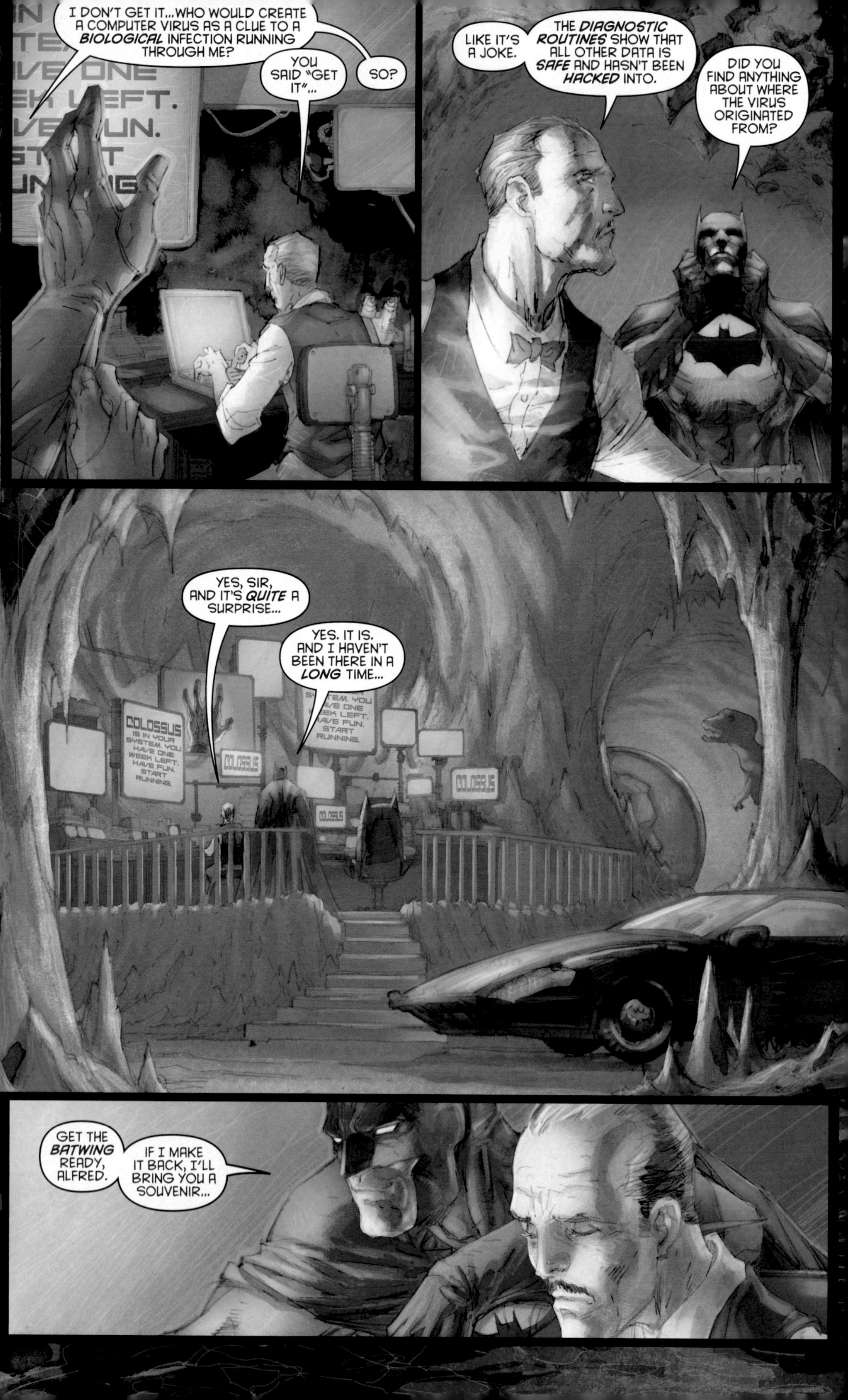
I DON'T GET IT...WHO WOULD CREATE A COMPUTER VIRUS AS A CLUE TO A BIOLOGICAL INFECTION RUNNING THROUGH ME?
YOU SAID "GET IT"...
SO?
LIKE IT'S A JOKE.
THE DIAGNOSTIC ROUTINES SHOW THAT ALL OTHER DATA IS SAFE AND HASN'T BEEN HACKED INTO.
DID YOU FIND ANYTHING ABOUT WHERE THE VIRUS ORIGINATED FROM?
YES, SIR, AND IT'S QUITE A SURPRISE...
YES. IT IS. AND I HAVEN'T BEEN THERE IN A LONG TIME...
COLOSSUS IS IN YOUR SYSTEM. YOU HAVE ONE WEEK LEFT. HAVE FUN. START RUNNING.
COLOSSUS
COLOSSUS
COLOSSUS
GET THE BATWING READY, ALFRED.
IF I MAKE IT BACK, I'LL BRING YOU A SOUVENIR...

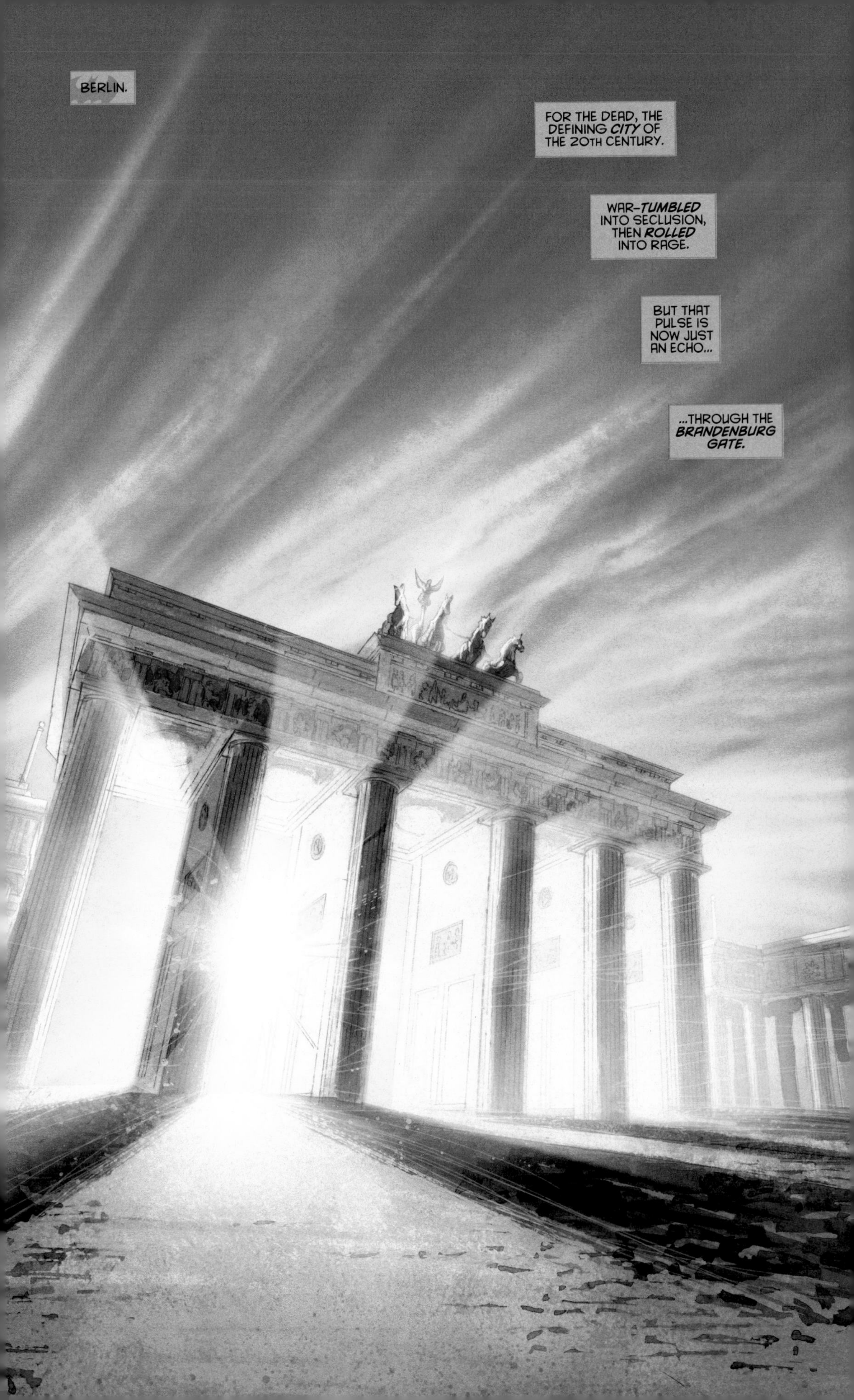
BERLIN.
FOR THE DEAD, THE DEFINING *CITY* OF THE 20TH CENTURY.
WAR-*TUMBLED* INTO SECLUSION, THEN *ROLLED* INTO RAGE.
BUT THAT PULSE IS NOW JUST AN ECHO...
...THROUGH THE ***BRANDENBURG GATE.***

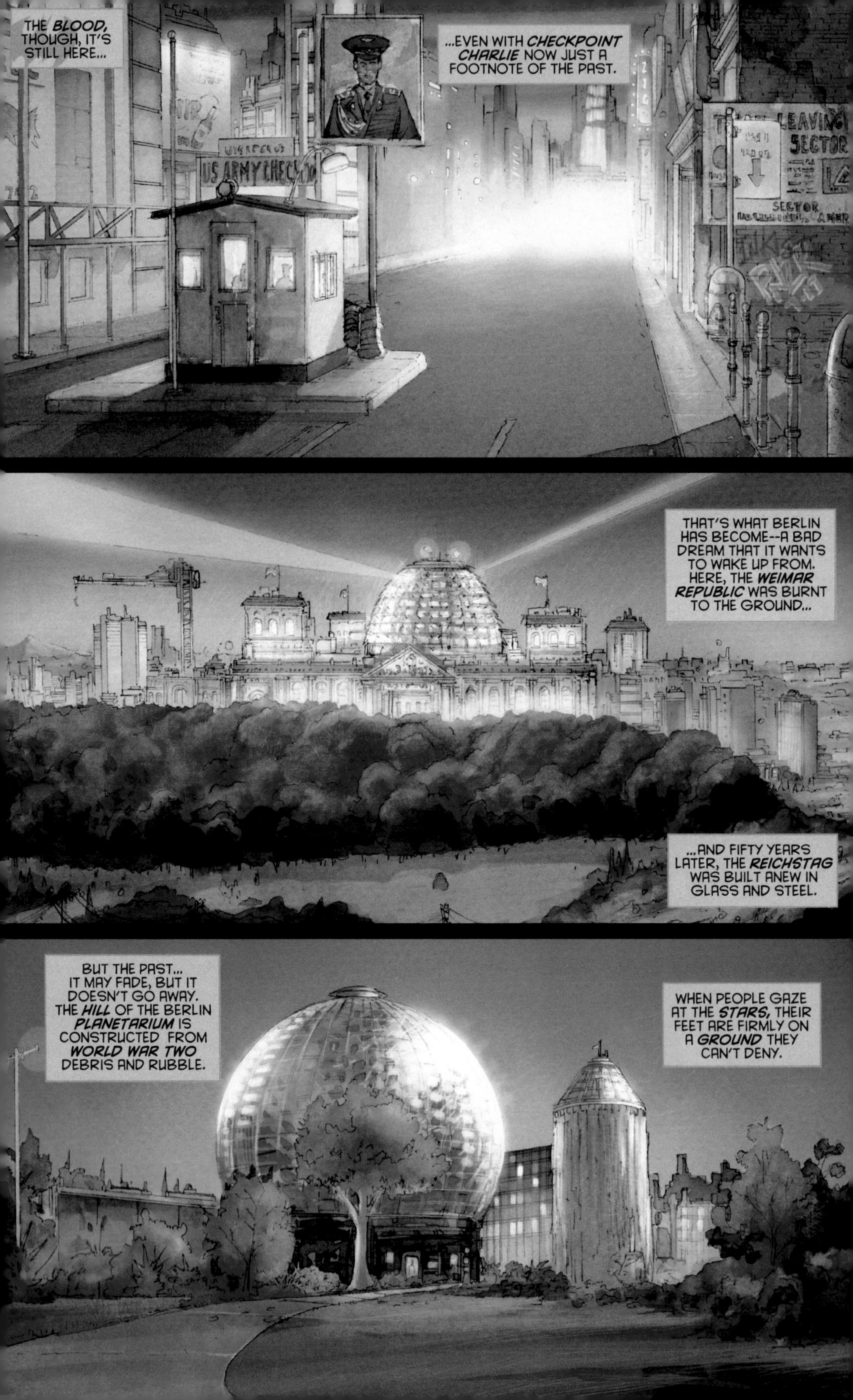
THE *BLOOD,* THOUGH, IT'S STILL HERE...
...EVEN WITH *CHECKPOINT CHARLIE* NOW JUST A FOOTNOTE OF THE PAST.
THAT'S WHAT BERLIN HAS BECOME--A BAD DREAM THAT IT WANTS TO WAKE UP FROM. HERE, THE *WEIMAR REPUBLIC* WAS BURNT TO THE GROUND...
...AND FIFTY YEARS LATER, THE *REICHSTAG* WAS BUILT ANEW IN GLASS AND STEEL.
BUT THE PAST... IT MAY FADE, BUT IT DOESN'T GO AWAY. THE *HILL* OF THE BERLIN *PLANETARIUM* IS CONSTRUCTED FROM *WORLD WAR TWO* DEBRIS AND RUBBLE.
WHEN PEOPLE GAZE AT THE *STARS,* THEIR FEET ARE FIRMLY ON A *GROUND* THEY CAN'T DENY.

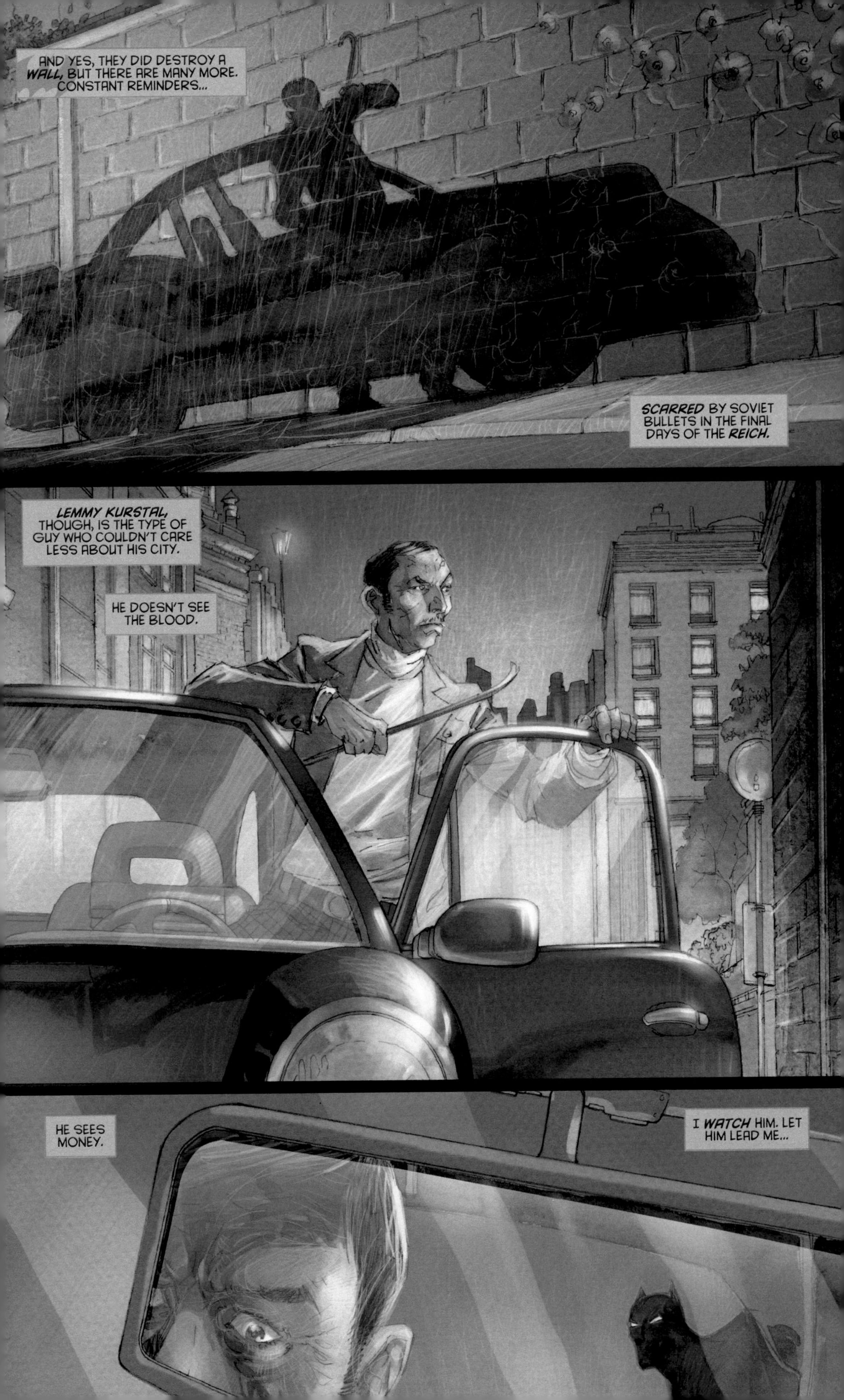

AND YES, THEY DID DESTROY A WALL, BUT THERE ARE MANY MORE. CONSTANT REMINDERS...
SCARRED BY SOVIET BULLETS IN THE FINAL DAYS OF THE REICH.
LEMMY KURSTAL, THOUGH, IS THE TYPE OF GUY WHO COULDN'T CARE LESS ABOUT HIS CITY.
HE DOESN'T SEE THE BLOOD.
HE SEES MONEY.
I WATCH HIM. LET HIM LEAD ME...

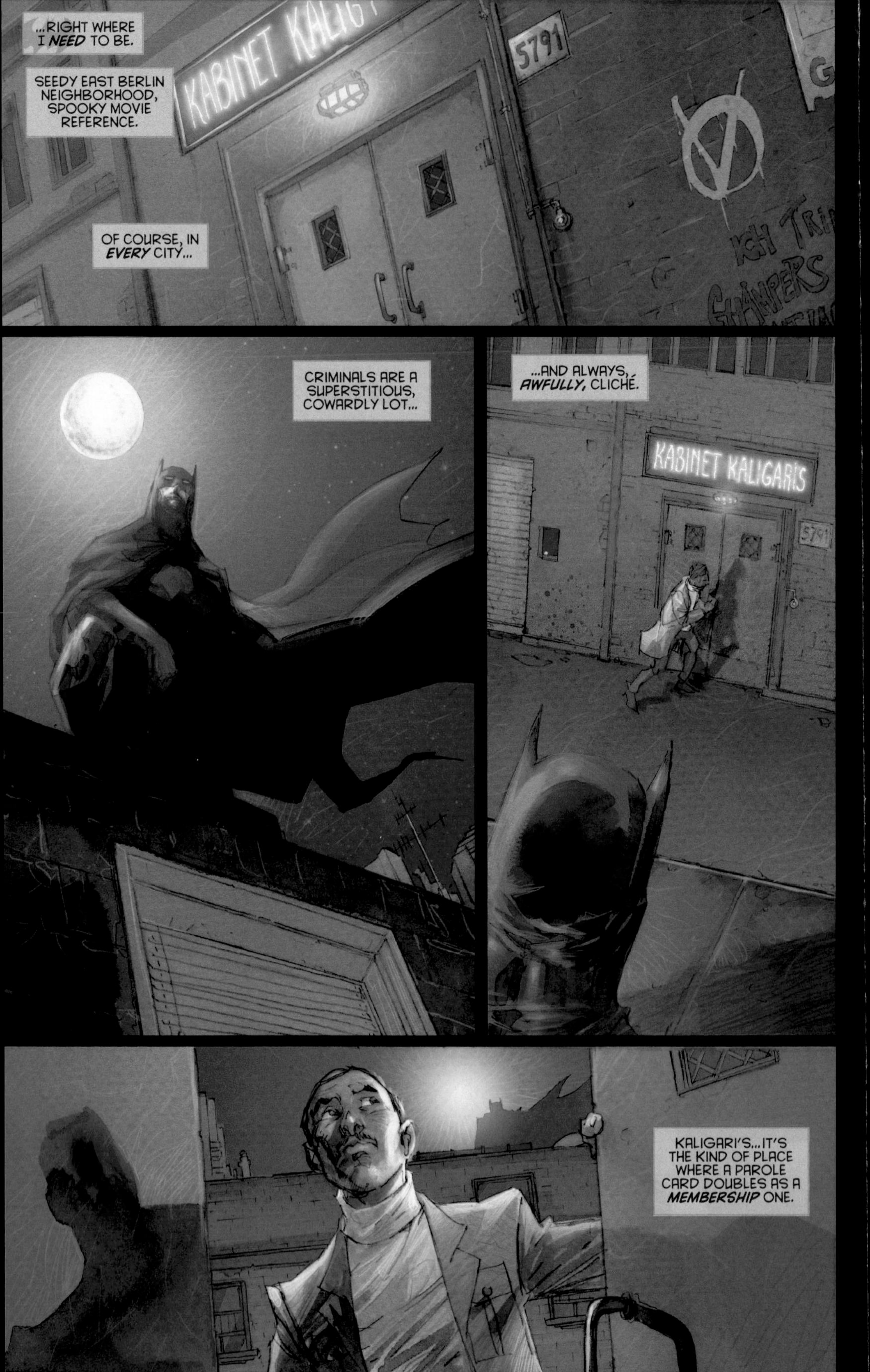
...RIGHT WHERE I *NEED* TO BE.
SEEDY EAST BERLIN NEIGHBORHOOD, SPOOKY MOVIE REFERENCE.
KABINET KALIG
5791
OF COURSE, IN *EVERY* CITY...
CRIMINALS ARE A SUPERSTITIOUS, COWARDLY LOT...
...AND ALWAYS, *AWFULLY,* CLICHÉ.
KABINET KALIGARIS
5791
KALIGARI'S...IT'S THE KIND OF PLACE WHERE A PAROLE CARD DOUBLES AS A *MEMBERSHIP* ONE.

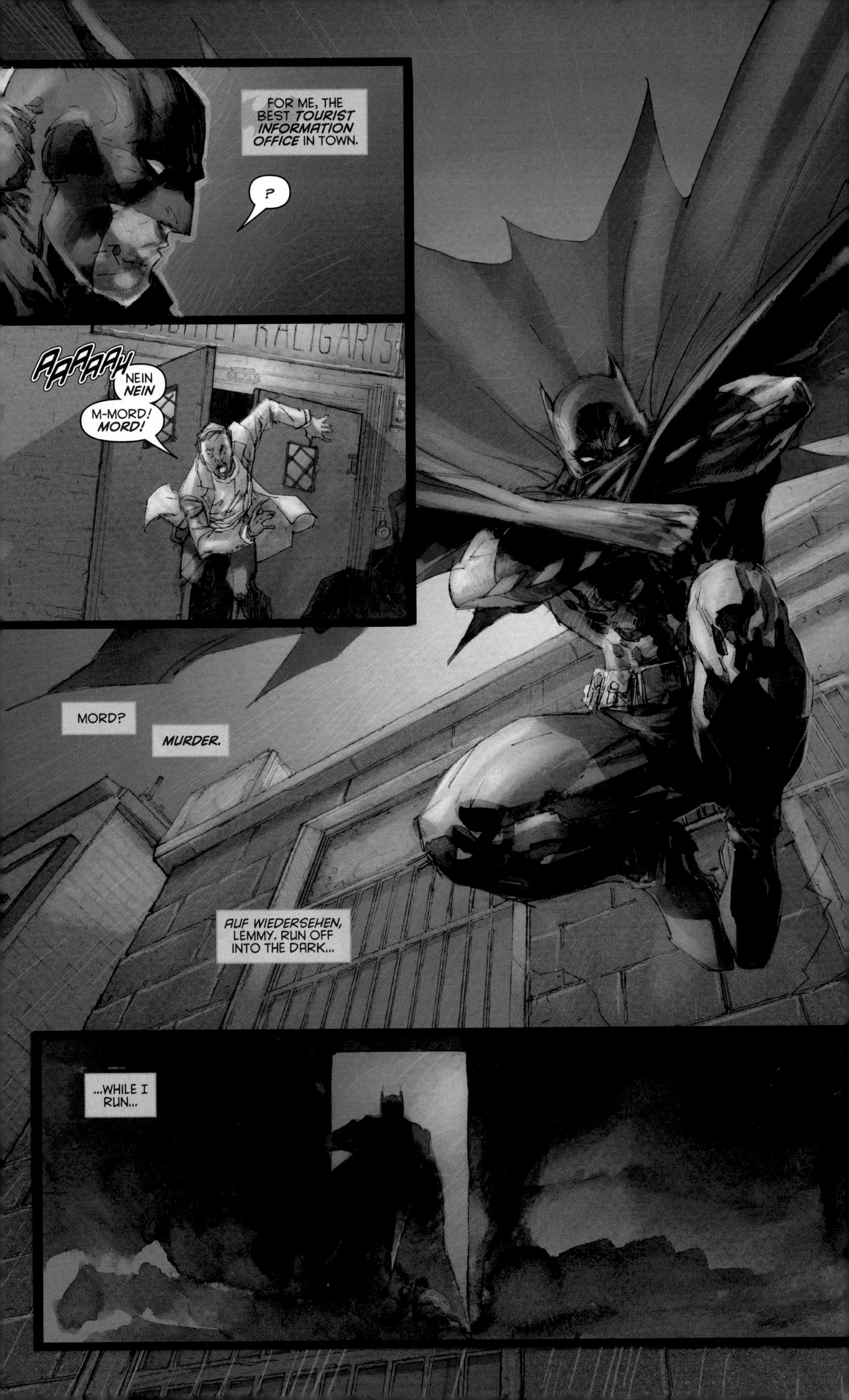

FOR ME, THE BEST TOURIST INFORMATION OFFICE IN TOWN.
?
AAAAAH
NEIN NEIN
M-MORD! MORD!
MORD?
MURDER.
AUF WIEDERSEHEN, LEMMY. RUN OFF INTO THE DARK...
...WHILE I RUN...

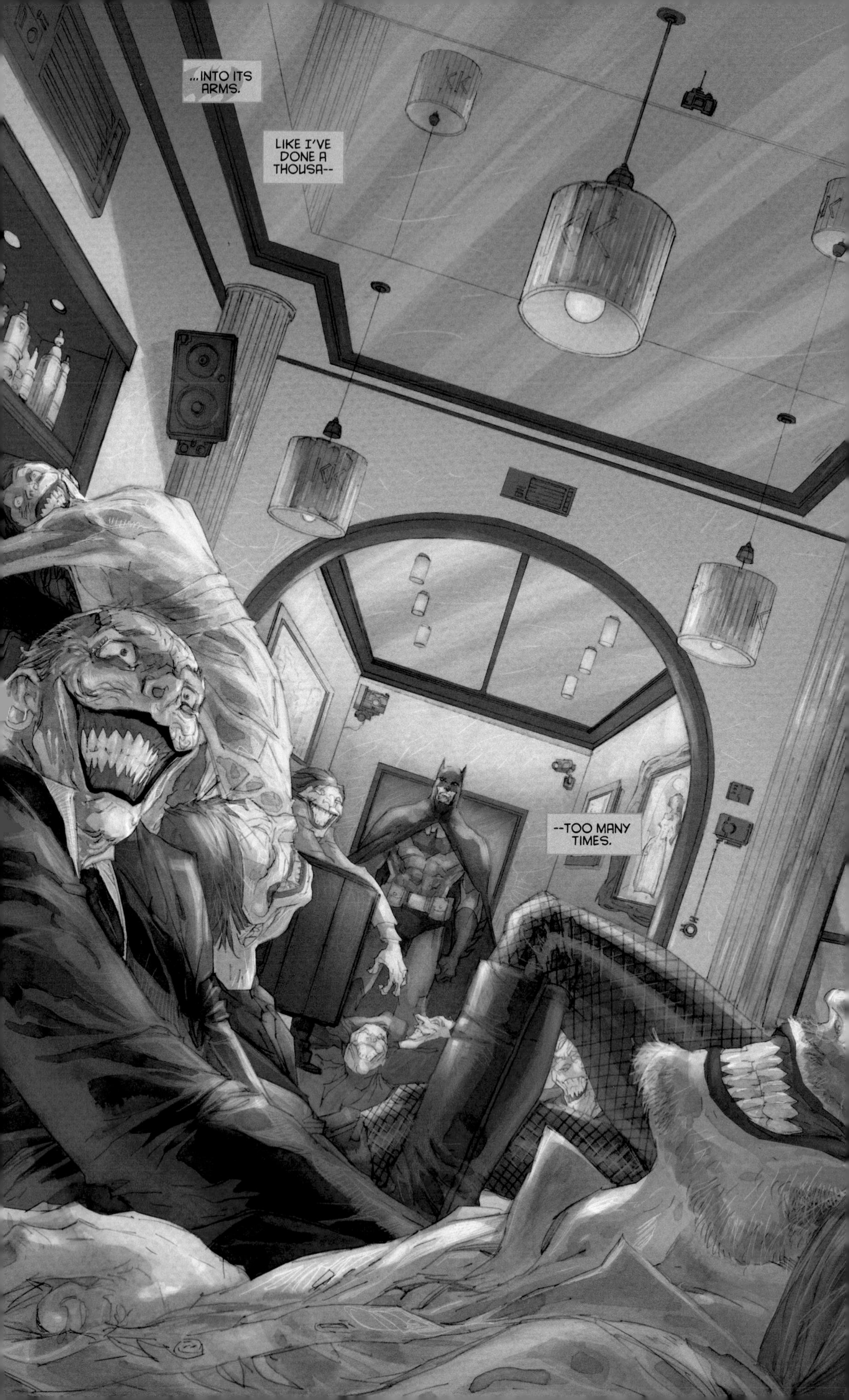
...INTO ITS ARMS.
LIKE I'VE DONE A THOUSA--
--TOO MANY TIMES.

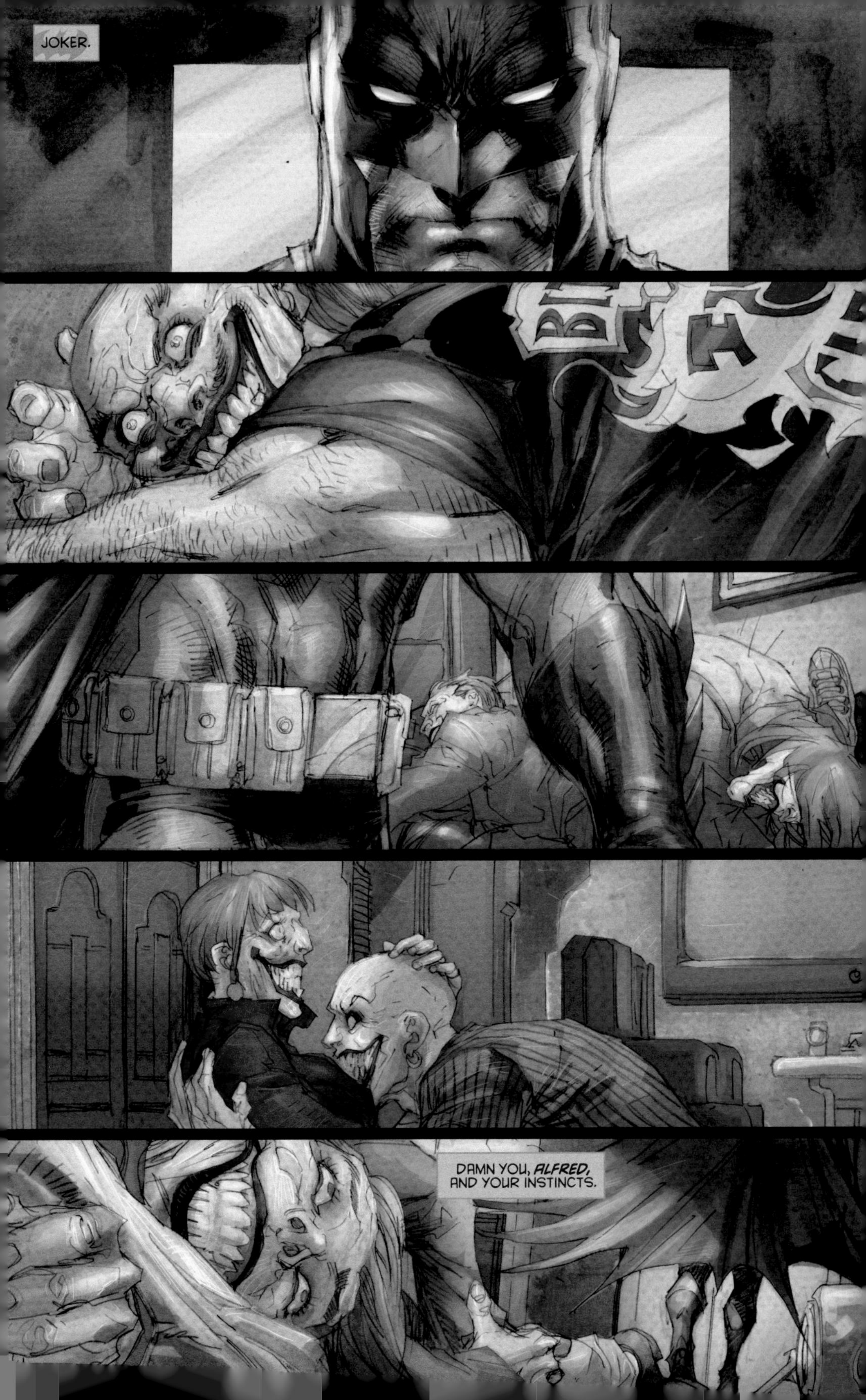
JOKER.
DAMN YOU, ALFRED, AND YOUR INSTINCTS.

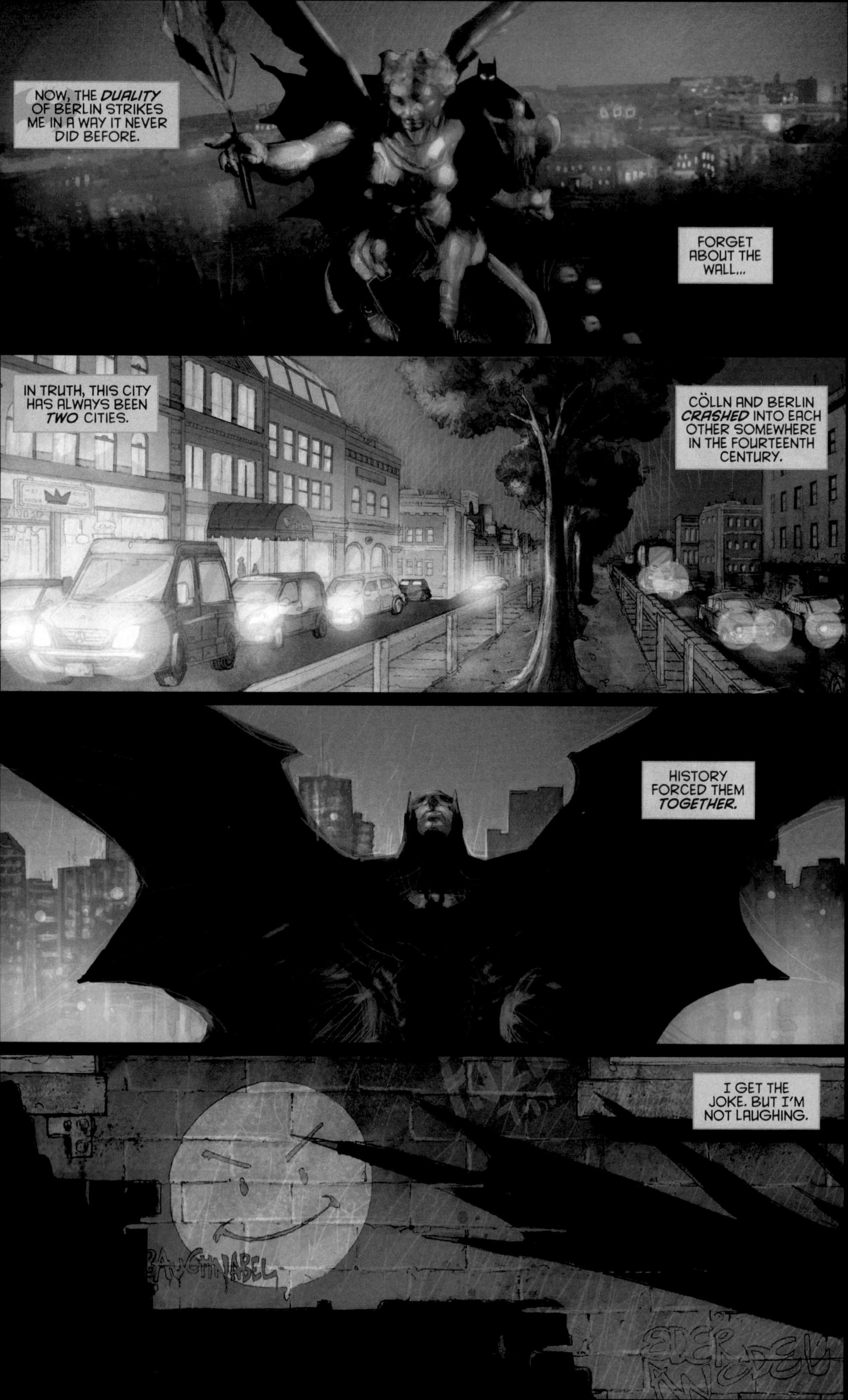
NOW, THE DUALITY OF BERLIN STRIKES ME IN A WAY IT NEVER DID BEFORE.
FORGET ABOUT THE WALL...
IN TRUTH, THIS CITY HAS ALWAYS BEEN TWO CITIES.
CÖLLN AND BERLIN CRASHED INTO EACH OTHER SOMEWHERE IN THE FOURTEENTH CENTURY.
HISTORY FORCED THEM TOGETHER.
I GET THE JOKE. BUT I'M NOT LAUGHING.

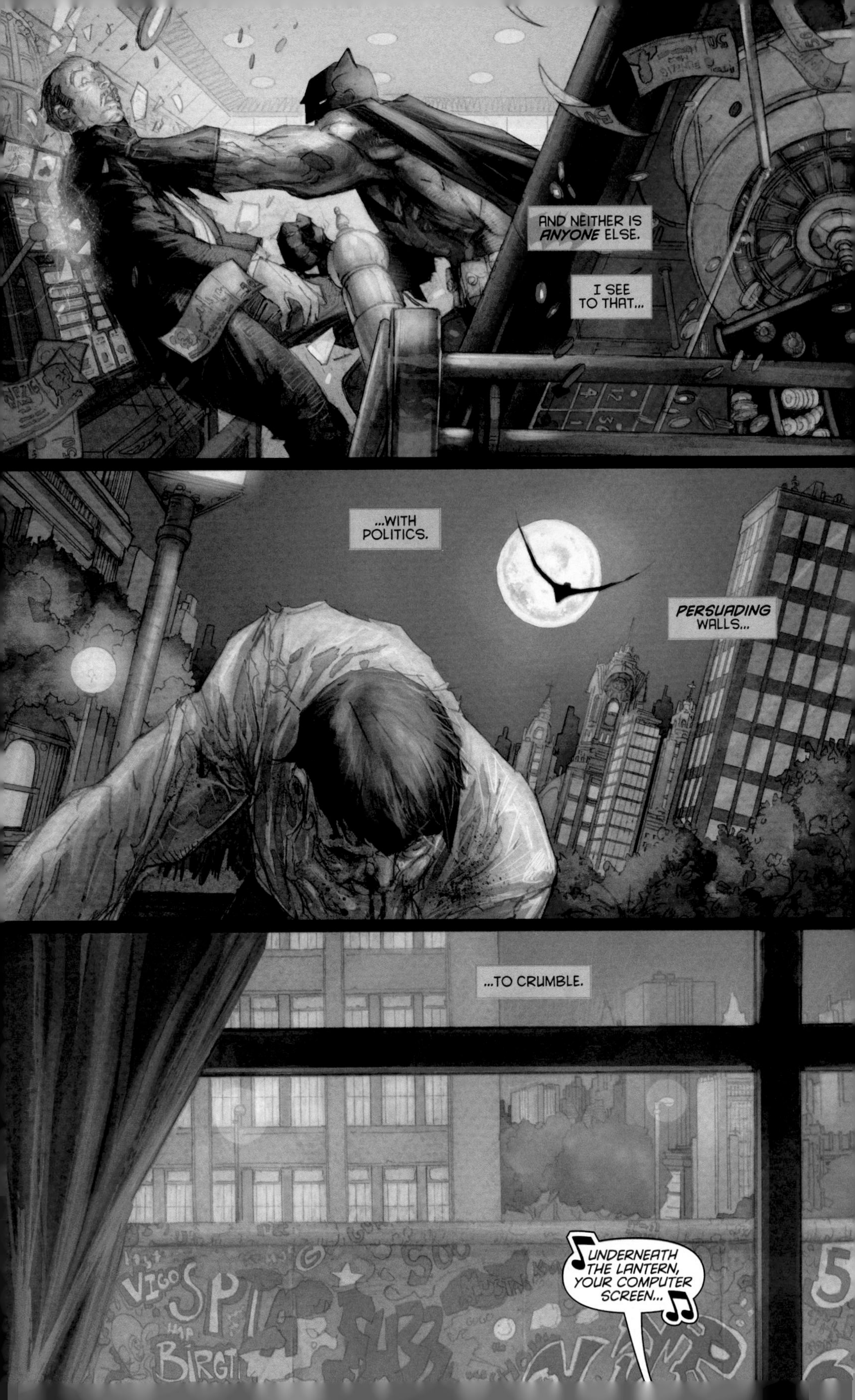
AND NEITHER IS ANYONE ELSE.
I SEE TO THAT...
...WITH POLITICS.
PERSUADING WALLS...
...TO CRUMBLE.
UNDERNEATH THE LANTERN, YOUR COMPUTER SCREEN...

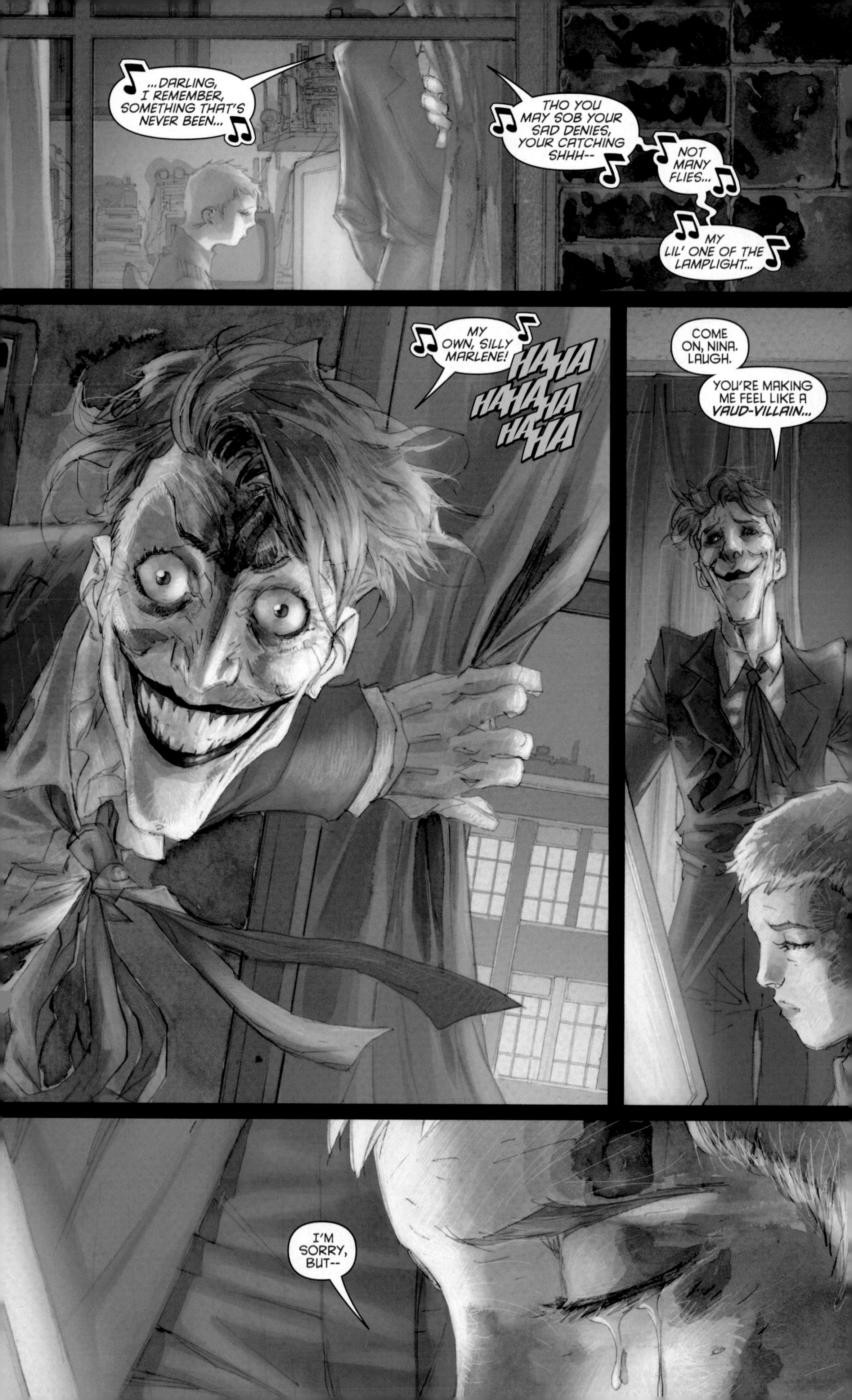

...DARLING, I REMEMBER, SOMETHING THAT'S NEVER BEEN...
THO YOU MAY SOB YOUR SAD DENIES, YOUR CATCHING SHHH--
NOT MANY FLIES...
MY LIL' ONE OF THE LAMPLIGHT...
MY OWN, SILLY MARLENE!
HAHA HAHAHAHA HAHA
COME ON, NINA. LAUGH.
YOU'RE MAKING ME FEEL LIKE A VAUD-VILLAIN...
I'M SORRY, BUT--

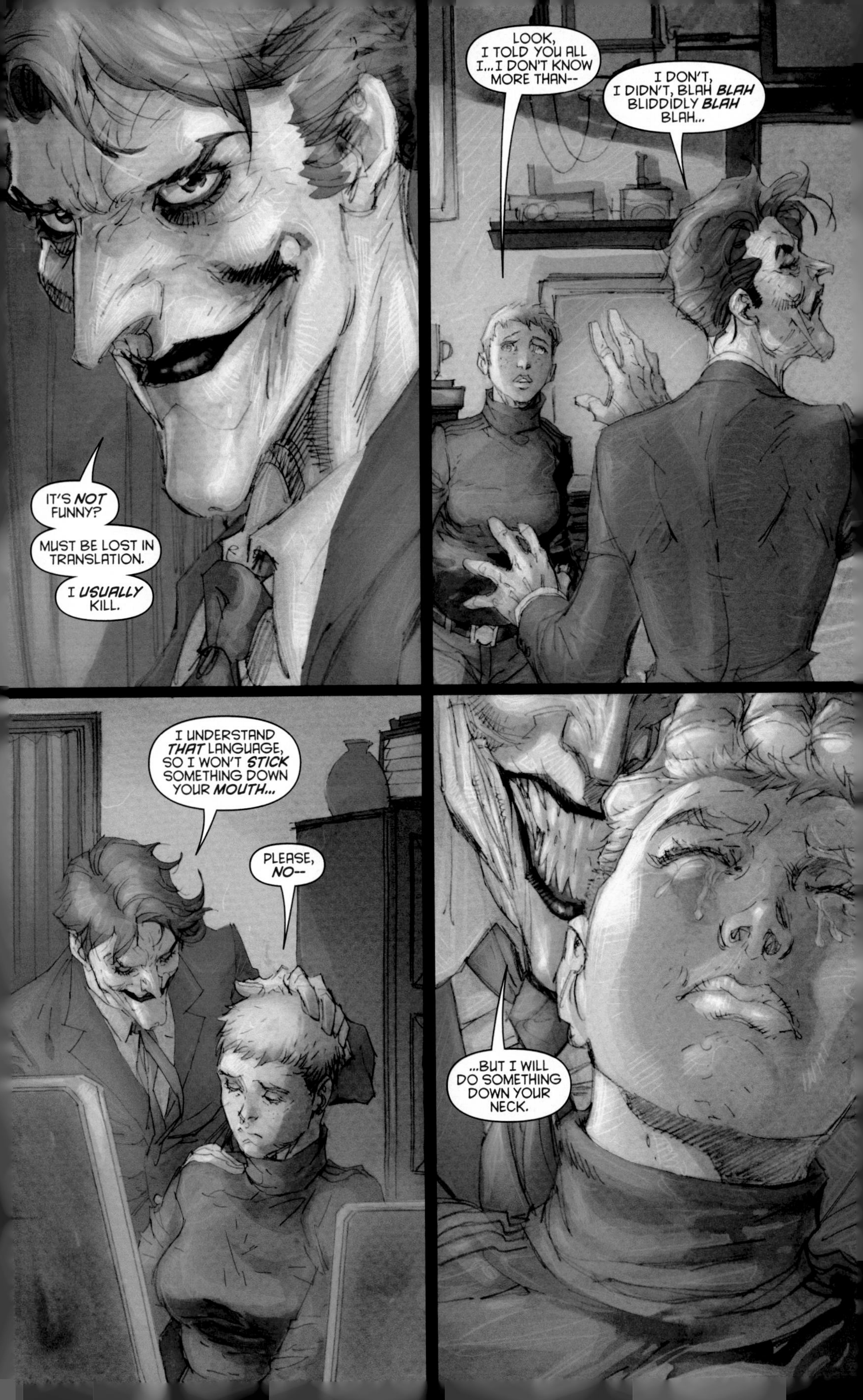
IT'S NOT FUNNY?
MUST BE LOST IN TRANSLATION.
I USUALLY KILL.
LOOK, I TOLD YOU ALL I...I DON'T KNOW MORE THAN--
I DON'T, I DIDN'T, BLAH BLAH BLIDDIDLY BLAH BLAH...
I UNDERSTAND THAT LANGUAGE, SO I WON'T STICK SOMETHING DOWN YOUR MOUTH...
PLEASE, NO--
...BUT I WILL DO SOMETHING DOWN YOUR NECK.

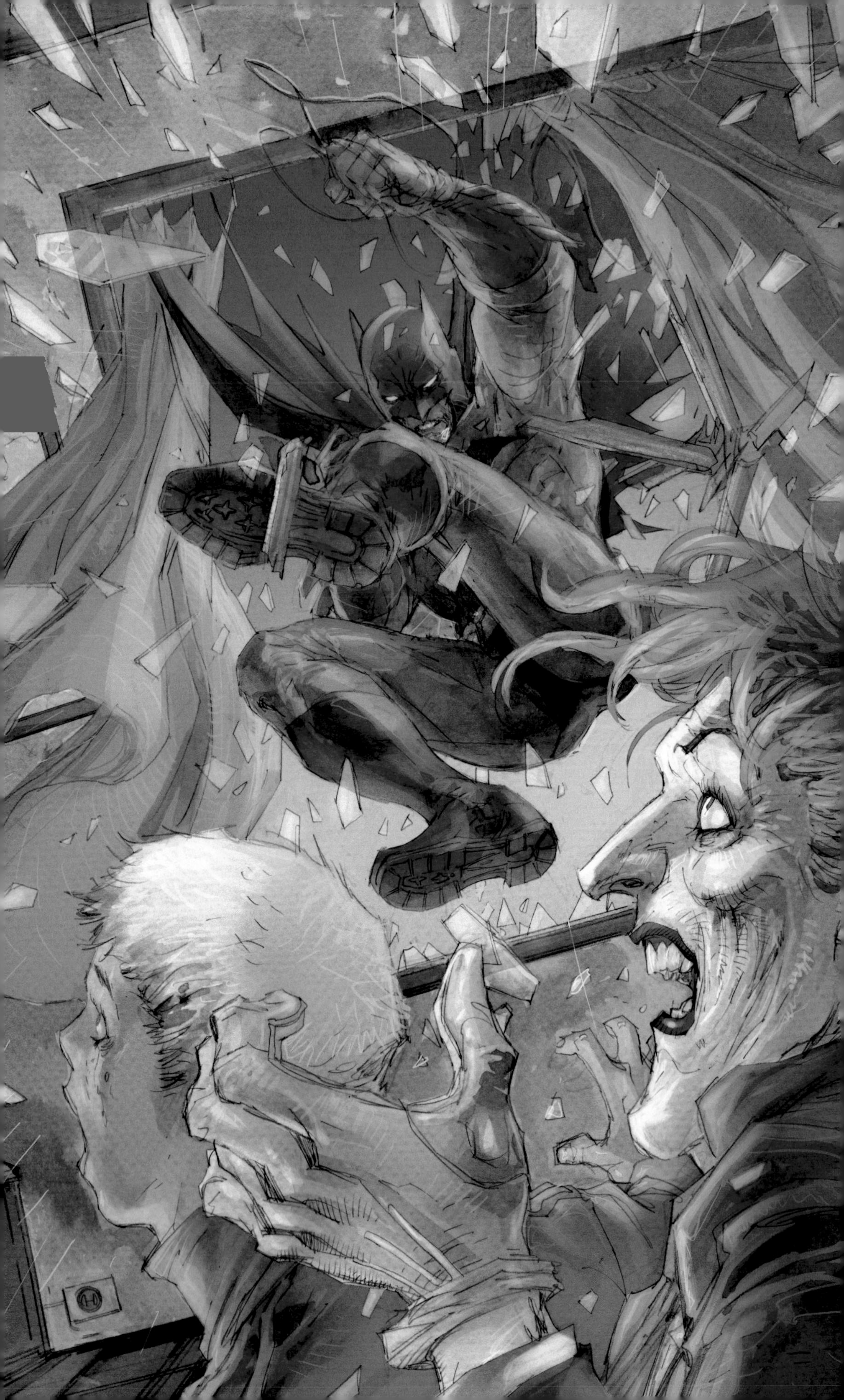

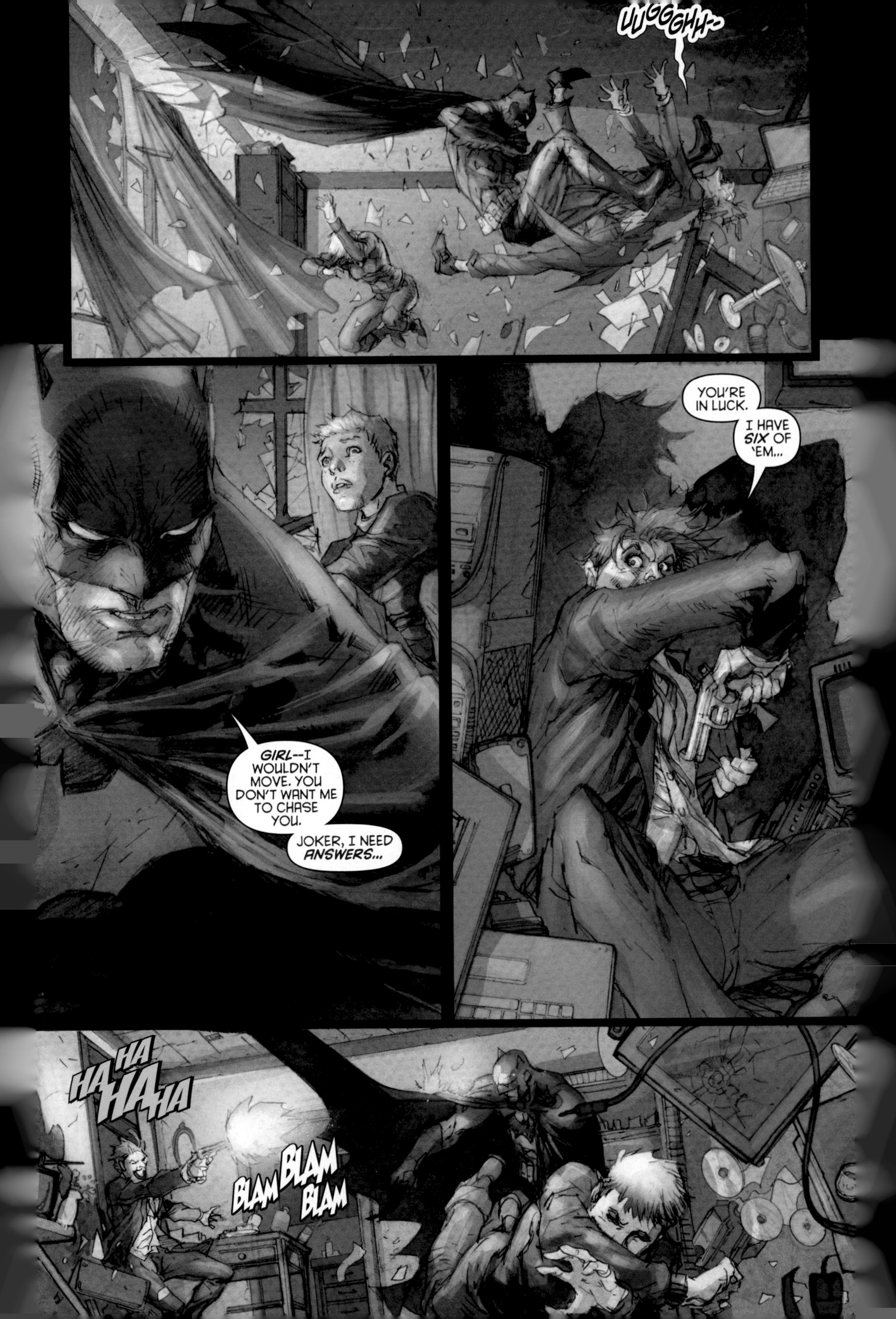
UUGGGHH-
GIRL--I WOULDN'T MOVE. YOU DON'T WANT ME TO CHASE YOU.
JOKER, I NEED ANSWERS...
YOU'RE IN LUCK.
I HAVE SIX OF 'EM...
HA HA HA HA
BLAM BLAM BLAM

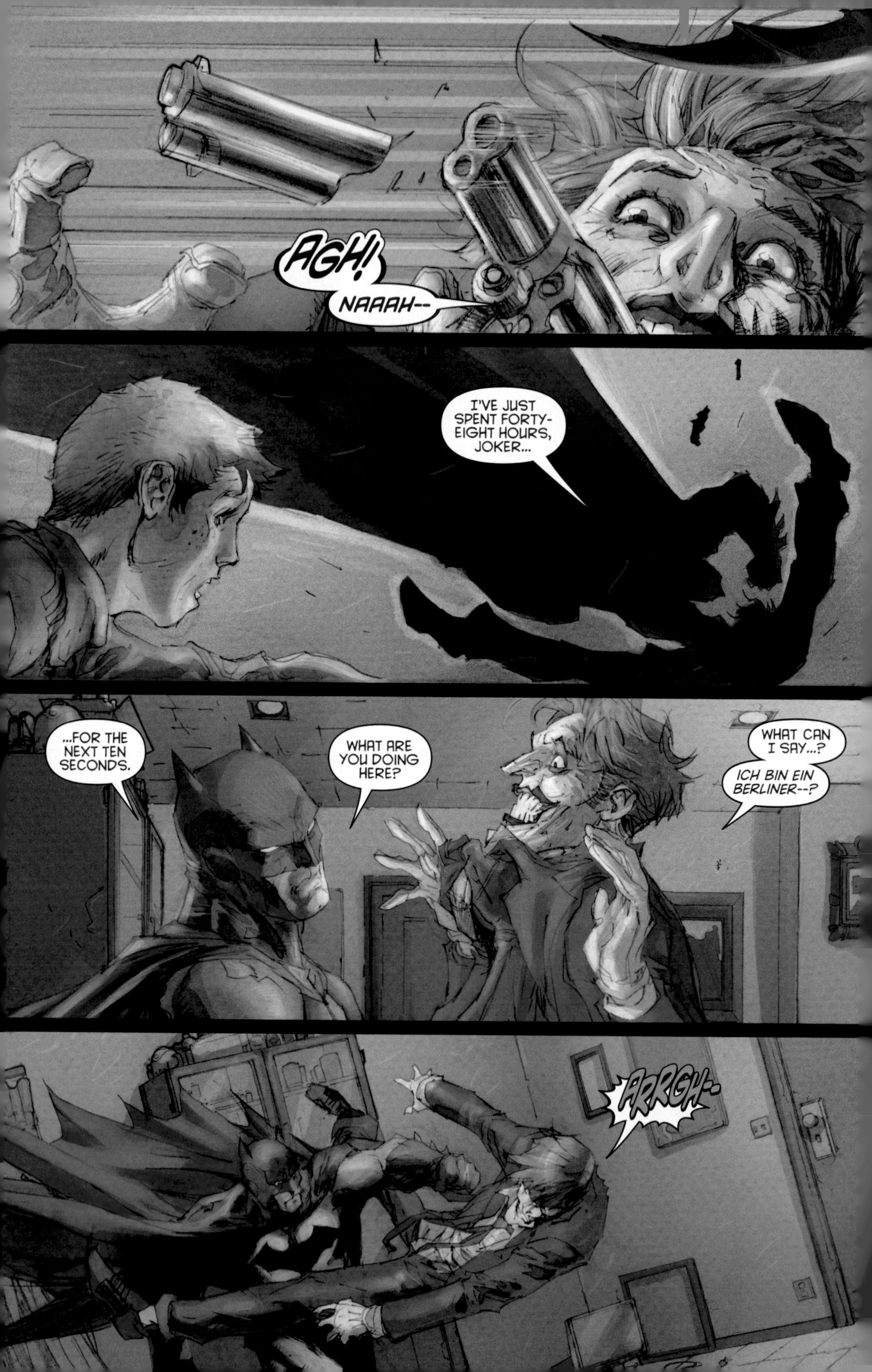
AGH!
NAAAH--
I'VE JUST SPENT FORTY-EIGHT HOURS, JOKER...
...FOR THE NEXT TEN SECONDS.
WHAT ARE YOU DOING HERE?
WHAT CAN I SAY...?
ICH BIN EIN BERLINER--?
ARRGH-

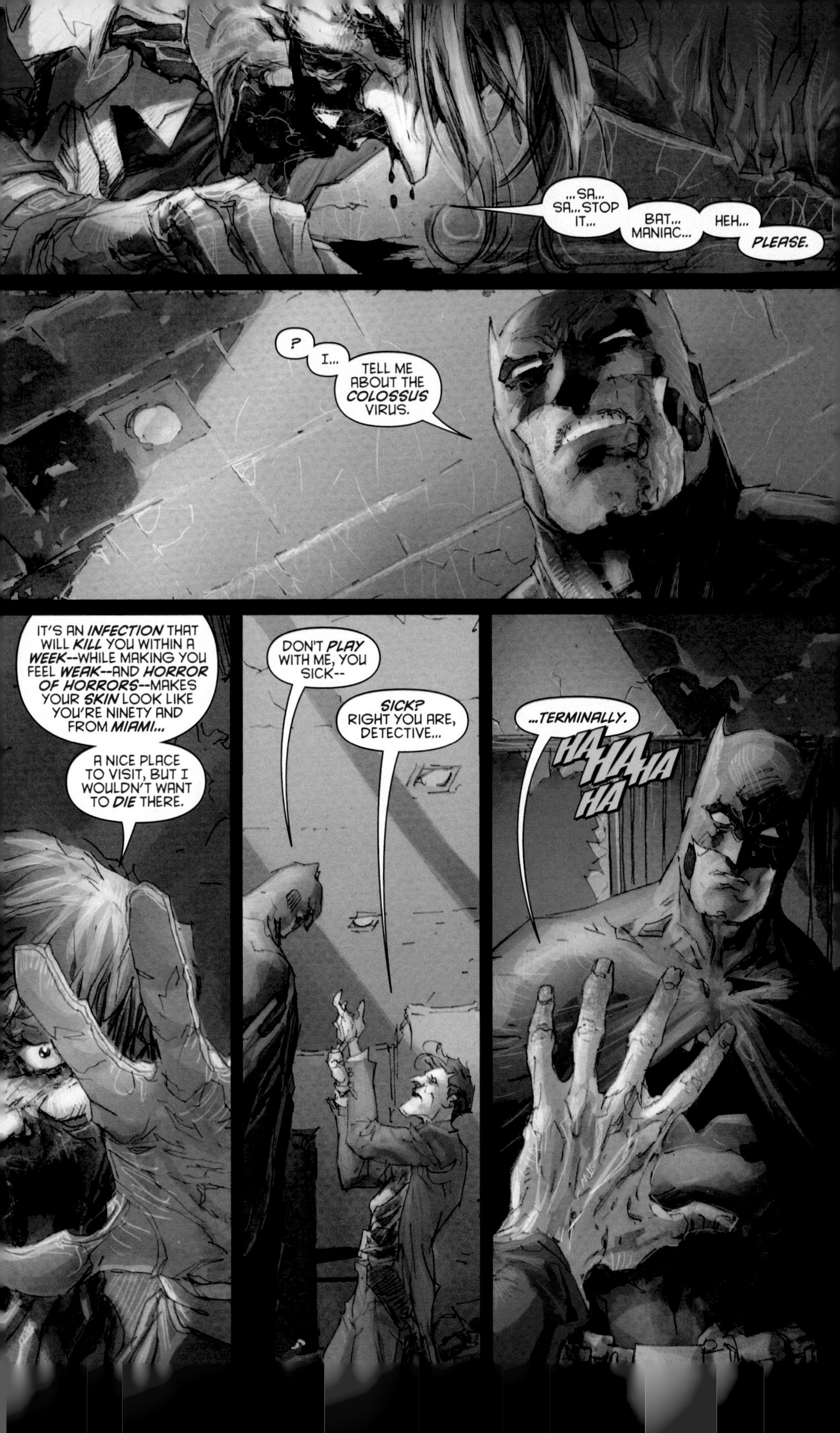

...SA... SA...STOP IT...
BAT... MANIAC...
HEH...
PLEASE.
?
I...
TELL ME ABOUT THE COLOSSUS VIRUS.
IT'S AN INFECTION THAT WILL KILL YOU WITHIN A WEEK--WHILE MAKING YOU FEEL WEAK--AND HORROR OF HORRORS--MAKES YOUR SKIN LOOK LIKE YOU'RE NINETY AND FROM MIAMI...
A NICE PLACE TO VISIT, BUT I WOULDN'T WANT TO DIE THERE.
DON'T PLAY WITH ME, YOU SICK--
SICK? RIGHT YOU ARE, DETECTIVE...
...TERMINALLY.
HA HA HA HA HA

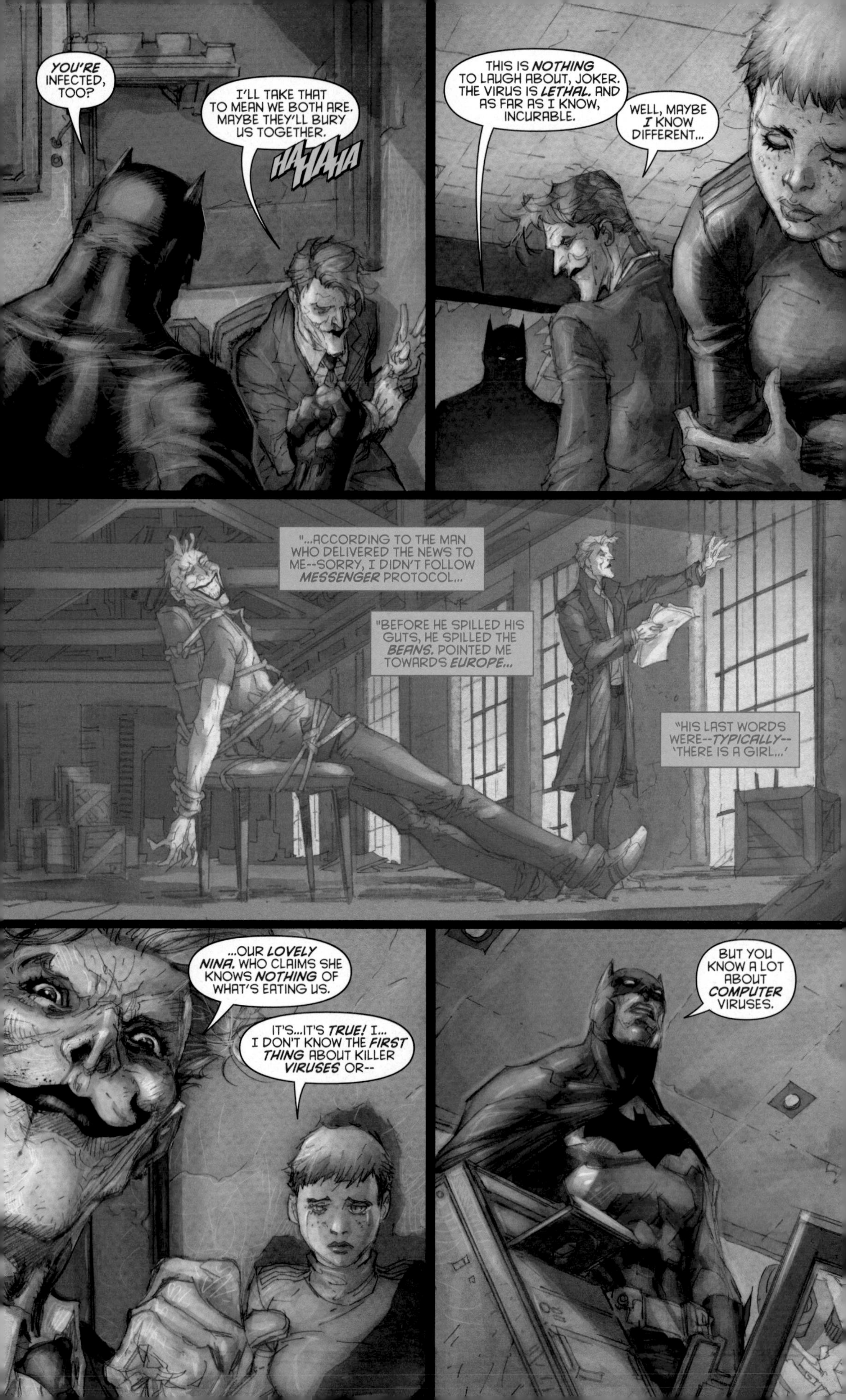

YOU'RE INFECTED, TOO?
I'LL TAKE THAT TO MEAN WE BOTH ARE. MAYBE THEY'LL BURY US TOGETHER.
HAHAHA
THIS IS NOTHING TO LAUGH ABOUT, JOKER. THE VIRUS IS LETHAL. AND AS FAR AS I KNOW, INCURABLE.
WELL, MAYBE I KNOW DIFFERENT...
"...ACCORDING TO THE MAN WHO DELIVERED THE NEWS TO ME--SORRY, I DIDN'T FOLLOW MESSENGER PROTOCOL...
"BEFORE HE SPILLED HIS GUTS, HE SPILLED THE BEANS. POINTED ME TOWARDS EUROPE...
"HIS LAST WORDS WERE--TYPICALLY--'THERE IS A GIRL...'
...OUR LOVELY NINA. WHO CLAIMS SHE KNOWS NOTHING OF WHAT'S EATING US.
IT'S...IT'S TRUE! I... I DON'T KNOW THE FIRST THING ABOUT KILLER VIRUSES OR--
BUT YOU KNOW A LOT ABOUT COMPUTER VIRUSES.

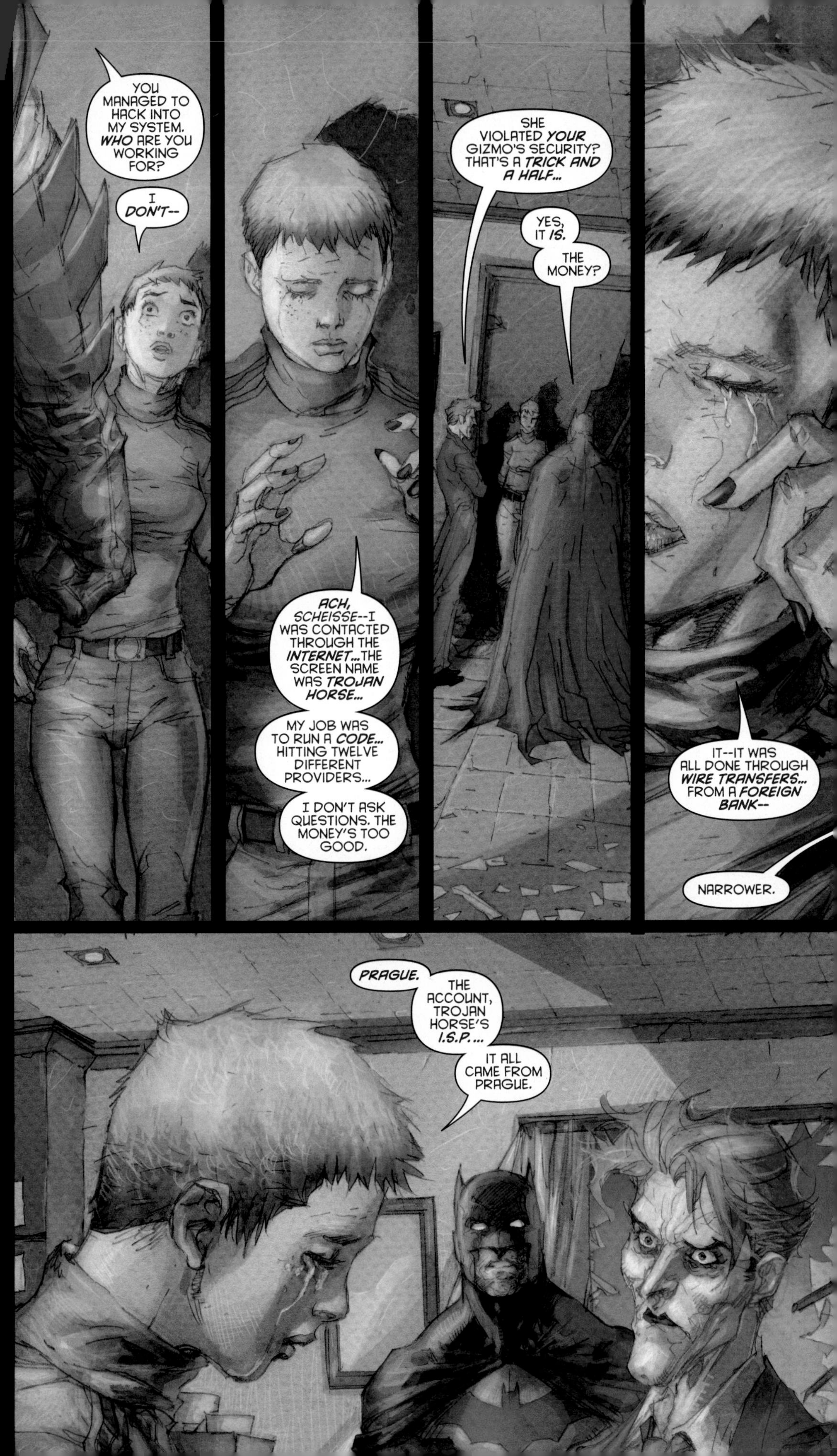

YOU MANAGED TO HACK INTO MY SYSTEM. *WHO* ARE YOU WORKING FOR?
I *DON'T*--
ACH, SCHEISSE--I WAS CONTACTED THROUGH THE *INTERNET*...THE SCREEN NAME WAS *TROJAN HORSE*...
MY JOB WAS TO RUN A *CODE*... HITTING TWELVE DIFFERENT PROVIDERS...
I DON'T ASK QUESTIONS. THE MONEY'S TOO GOOD.
SHE VIOLATED *YOUR* GIZMO'S SECURITY? THAT'S A *TRICK AND A HALF*...
YES, IT *IS*.
THE MONEY?
IT--IT WAS ALL DONE THROUGH *WIRE TRANSFERS*... FROM A *FOREIGN BANK*--
NARROWER.
PRAGUE.
THE ACCOUNT, TROJAN HORSE'S *I.S.P.*...
IT ALL CAME FROM PRAGUE.

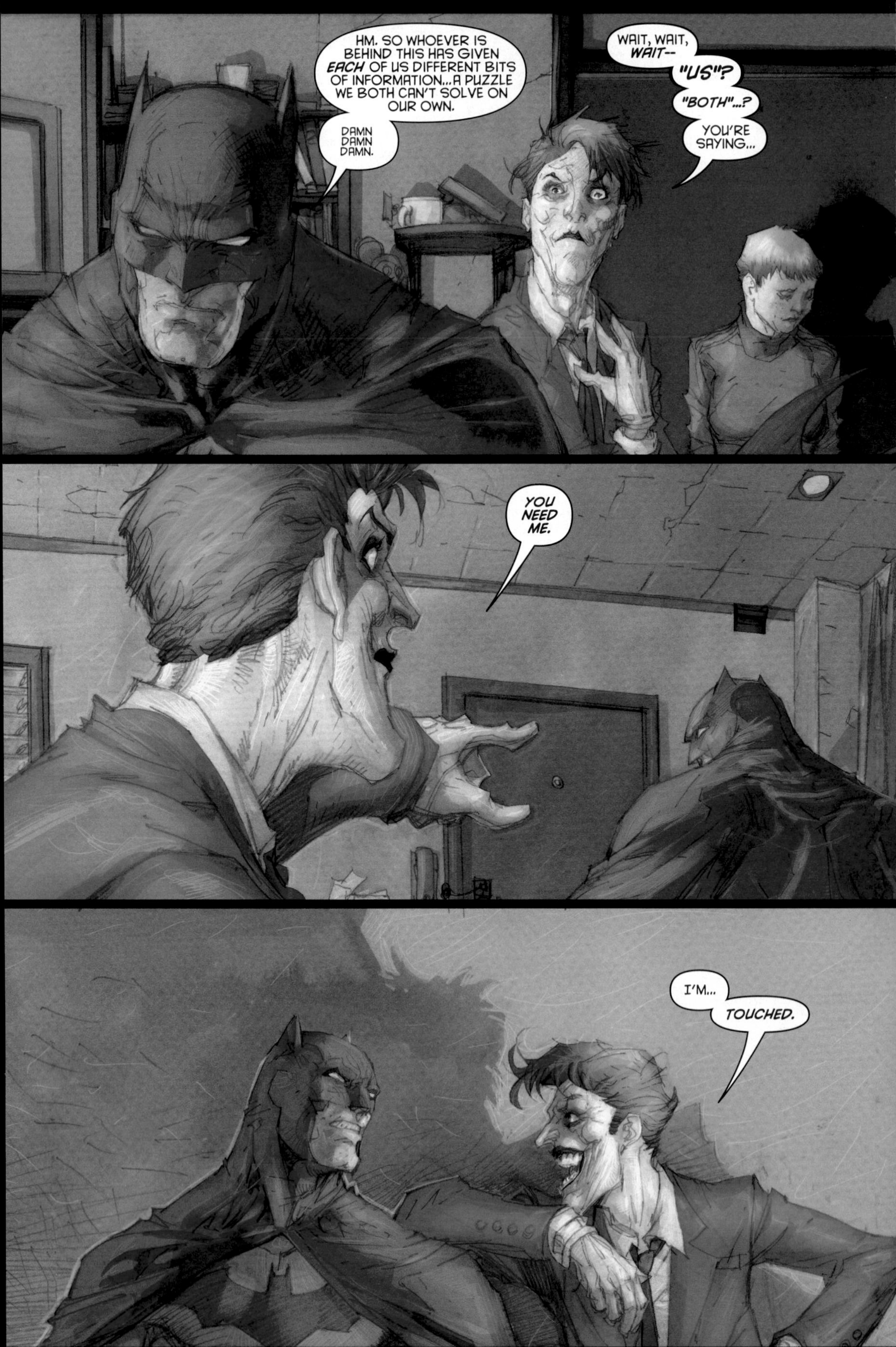
HM. SO WHOEVER IS BEHIND THIS HAS GIVEN EACH OF US DIFFERENT BITS OF INFORMATION...A PUZZLE WE BOTH CAN'T SOLVE ON OUR OWN.
DAMN DAMN DAMN.
WAIT, WAIT, WAIT--
"US"?
"BOTH"...?
YOU'RE SAYING...
YOU NEED ME.
I'M...
TOUCHED.

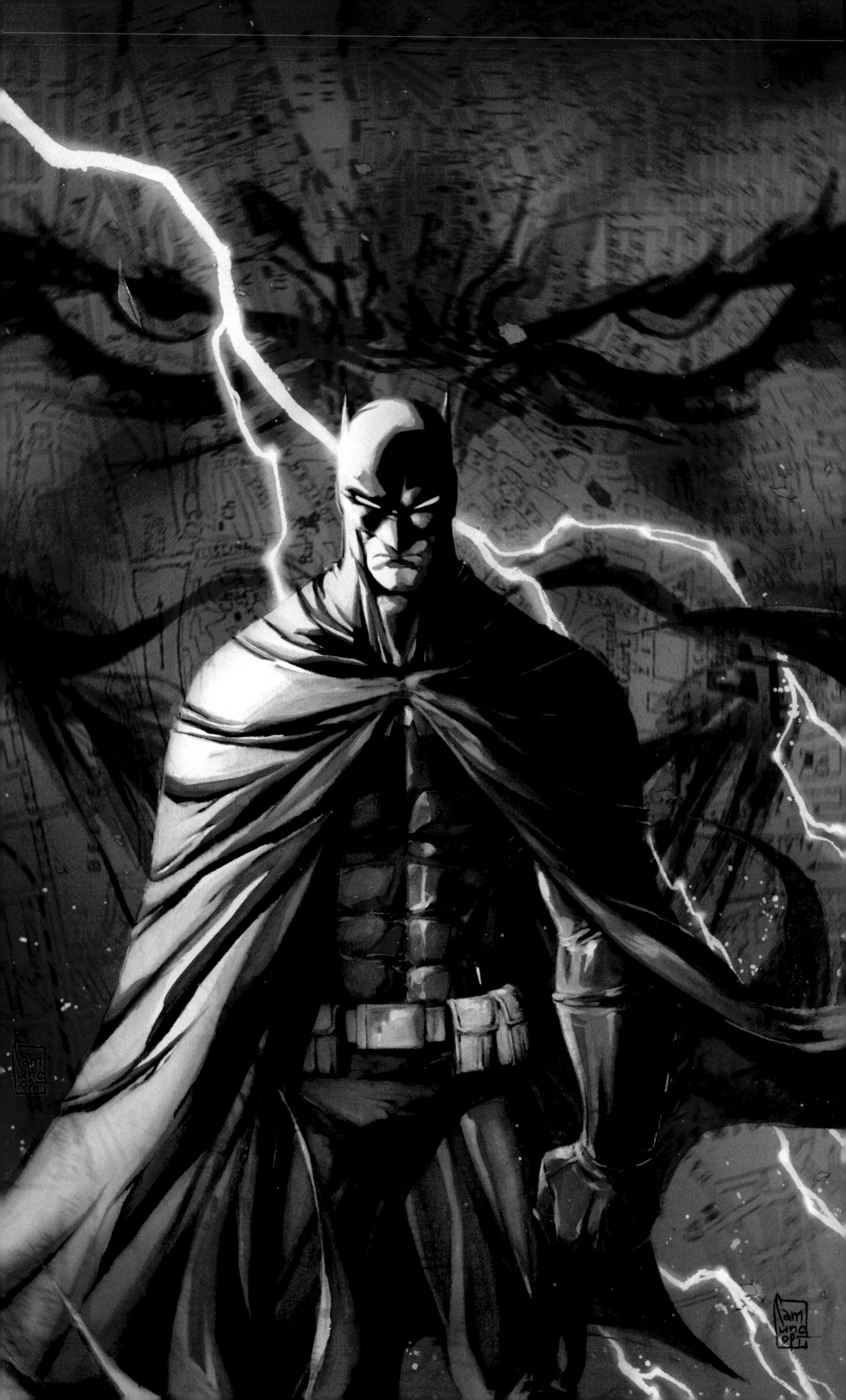

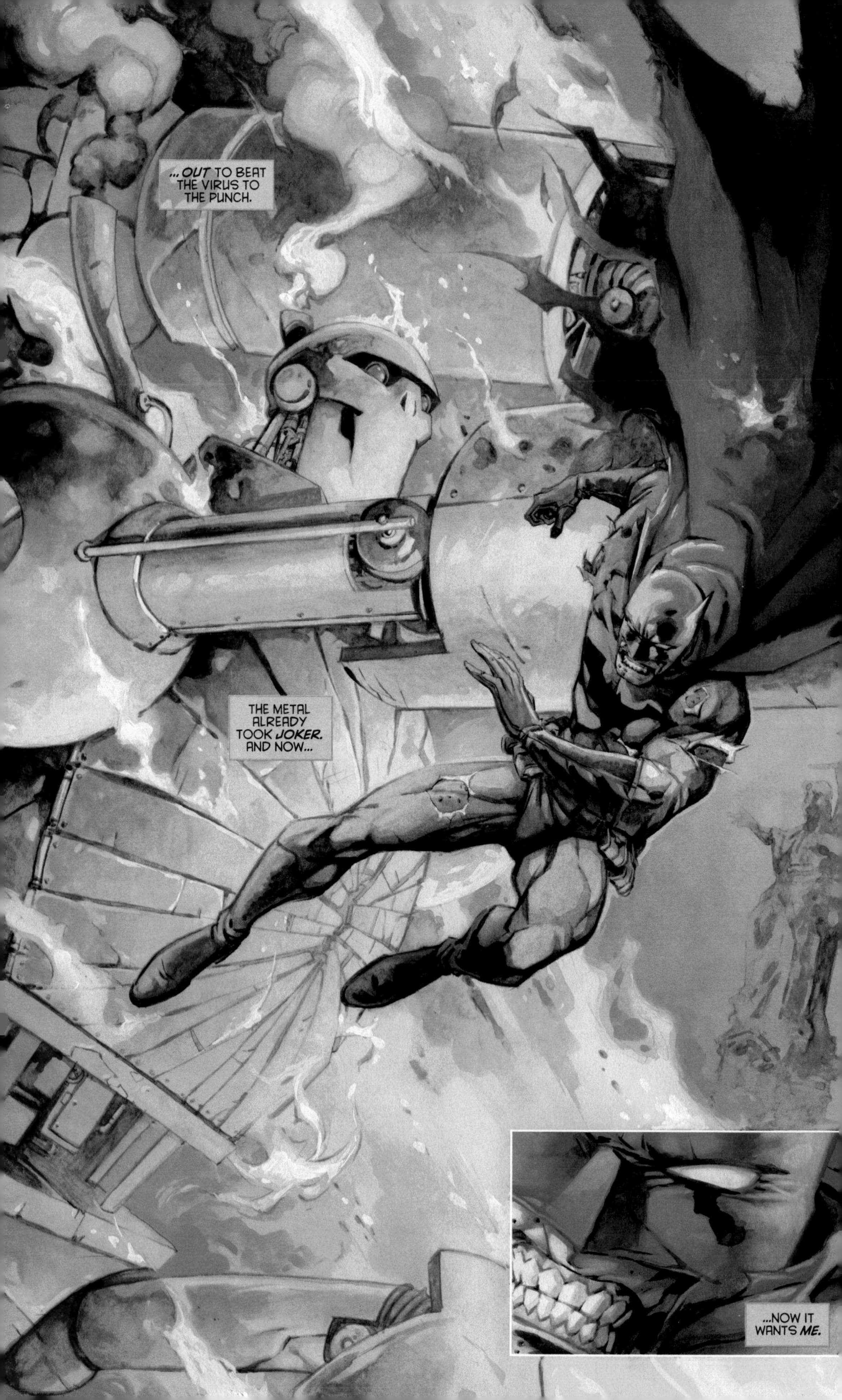

...OUT TO BEAT THE VIRUS TO THE PUNCH.
THE METAL ALREADY TOOK JOKER. AND NOW...
...NOW IT WANTS ME.

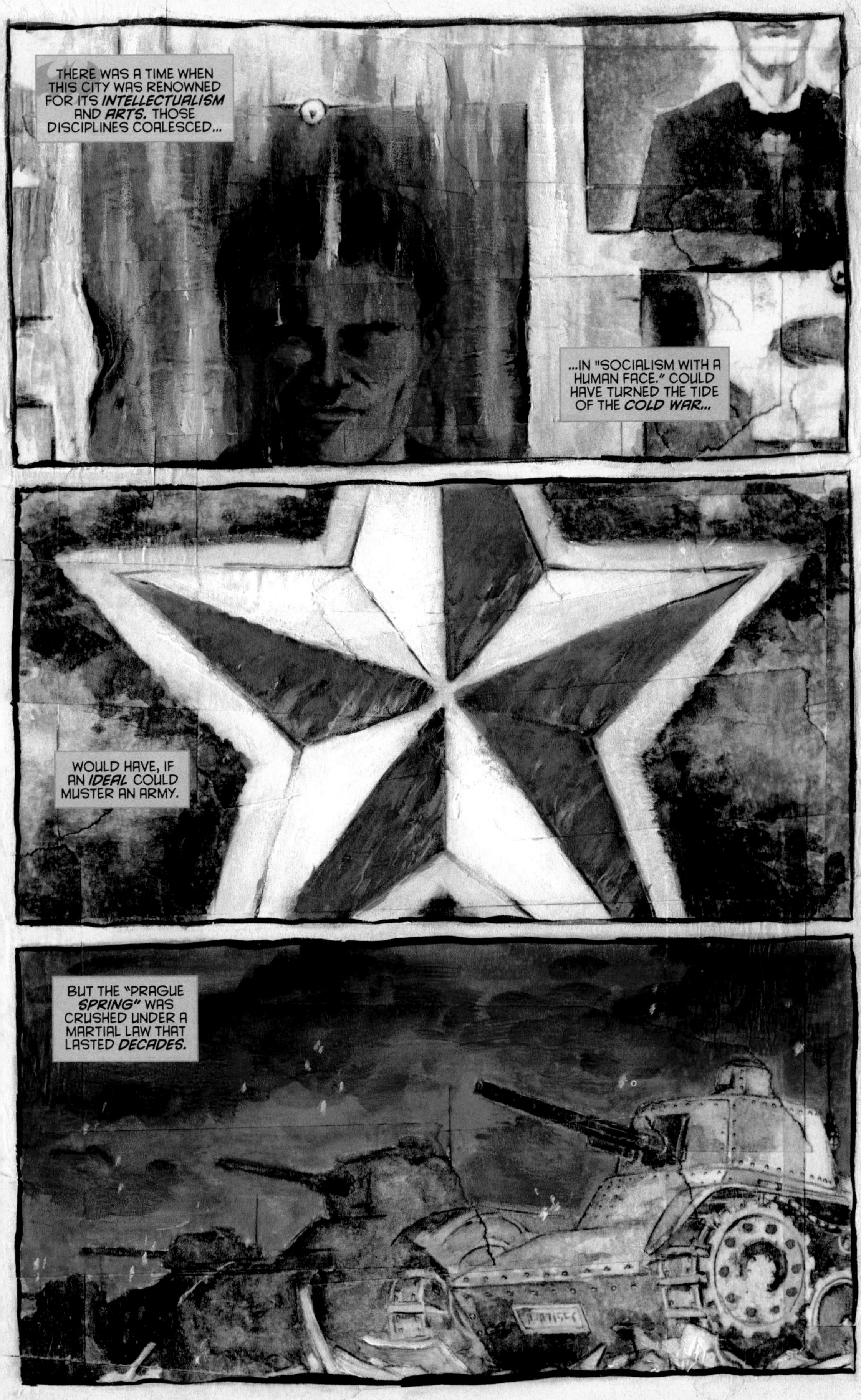
THERE WAS A TIME WHEN THIS CITY WAS RENOWNED FOR ITS *INTELLECTUALISM* AND *ARTS.* THOSE DISCIPLINES COALESCED...
...IN "SOCIALISM WITH A HUMAN FACE." COULD HAVE TURNED THE TIDE OF THE *COLD WAR...*
WOULD HAVE, IF AN *IDEAL* COULD MUSTER AN ARMY.
BUT THE "PRAGUE *SPRING*" WAS CRUSHED UNDER A MARTIAL LAW THAT LASTED *DECADES.*

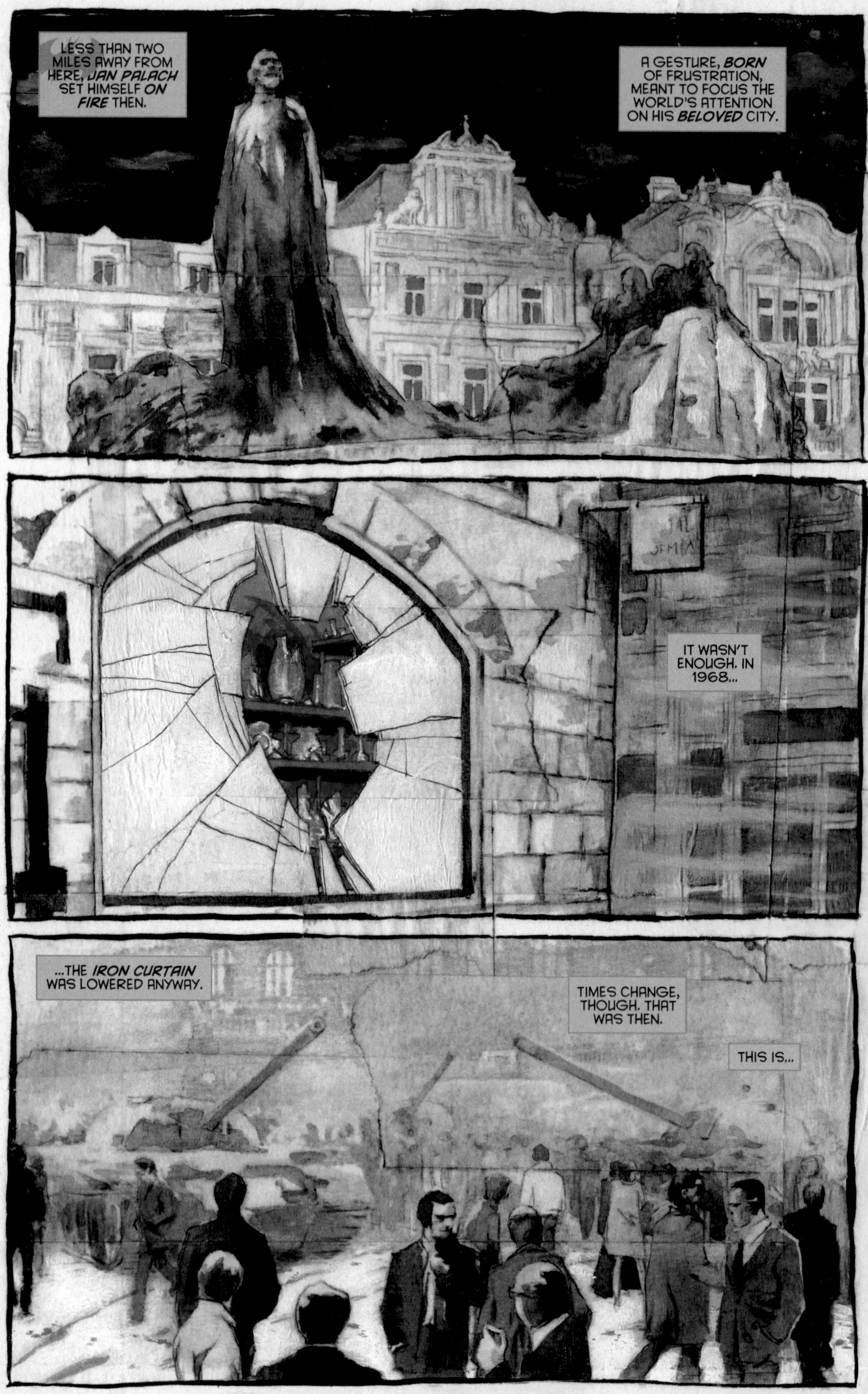
LESS THAN TWO MILES AWAY FROM HERE, JAN PALACH SET HIMSELF ON FIRE THEN.
A GESTURE, BORN OF FRUSTRATION, MEANT TO FOCUS THE WORLD'S ATTENTION ON HIS BELOVED CITY.
IT WASN'T ENOUGH. IN 1968...
...THE IRON CURTAIN WAS LOWERED ANYWAY.
TIMES CHANGE, THOUGH. THAT WAS THEN.
THIS IS...

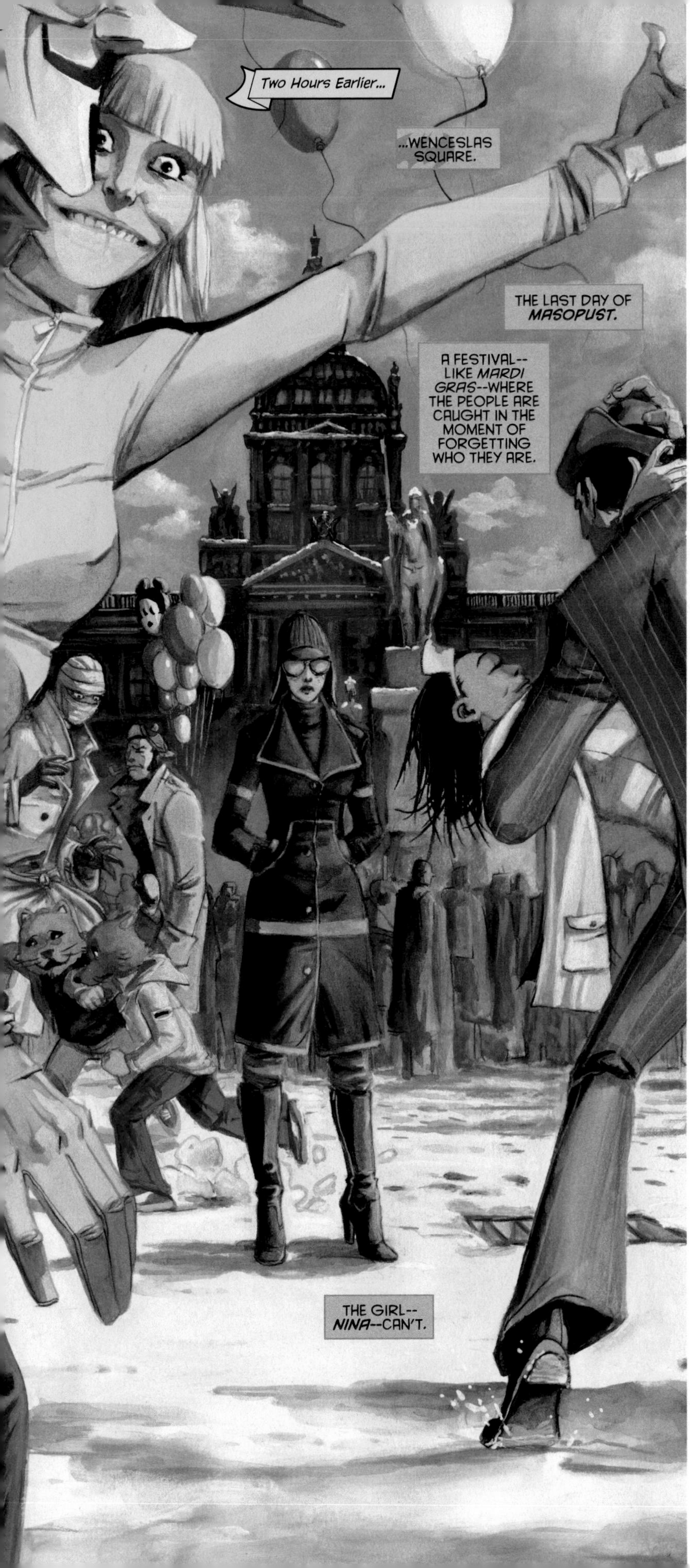
Two Hours Earlier...
...WENCESLAS SQUARE.
THE LAST DAY OF MASOPUST.
A FESTIVAL--LIKE MARDI GRAS--WHERE THE PEOPLE ARE CAUGHT IN THE MOMENT OF FORGETTING WHO THEY ARE.
THE GIRL--NINA--CAN'T.

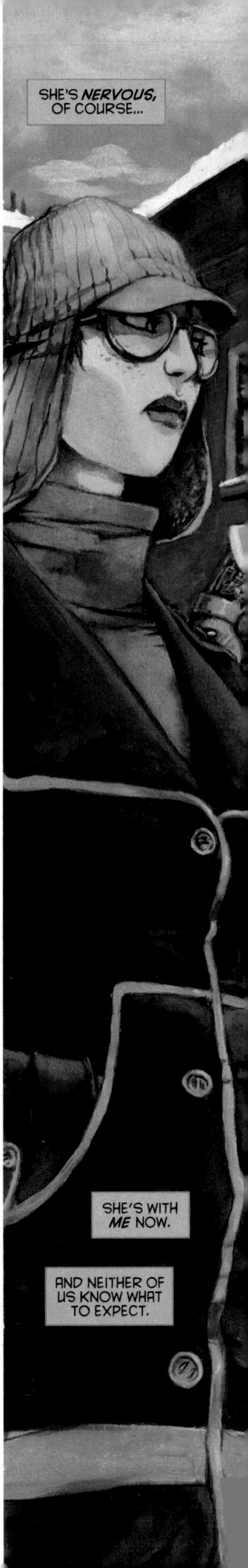
SHE'S NERVOUS, OF COURSE...
SHE'S WITH ME NOW.
AND NEITHER OF US KNOW WHAT TO EXPECT.

WHAT I DO KNOW IS THE *VIRUS* IS SLOWLY TAKING ITS TOLL.

I'VE COME ALL THE WAY TO *EUROPE* TO HUNT DOWN WHOEVER'S RESPONSIBLE FOR INFECTING ME.

OH, AND A CURE. *FAR* FROM GOTHAM...

...TRAPPED IN A GAME OF GLOBAL *HOPSCOTCH* THAT STARTED IN BERLIN.

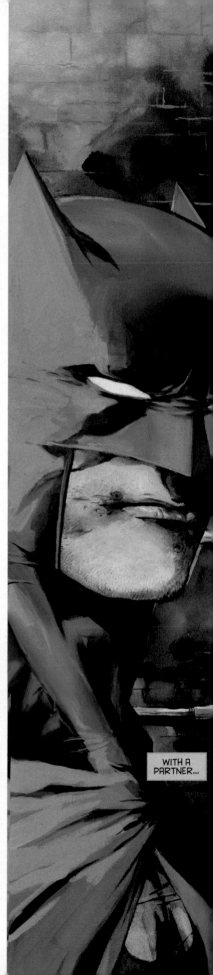

WITH A PARTNER...

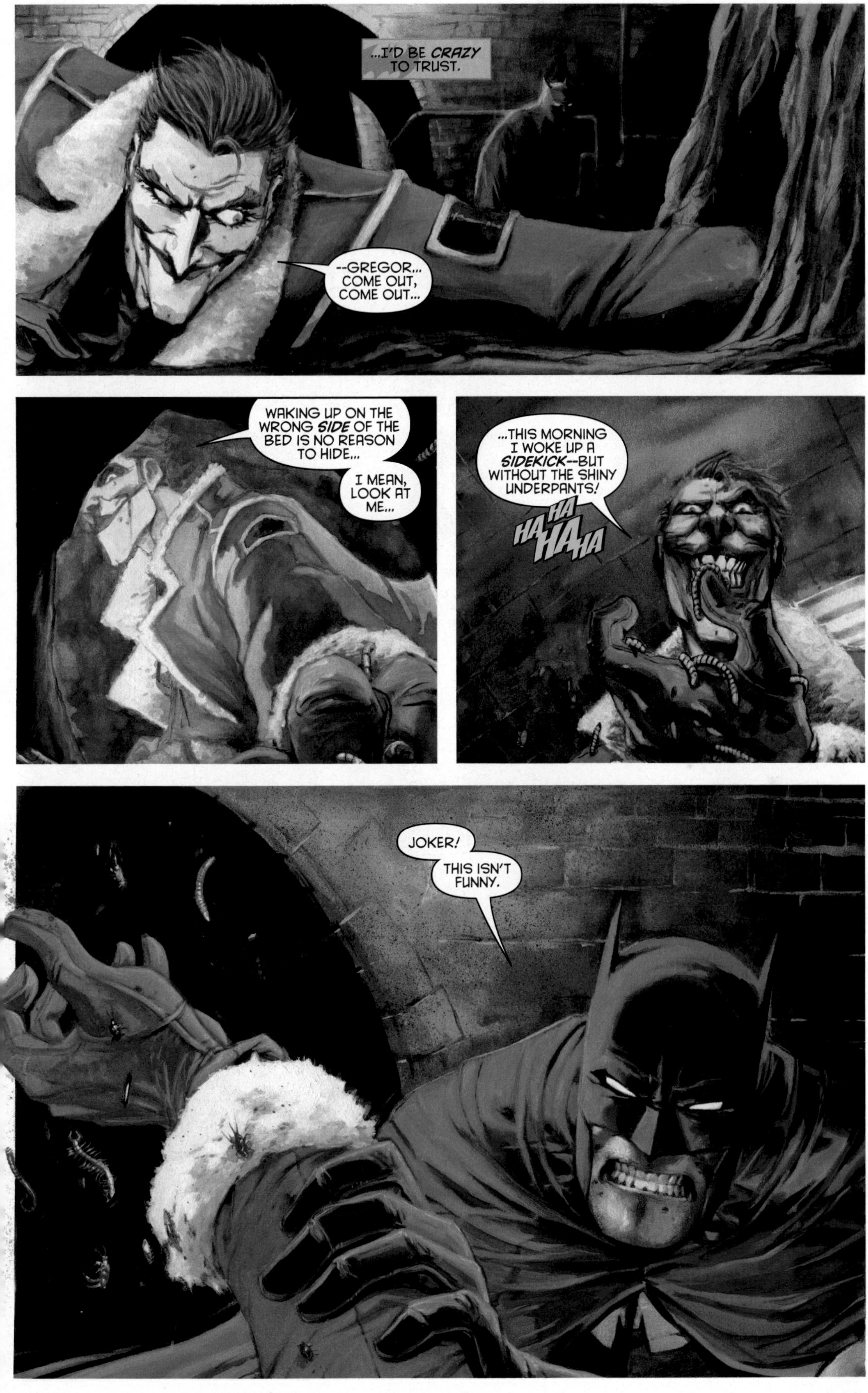
...I'D BE CRAZY TO TRUST.
--GREGOR... COME OUT, COME OUT...
WAKING UP ON THE WRONG SIDE OF THE BED IS NO REASON TO HIDE...
I MEAN, LOOK AT ME...
...THIS MORNING I WOKE UP A SIDEKICK--BUT WITHOUT THE SHINY UNDERPANTS!
HA HA HA HA
JOKER!
THIS ISN'T FUNNY.

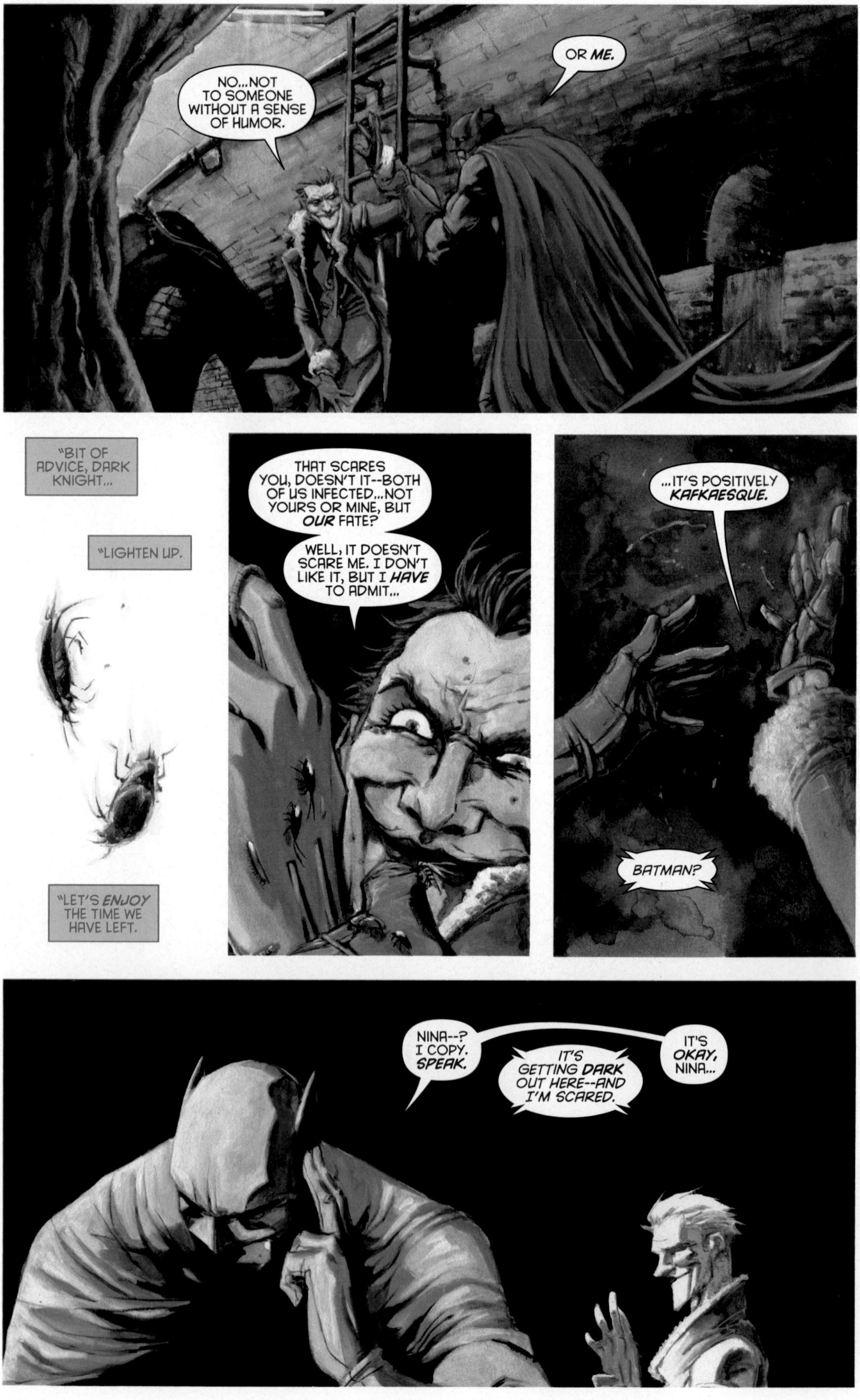
NO...NOT TO SOMEONE WITHOUT A SENSE OF HUMOR.
OR ME.
"BIT OF ADVICE, DARK KNIGHT...
"LIGHTEN UP.
"LET'S ENJOY THE TIME WE HAVE LEFT.
THAT SCARES YOU, DOESN'T IT--BOTH OF US INFECTED...NOT YOURS OR MINE, BUT OUR FATE?
WELL, IT DOESN'T SCARE ME. I DON'T LIKE IT, BUT I HAVE TO ADMIT...
...IT'S POSITIVELY KAFKAESQUE.
BATMAN?
NINA--? I COPY. SPEAK.
IT'S GETTING DARK OUT HERE--AND I'M SCARED.
IT'S OKAY, NINA...

...DEEP BREATH.

I'D FEEL SAFER TAKING ONE IN THE SEWER *YOU'RE* IN. OUT HERE, I'M SURROUNDED.

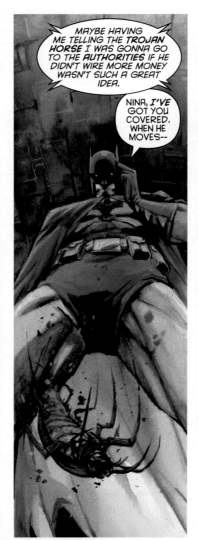

MAYBE HAVING ME TELLING THE *TROJAN HORSE* I WAS GONNA GO TO THE *AUTHORITIES* IF HE DIDN'T WIRE MORE MONEY WASN'T SUCH A GREAT IDEA.

NINA, *I'VE* GOT YOU COVERED. WHEN HE MOVES--

HE? THE TROJAN HORSE COULD BE ANYONE--

--A CHILD, A *WOMAN*... ANYONE--! WE COMMUNICATED THROUGH THE NET--

"--OUR MACHINES...

"MEIN GOTT--"

WHAT? NINA--WHAT'S GOING ON--?!

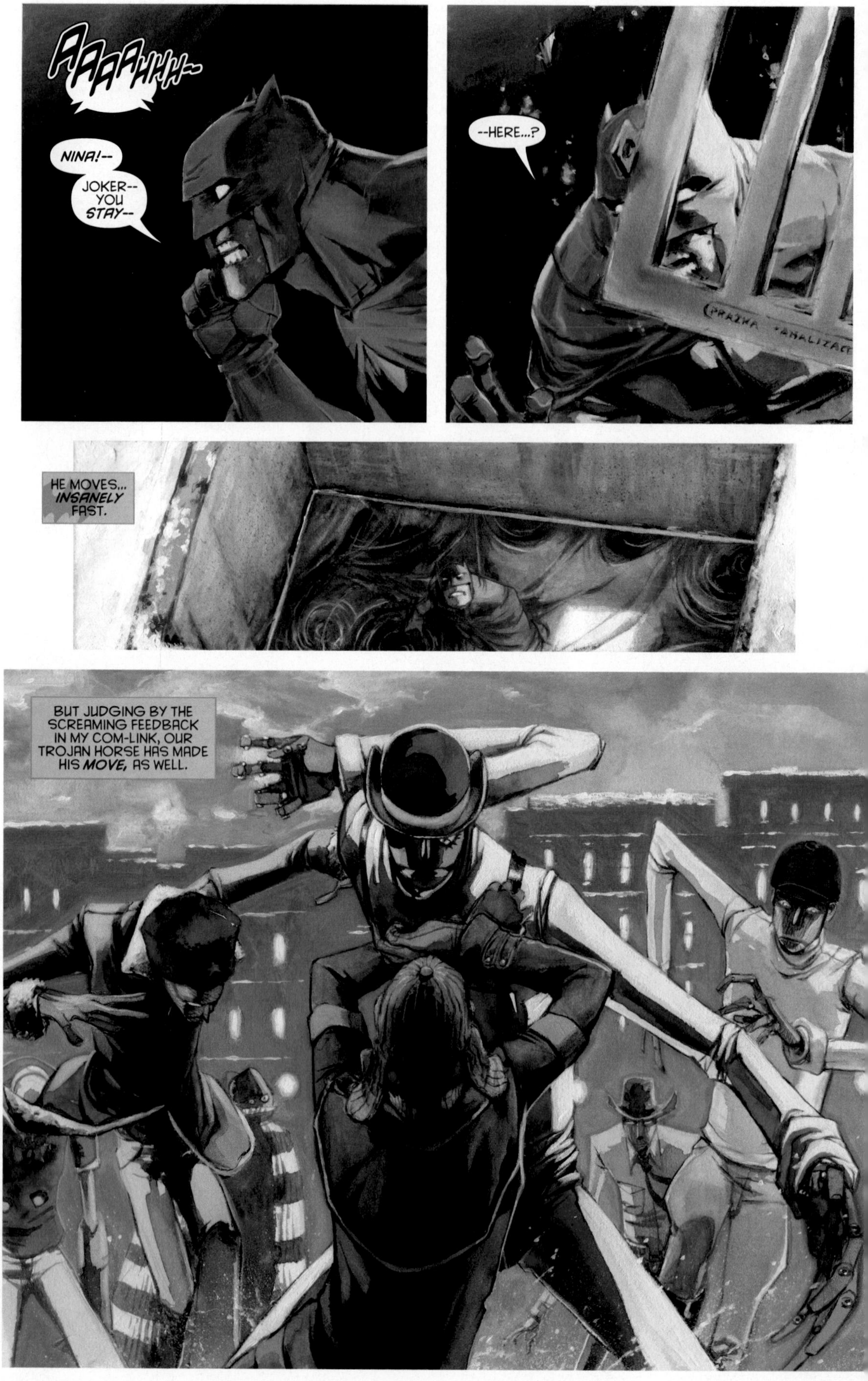
AAAAHHH--
NINA!--
JOKER--
YOU
STAY--
--HERE...?
HE MOVES...
INSANELY
FAST.
BUT JUDGING BY THE
SCREAMING FEEDBACK
IN MY COM-LINK, OUR
TROJAN HORSE HAS MADE
HIS MOVE, AS WELL.

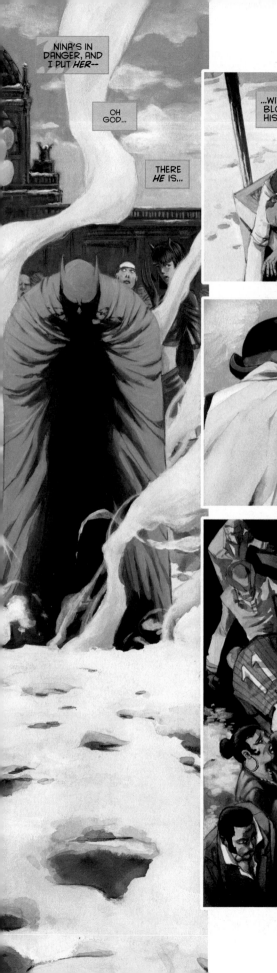

NINA'S IN DANGER, AND I PUT *HER*--

OH GOD...

THERE *HE* IS...

...WITH MORE BLOOD ON HIS HANDS.

BATMAN! *HELP!!!*

I TRY...*TOO CROWDED*-- THE FEVER, IT'S SLOWING ME DOWN...

JOKER IS...

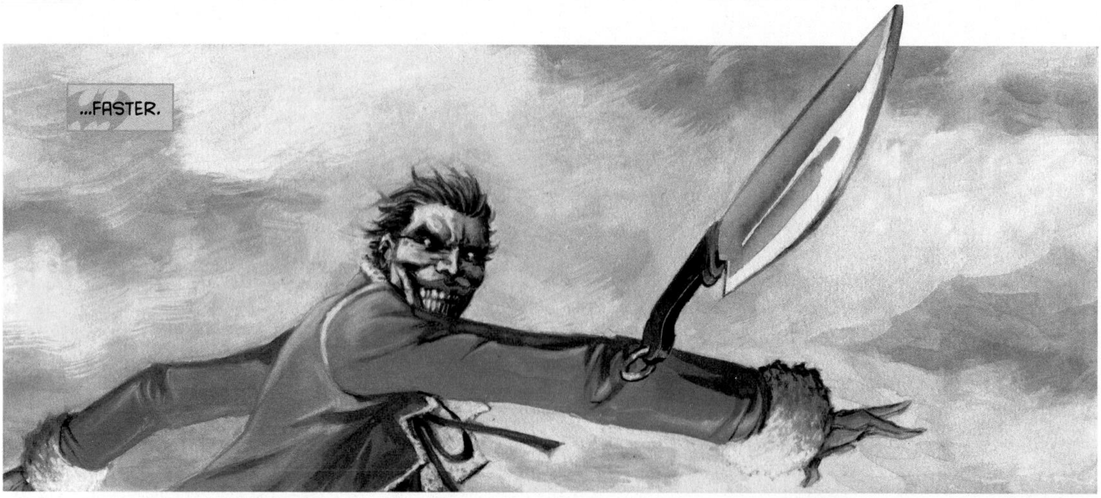
...FASTER.
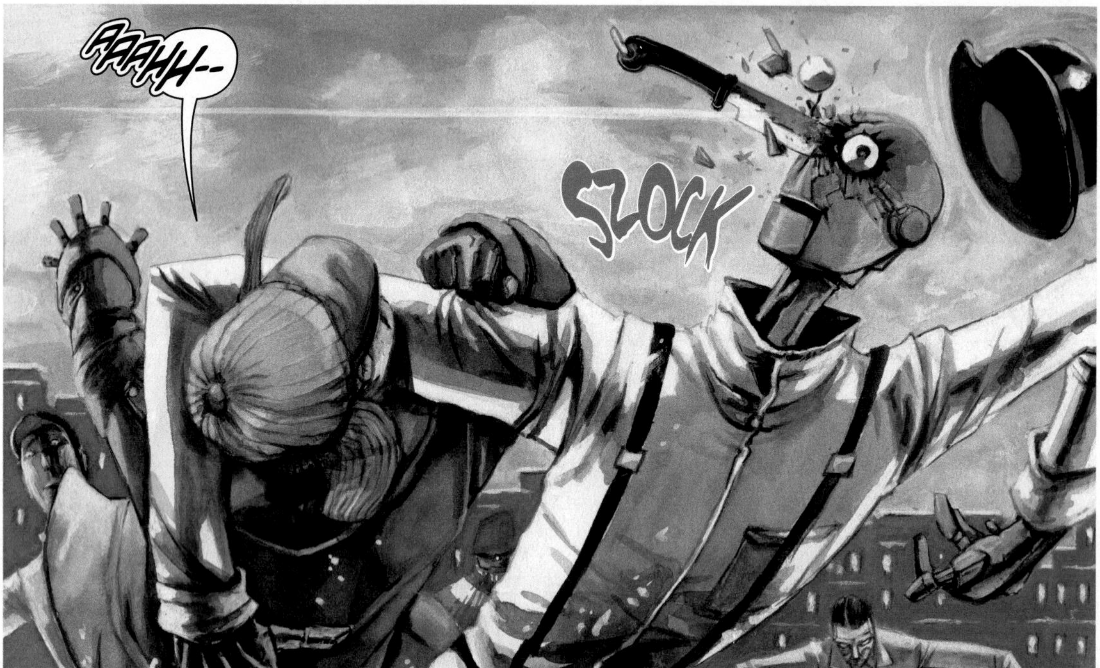
AAAHH--
SZLOCK
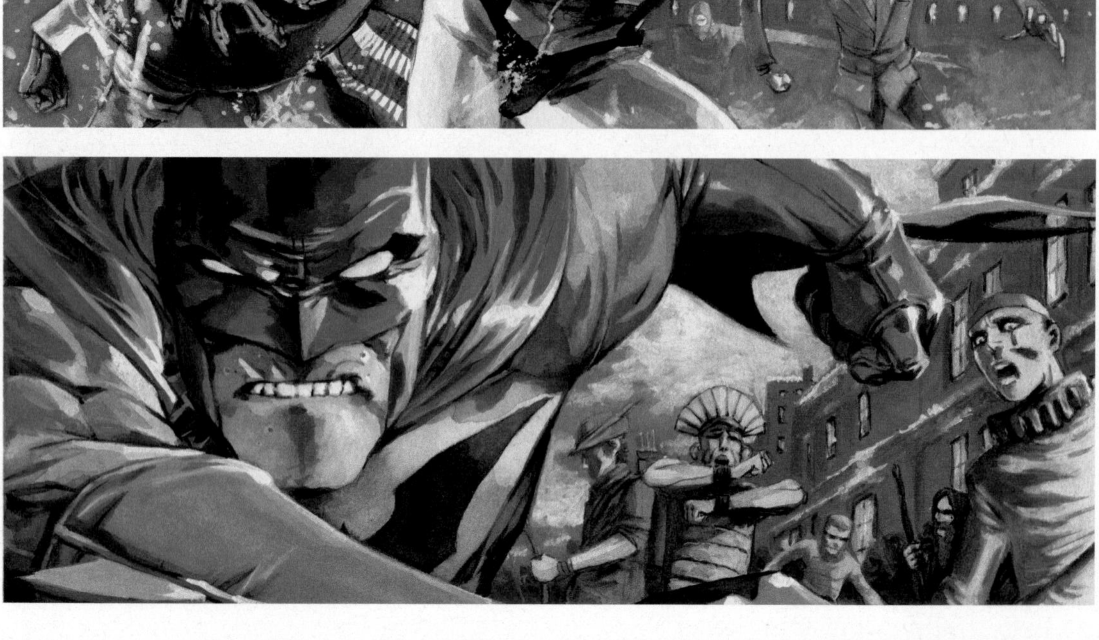

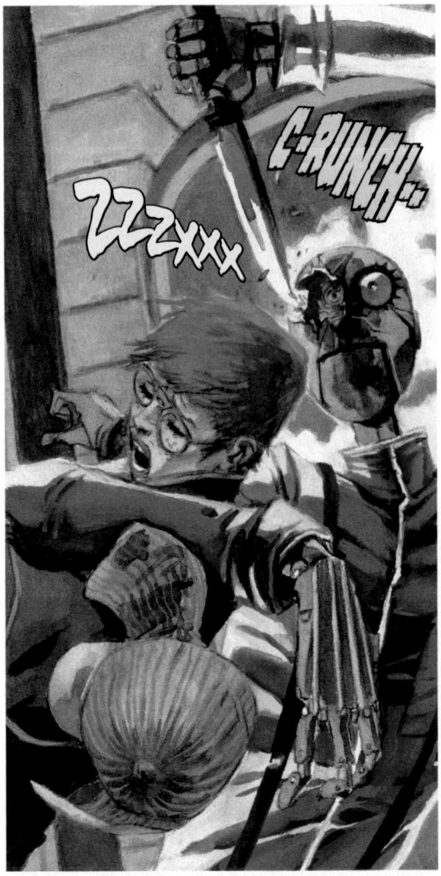
ZZZXXX
C-RUNCH..

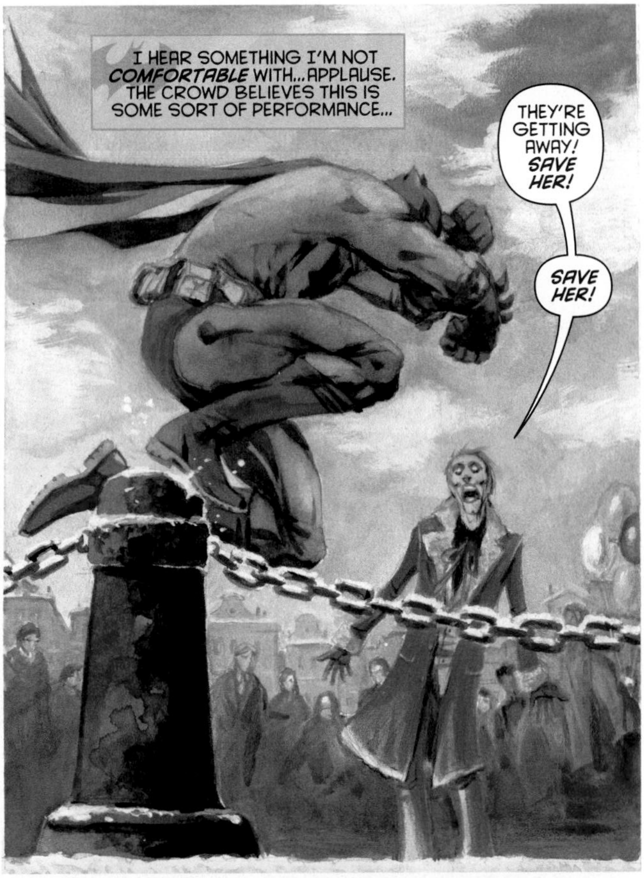
I HEAR SOMETHING I'M NOT COMFORTABLE WITH... APPLAUSE. THE CROWD BELIEVES THIS IS SOME SORT OF PERFORMANCE...
THEY'RE GETTING AWAY! SAVE HER!
SAVE HER!

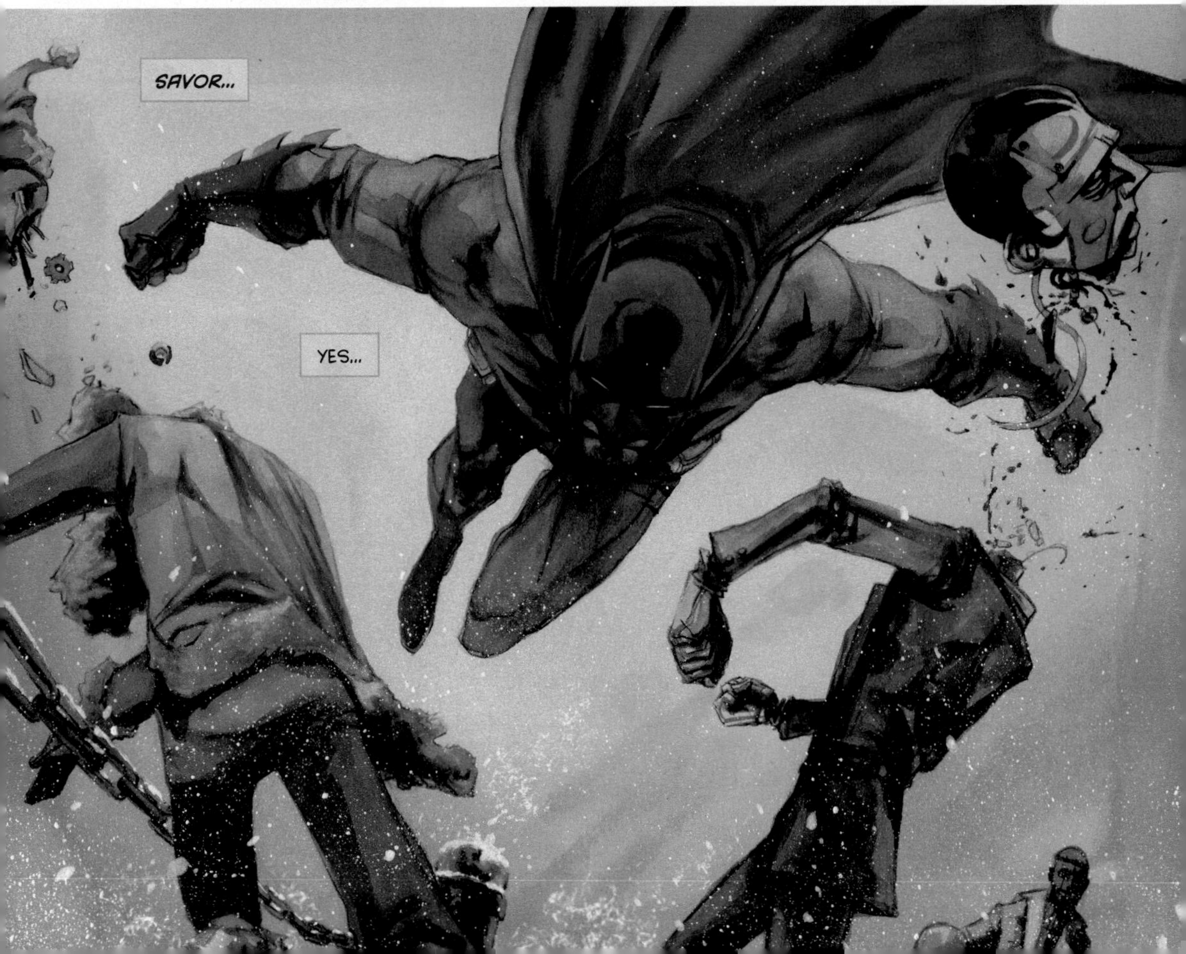
SAVOR...
YES...

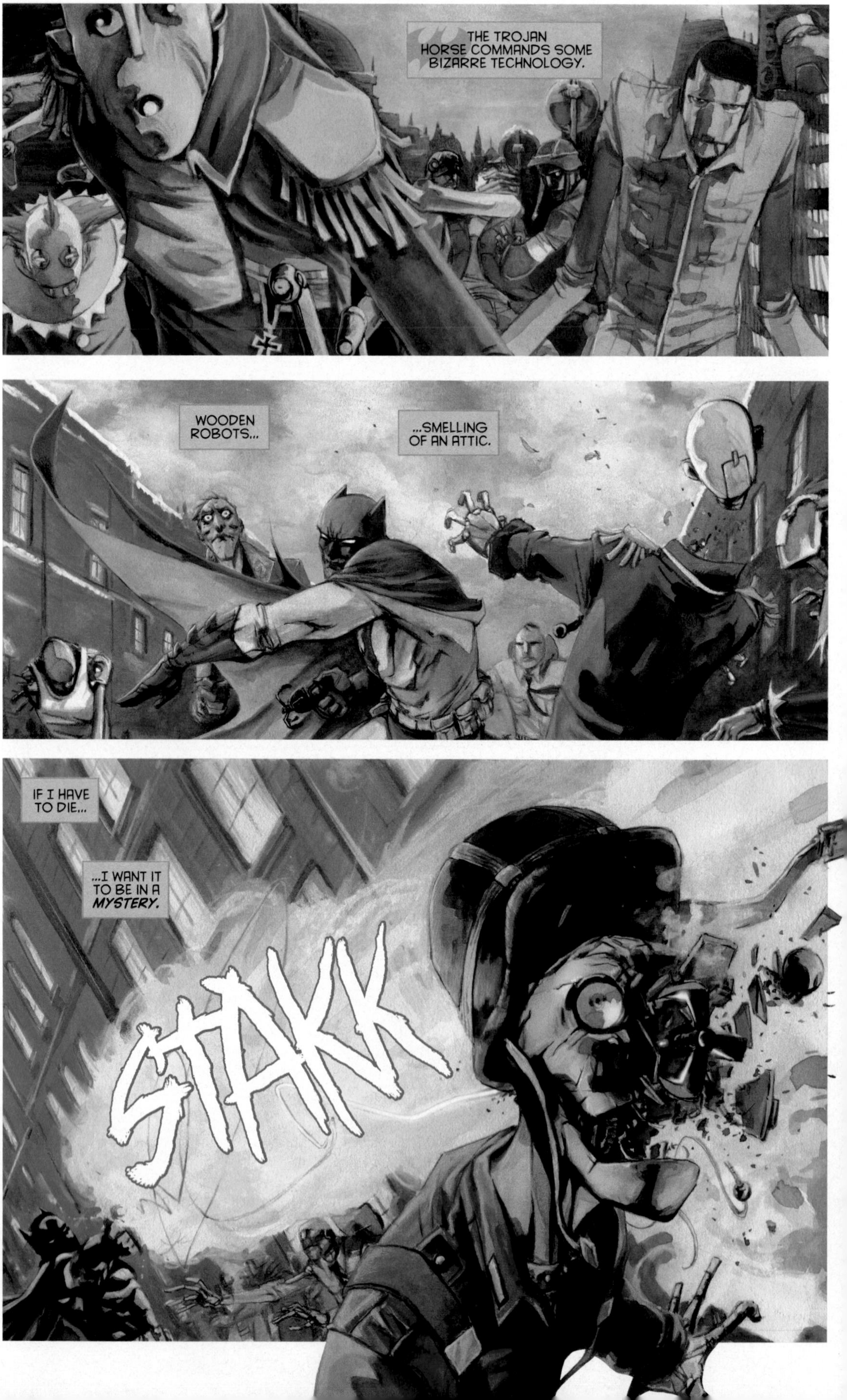
THE TROJAN HORSE COMMANDS SOME BIZARRE TECHNOLOGY.
WOODEN ROBOTS...
...SMELLING OF AN ATTIC.
IF I HAVE TO DIE...
...I WANT IT TO BE IN A *MYSTERY.*
STAKK

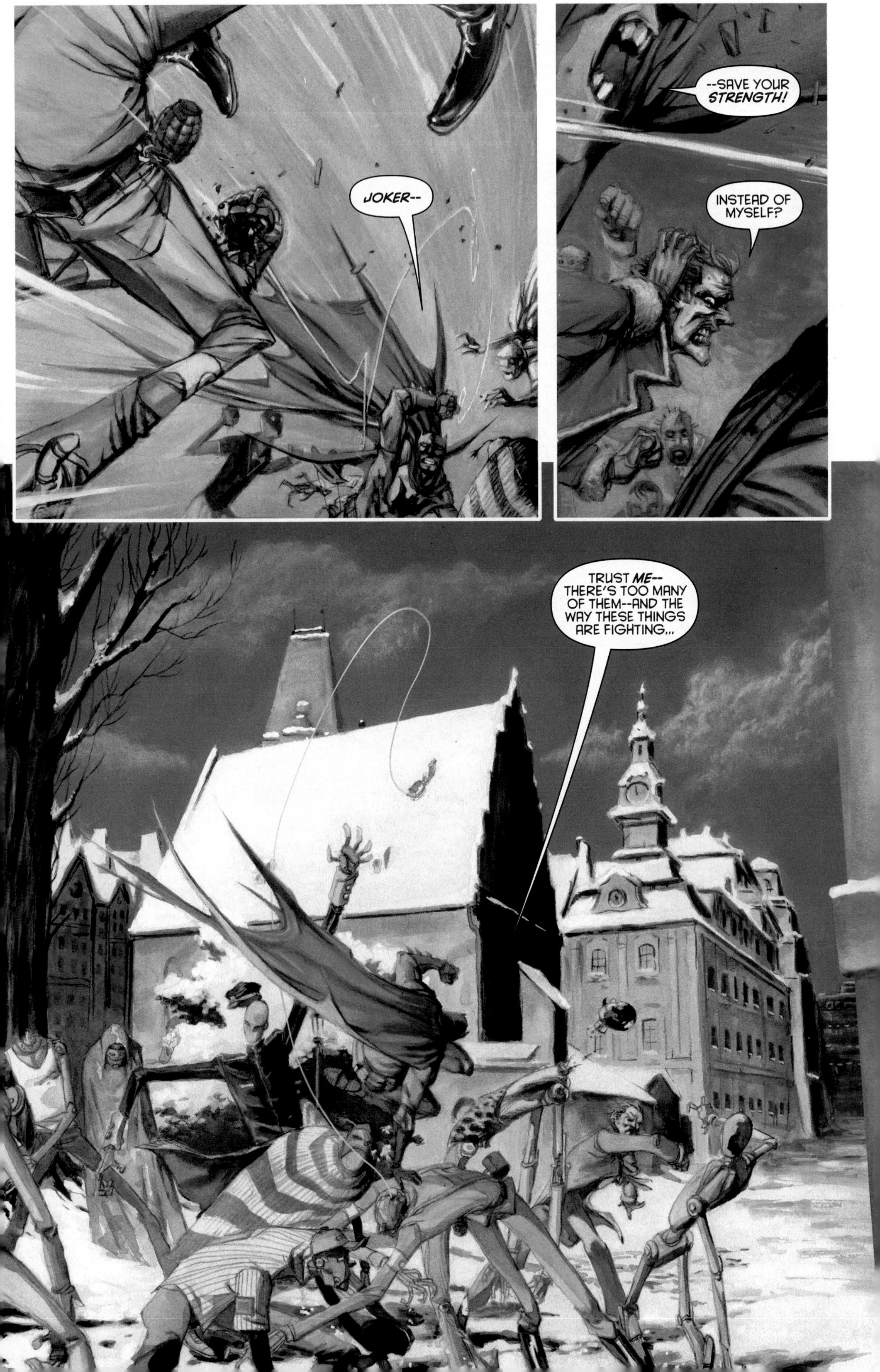
JOKER--
--SAVE YOUR STRENGTH!
INSTEAD OF MYSELF?
TRUST ME-- THERE'S TOO MANY OF THEM--AND THE WAY THESE THINGS ARE FIGHTING...

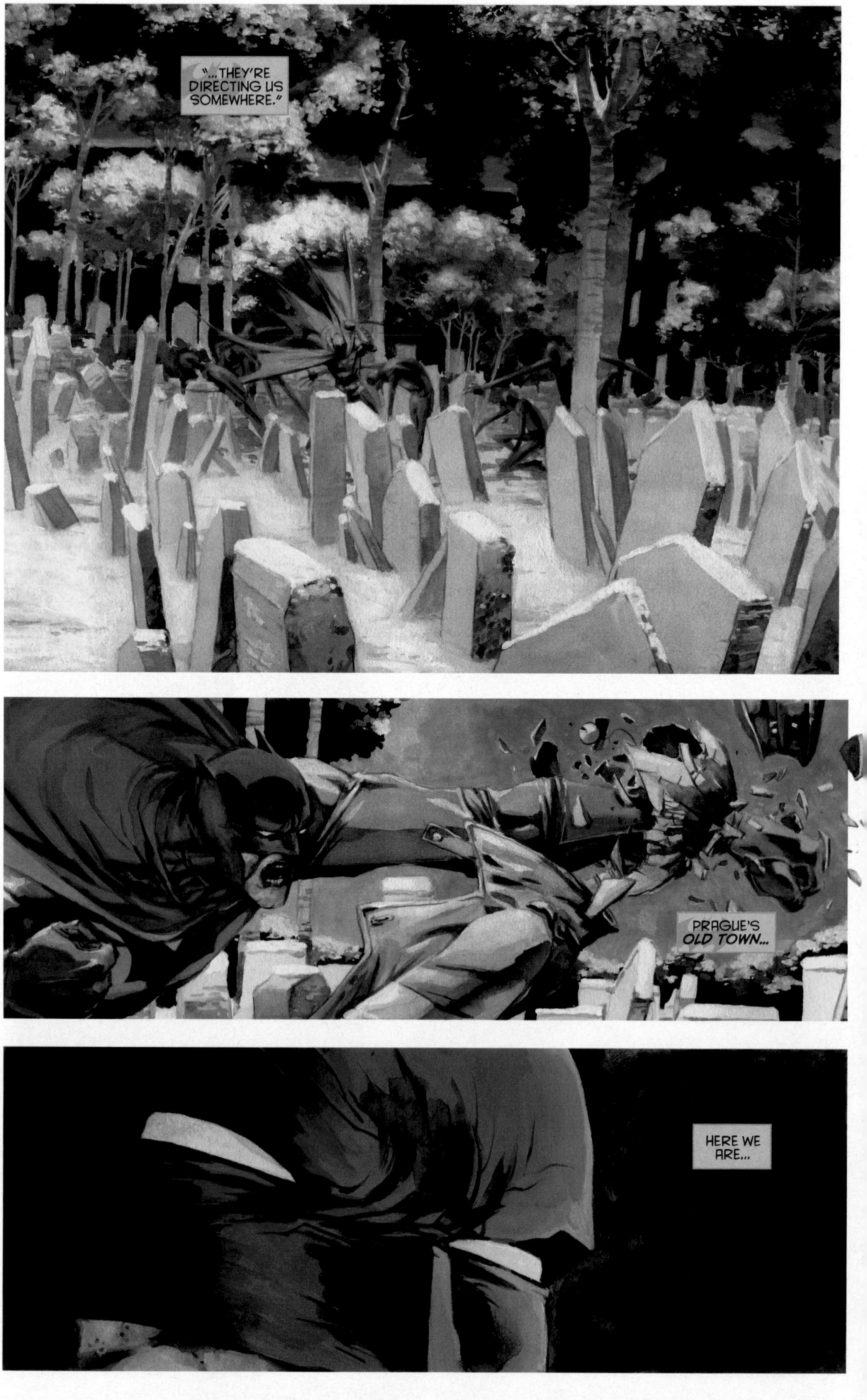
"...THEY'RE DIRECTING US SOMEWHERE."
PRAGUE'S *OLD TOWN*...
HERE WE ARE...

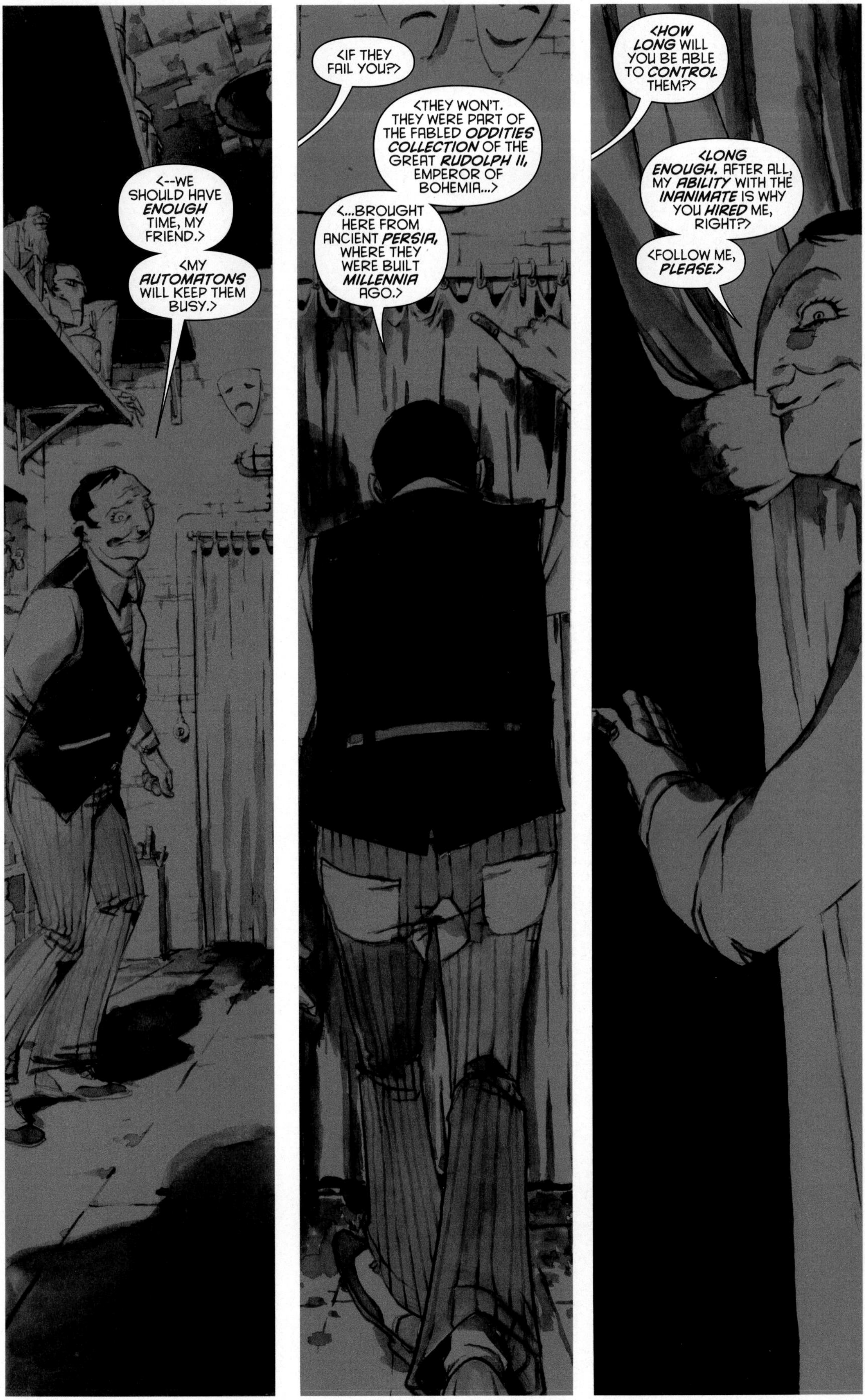
<--WE SHOULD HAVE ENOUGH TIME, MY FRIEND.>
<MY AUTOMATONS WILL KEEP THEM BUSY.>
<IF THEY FAIL YOU?>
<THEY WON'T. THEY WERE PART OF THE FABLED ODDITIES COLLECTION OF THE GREAT RUDOLPH II, EMPEROR OF BOHEMIA...>
<...BROUGHT HERE FROM ANCIENT PERSIA, WHERE THEY WERE BUILT MILLENNIA AGO.>
<HOW LONG WILL YOU BE ABLE TO CONTROL THEM?>
<LONG ENOUGH. AFTER ALL, MY ABILITY WITH THE INANIMATE IS WHY YOU HIRED ME, RIGHT?>
<FOLLOW ME, PLEASE.>

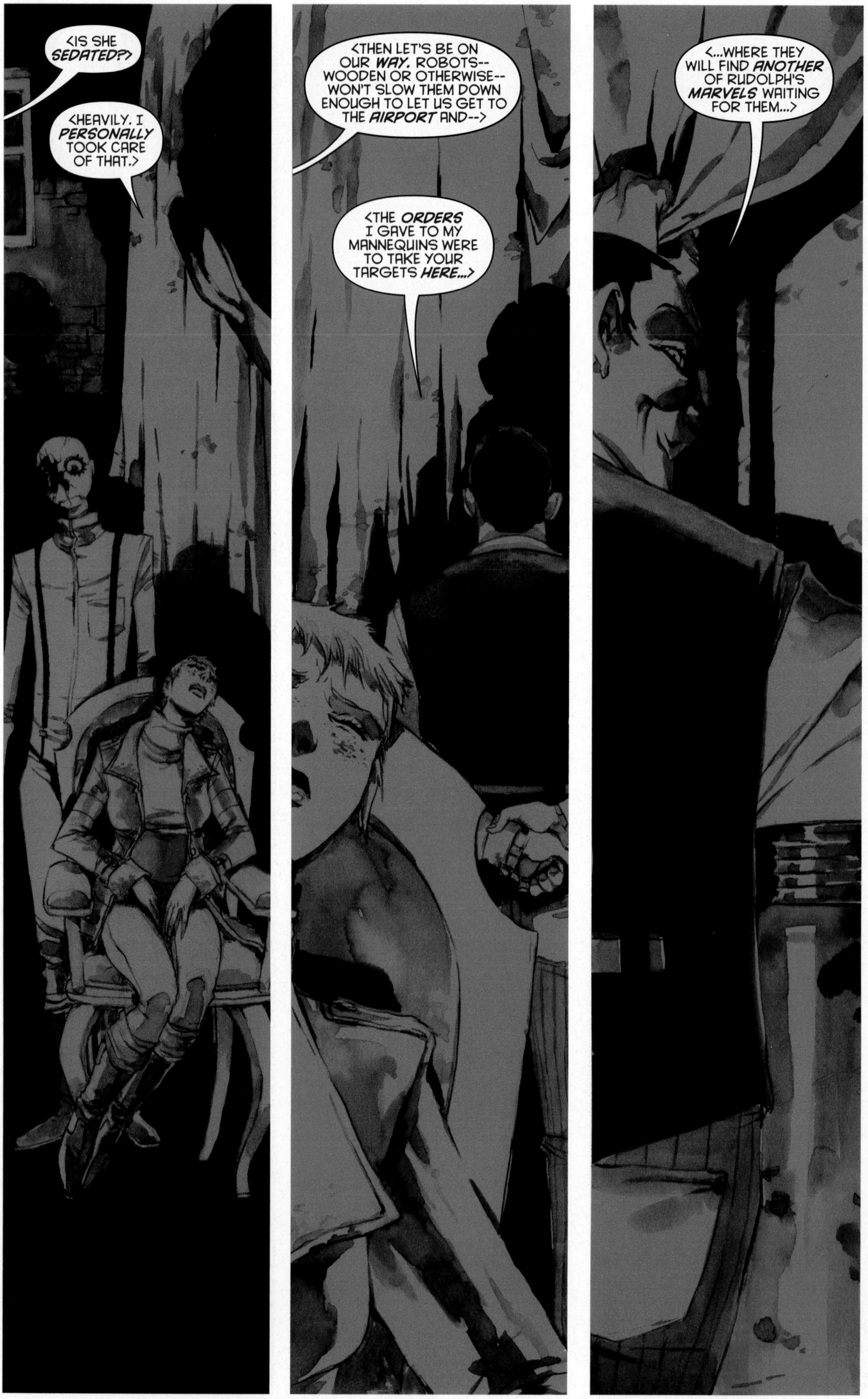
<IS SHE SEDATED?>
<HEAVILY. I PERSONALLY TOOK CARE OF THAT.>
<THEN LET'S BE ON OUR WAY. ROBOTS-- WOODEN OR OTHERWISE-- WON'T SLOW THEM DOWN ENOUGH TO LET US GET TO THE AIRPORT AND-->
<THE ORDERS I GAVE TO MY MANNEQUINS WERE TO TAKE YOUR TARGETS HERE...>
<...WHERE THEY WILL FIND ANOTHER OF RUDOLPH'S MARVELS WAITING FOR THEM...>

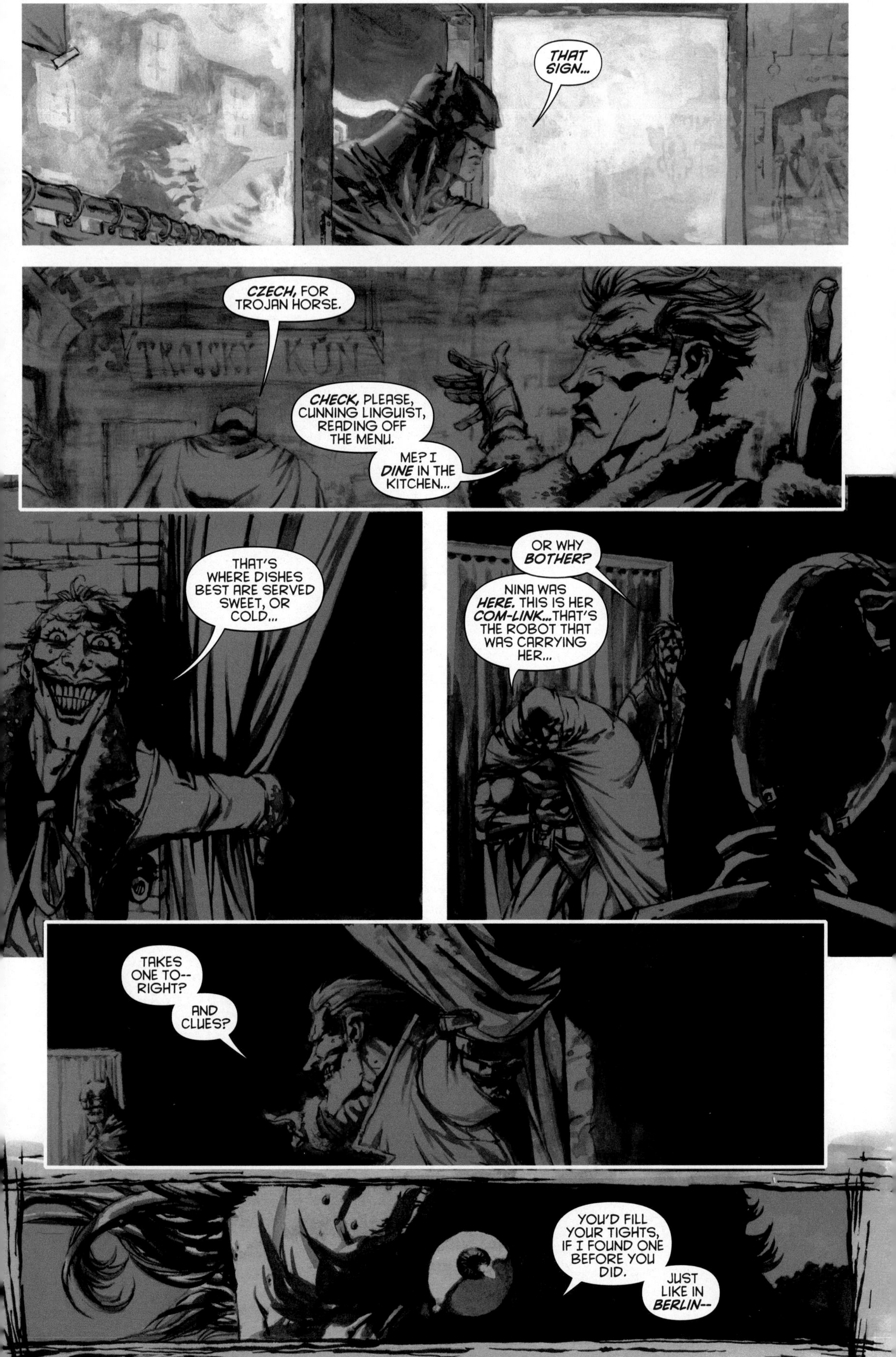
THAT SIGN...
CZECH, FOR TROJAN HORSE.
TROJSKÝ KŮŇ
CHECK, PLEASE, CUNNING LINGUIST, READING OFF THE MENU.
ME? I DINE IN THE KITCHEN...
THAT'S WHERE DISHES BEST ARE SERVED SWEET, OR COLD...
OR WHY BOTHER?
NINA WAS HERE. THIS IS HER COM-LINK...THAT'S THE ROBOT THAT WAS CARRYING HER...
TAKES ONE TO--RIGHT?
AND CLUES?
YOU'D FILL YOUR TIGHTS, IF I FOUND ONE BEFORE YOU DID.
JUST LIKE IN BERLIN--

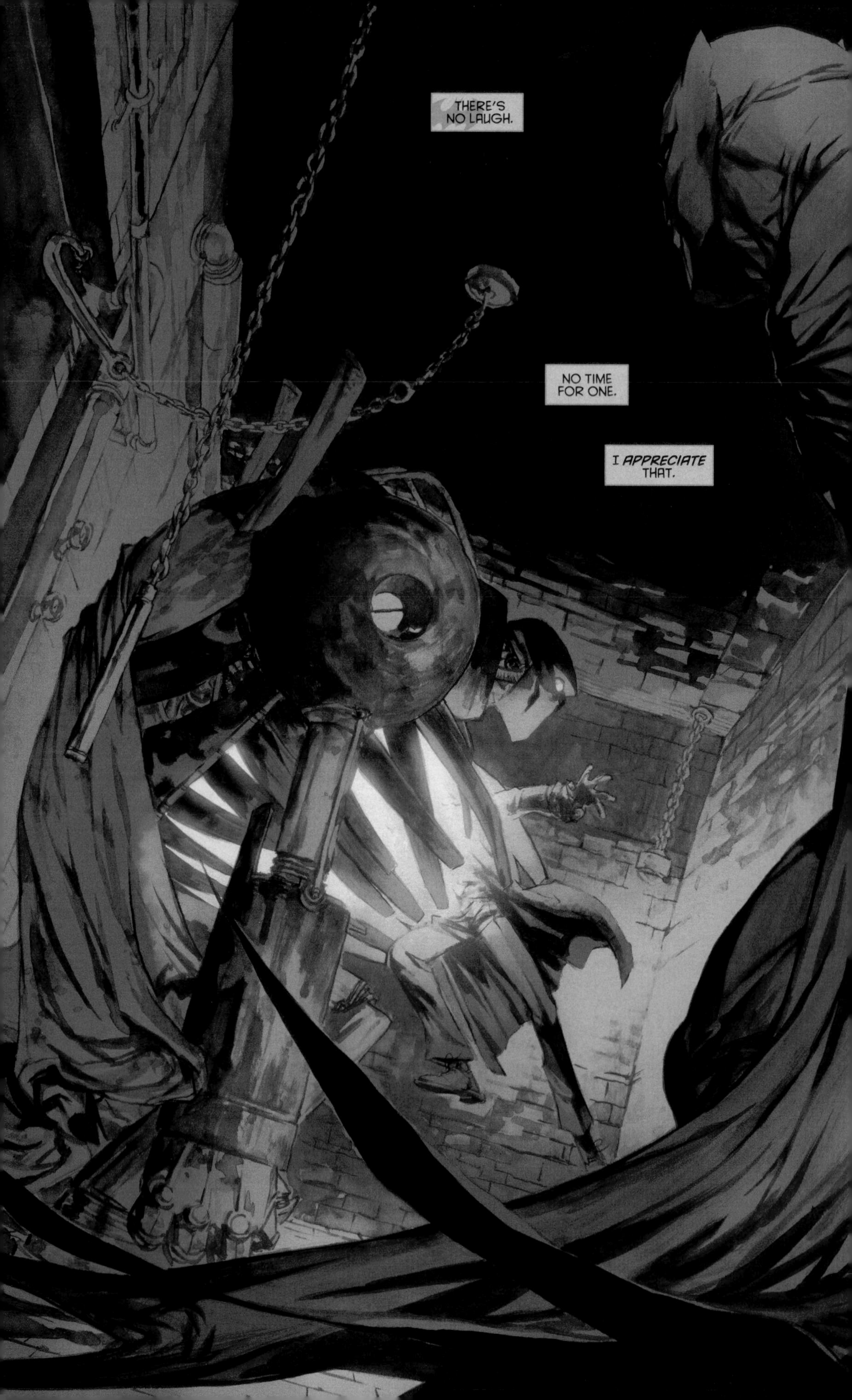
THERE'S NO LAUGH.
NO TIME FOR ONE.
I *APPRECIATE* THAT.

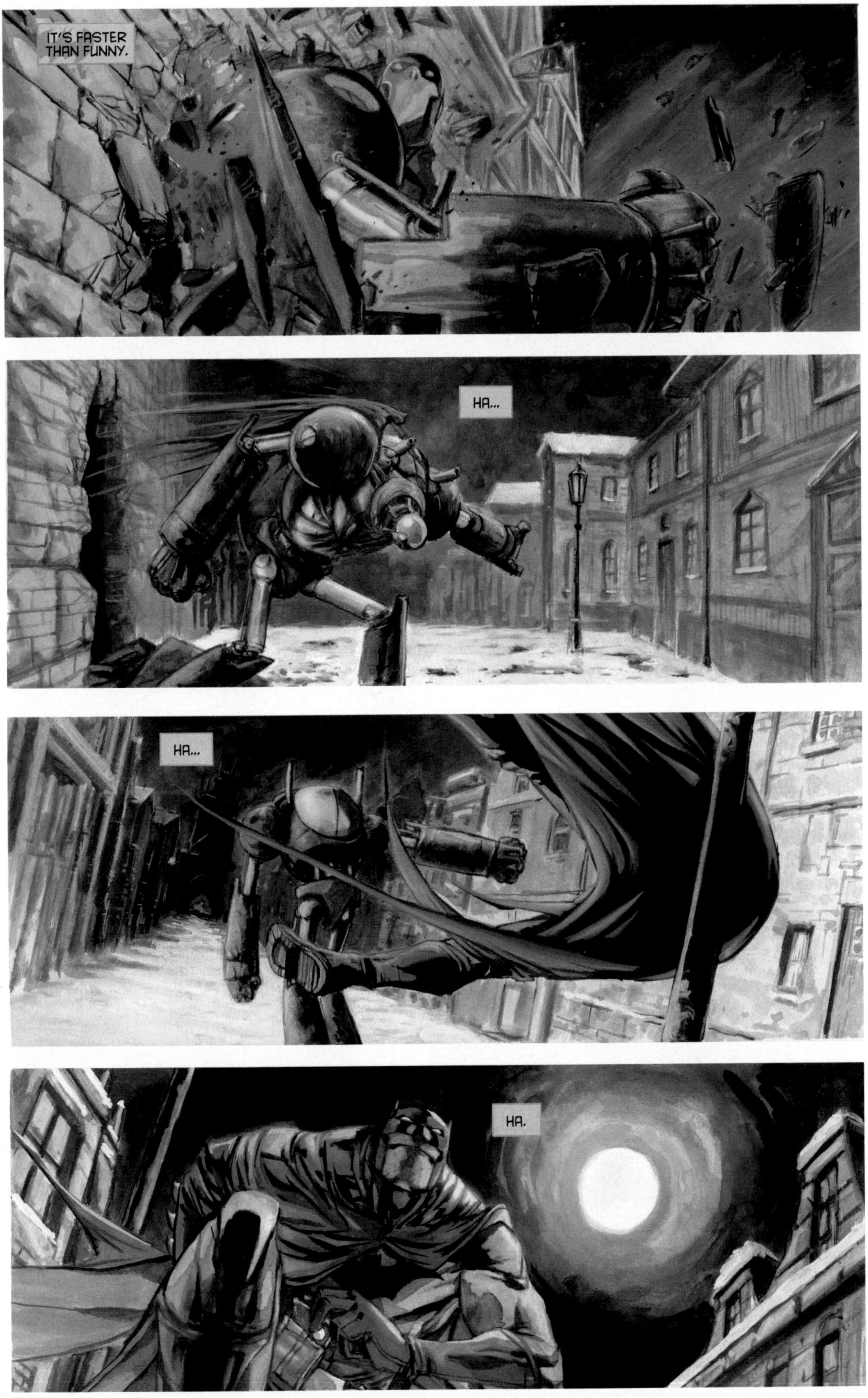
IT'S FASTER THAN FUNNY.
HA...
HA...
HA.

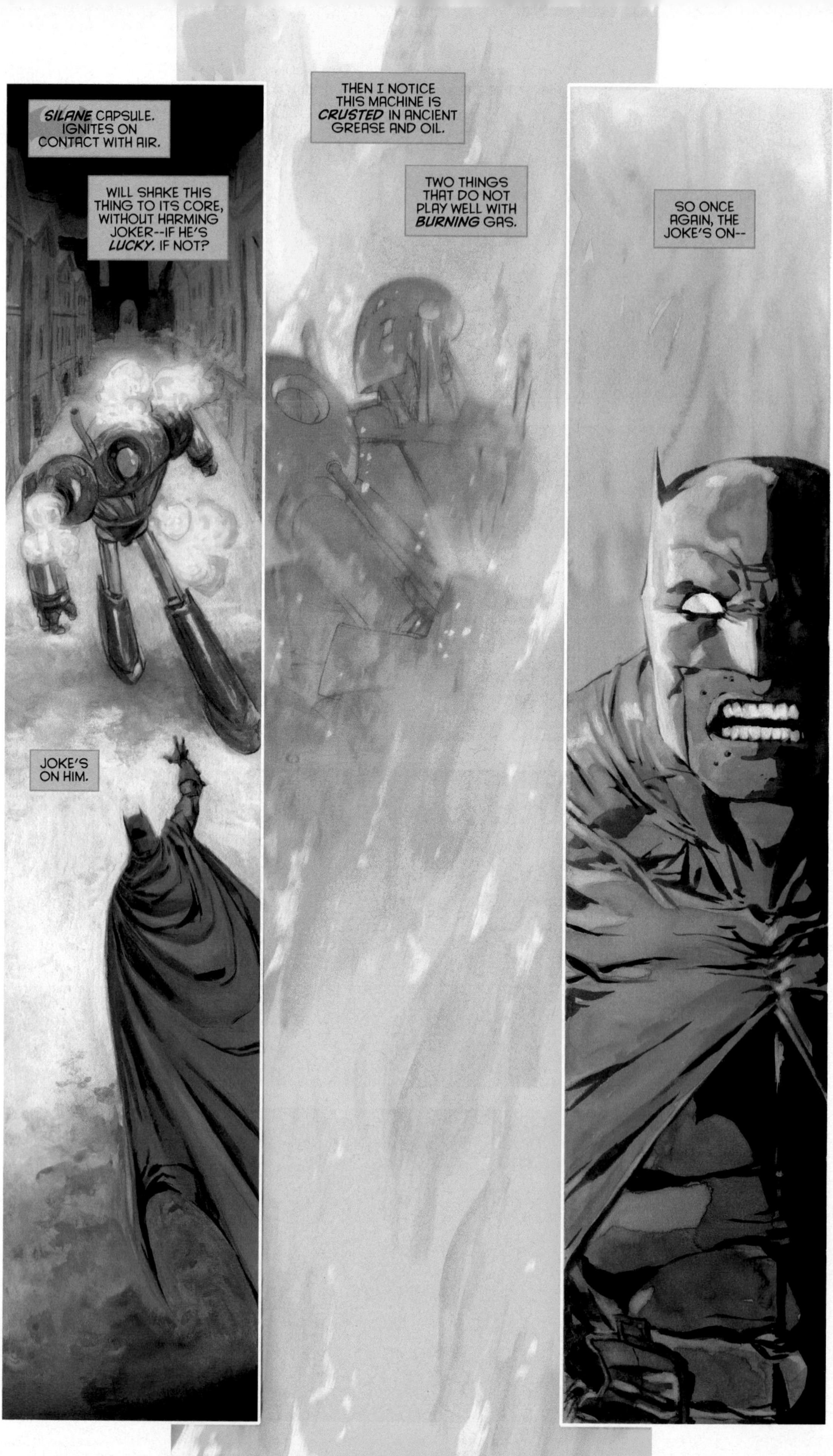
SILANE CAPSULE. IGNITES ON CONTACT WITH AIR.
WILL SHAKE THIS THING TO ITS CORE, WITHOUT HARMING JOKER--IF HE'S LUCKY. IF NOT?
JOKE'S ON HIM.
THEN I NOTICE THIS MACHINE IS CRUSTED IN ANCIENT GREASE AND OIL.
TWO THINGS THAT DO NOT PLAY WELL WITH BURNING GAS.
SO ONCE AGAIN, THE JOKE'S ON--

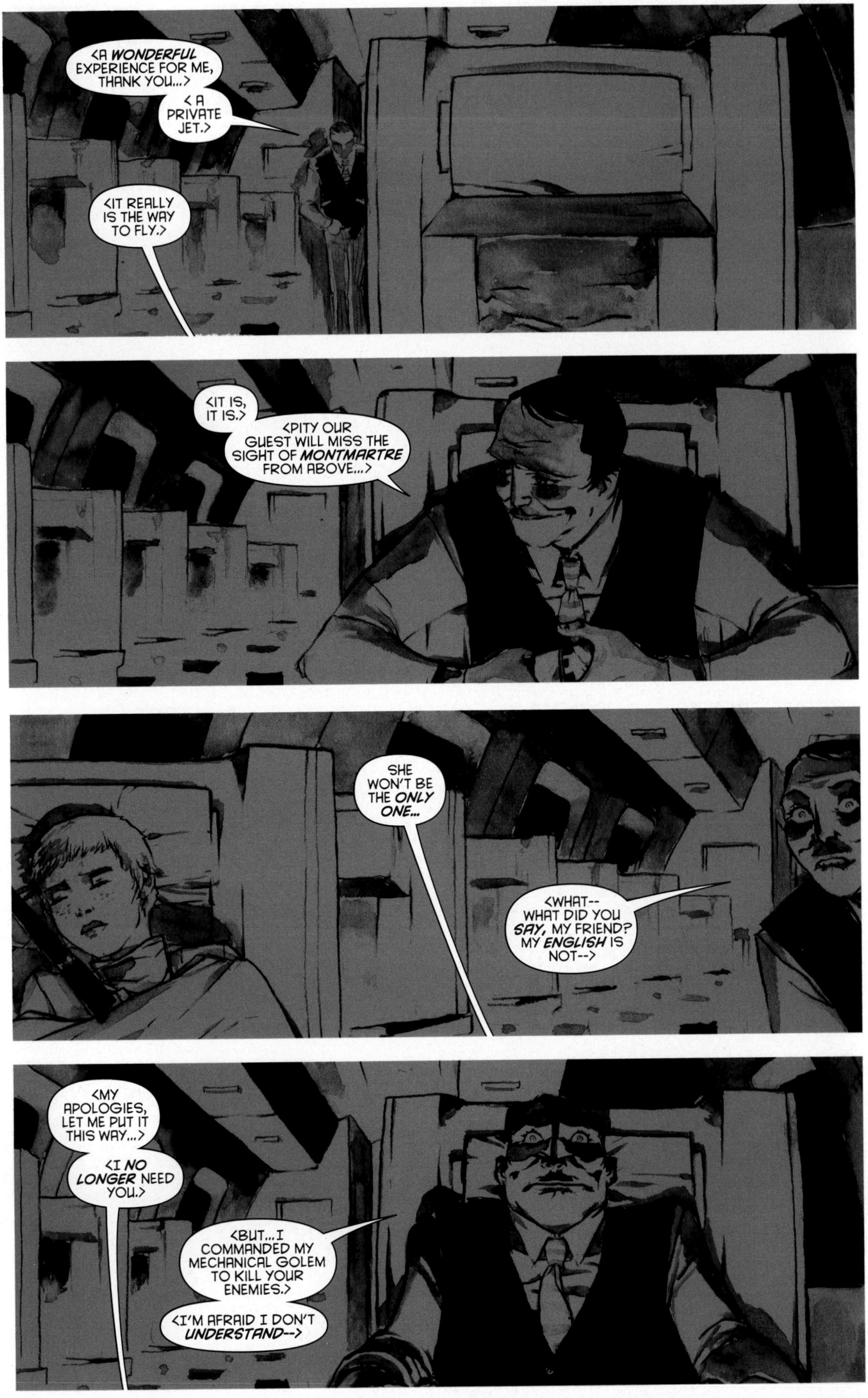
<A WONDERFUL EXPERIENCE FOR ME, THANK YOU...>
<A PRIVATE JET.>
<IT REALLY IS THE WAY TO FLY.>
<IT IS, IT IS.>
<PITY OUR GUEST WILL MISS THE SIGHT OF MONTMARTRE FROM ABOVE...>
SHE WON'T BE THE ONLY ONE...
<WHAT-- WHAT DID YOU SAY, MY FRIEND? MY ENGLISH IS NOT-->
<MY APOLOGIES, LET ME PUT IT THIS WAY...>
<I NO LONGER NEED YOU.>
<BUT...I COMMANDED MY MECHANICAL GOLEM TO KILL YOUR ENEMIES.>
<I'M AFRAID I DON'T UNDERSTAND-->

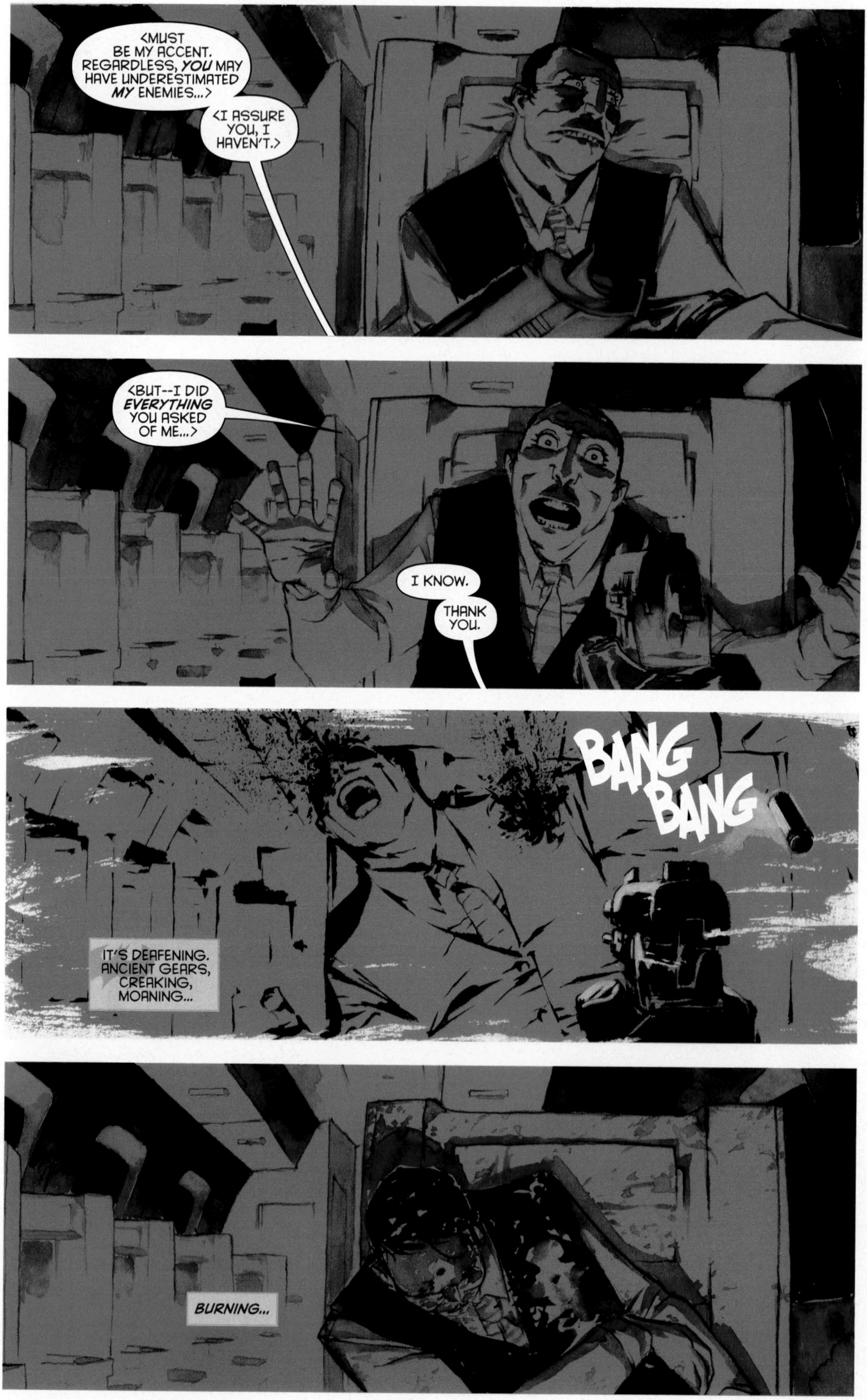

<MUST BE MY ACCENT. REGARDLESS, *YOU* MAY HAVE UNDERESTIMATED *MY* ENEMIES...>
<I ASSURE YOU, I HAVEN'T.>
<BUT--I DID *EVERYTHING* YOU ASKED OF ME...>
I KNOW.
THANK YOU.
BANG BANG
IT'S DEAFENING. ANCIENT GEARS, CREAKING, MOANING...
BURNING...

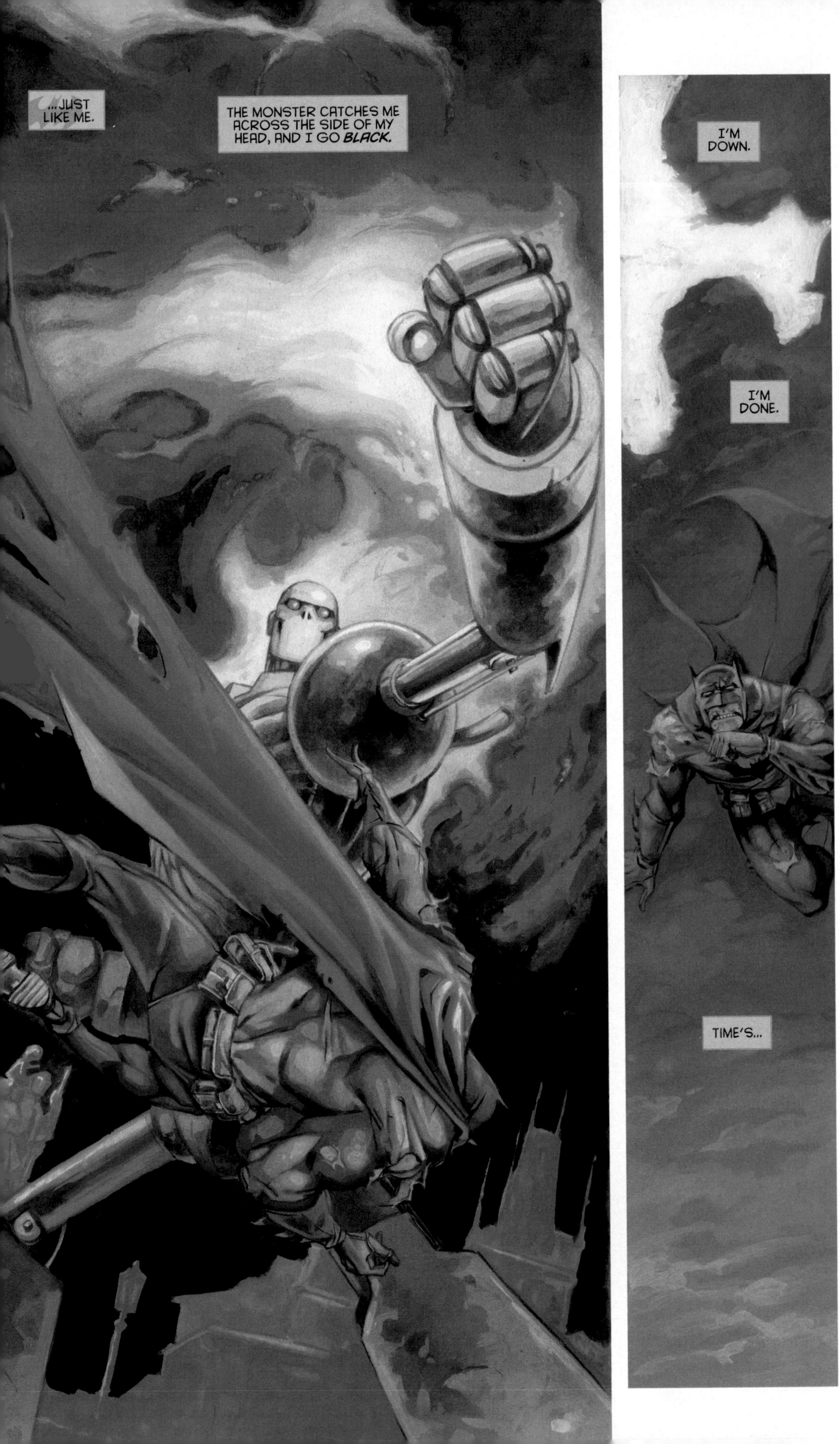
...JUST LIKE ME.
THE MONSTER CATCHES ME ACROSS THE SIDE OF MY HEAD, AND I GO *BLACK.*
I'M DOWN.
I'M DONE.
TIME'S...

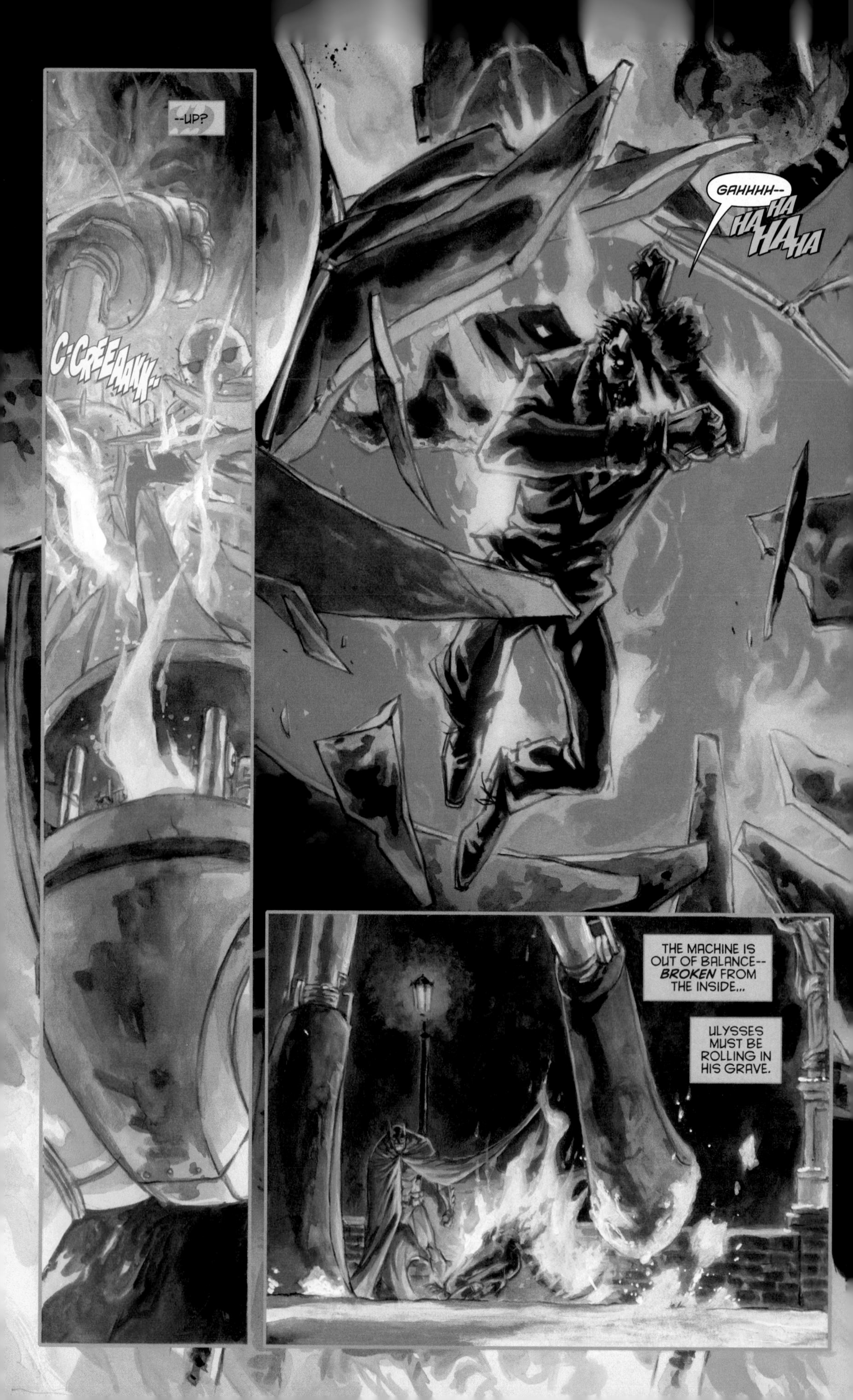
--UP?
C-CREEAAKK--
GAHHHH--
HA HA HA HA
THE MACHINE IS OUT OF BALANCE-- BROKEN FROM THE INSIDE...
ULYSSES MUST BE ROLLING IN HIS GRAVE.

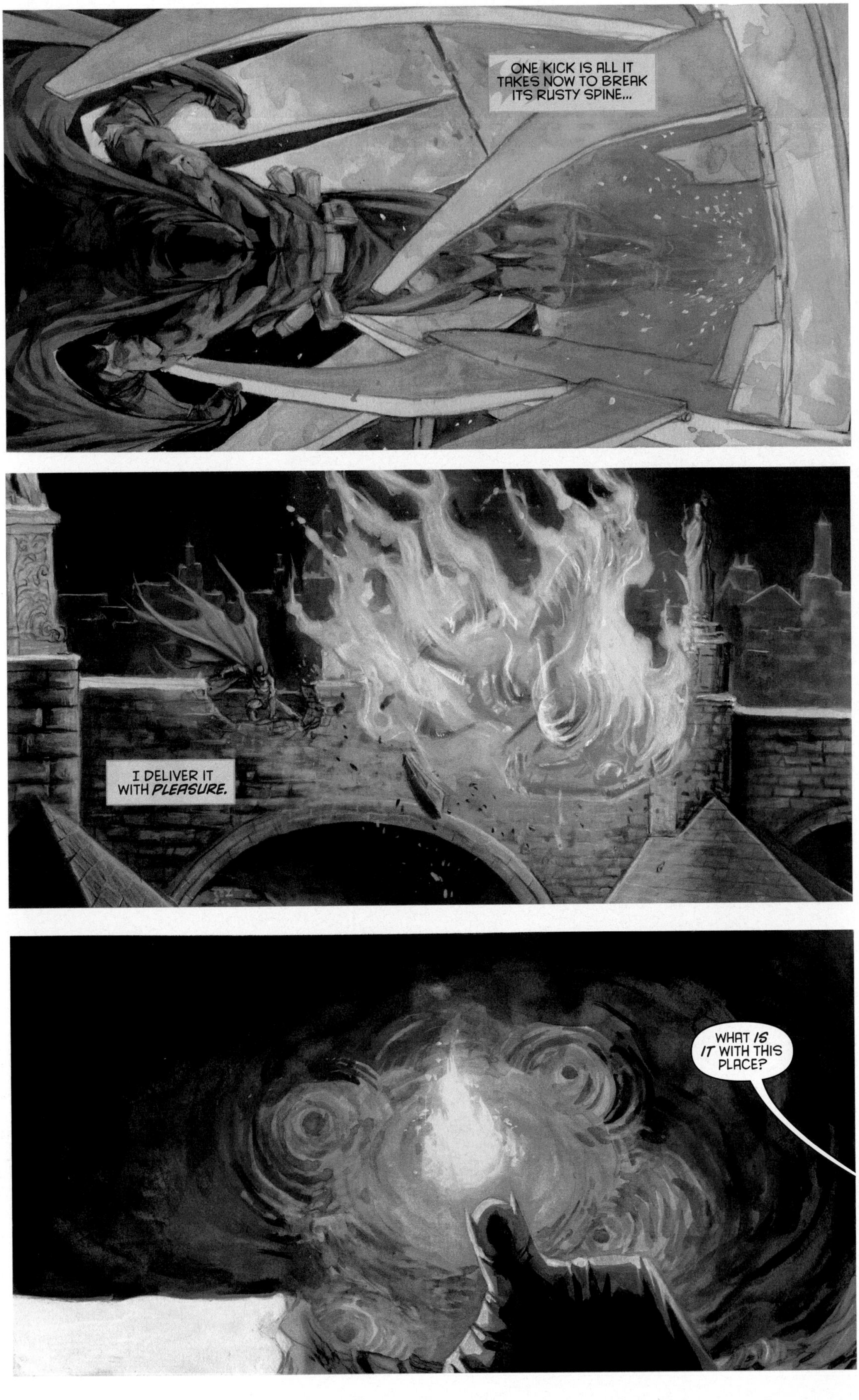
ONE KICK IS ALL IT TAKES NOW TO BREAK ITS RUSTY SPINE...
I DELIVER IT WITH *PLEASURE.*
WHAT *IS IT* WITH THIS PLACE?

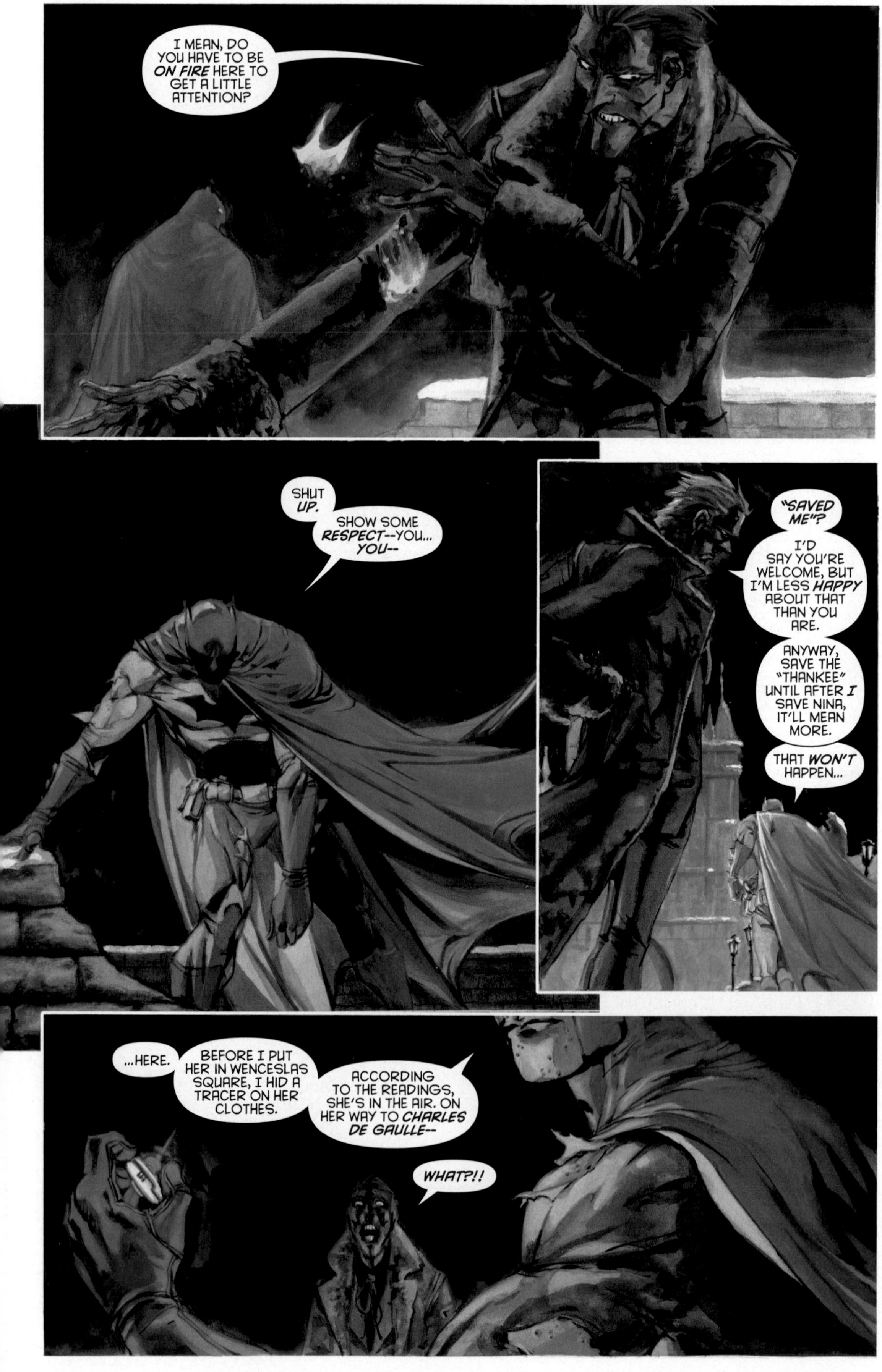

I MEAN, DO YOU HAVE TO BE ON FIRE HERE TO GET A LITTLE ATTENTION?
SHUT UP.
SHOW SOME RESPECT--YOU... YOU--
"SAVED ME"?
I'D SAY YOU'RE WELCOME, BUT I'M LESS HAPPY ABOUT THAT THAN YOU ARE.
ANYWAY, SAVE THE "THANKEE" UNTIL AFTER I SAVE NINA, IT'LL MEAN MORE.
THAT WON'T HAPPEN...
...HERE.
BEFORE I PUT HER IN WENCESLAS SQUARE, I HID A TRACER ON HER CLOTHES.
ACCORDING TO THE READINGS, SHE'S IN THE AIR. ON HER WAY TO CHARLES DE GAULLE--
WHAT?!!

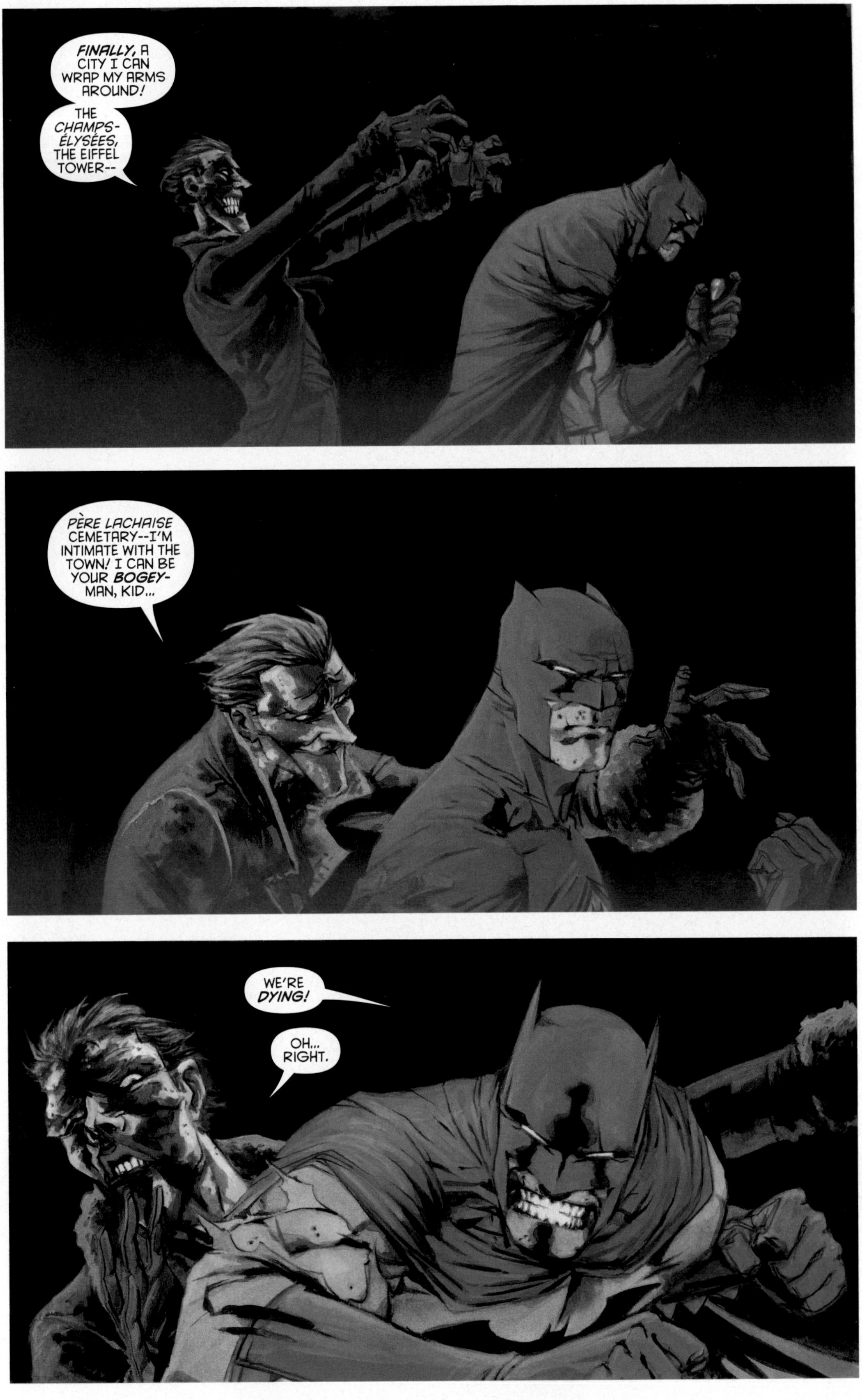
FINALLY, A CITY I CAN WRAP MY ARMS AROUND!
THE CHAMPS-ÉLYSÉES, THE EIFFEL TOWER--
PÈRE LACHAISE CEMETARY--I'M INTIMATE WITH THE TOWN! I CAN BE YOUR BOGEY-MAN, KID...
WE'RE DYING!
OH... RIGHT.

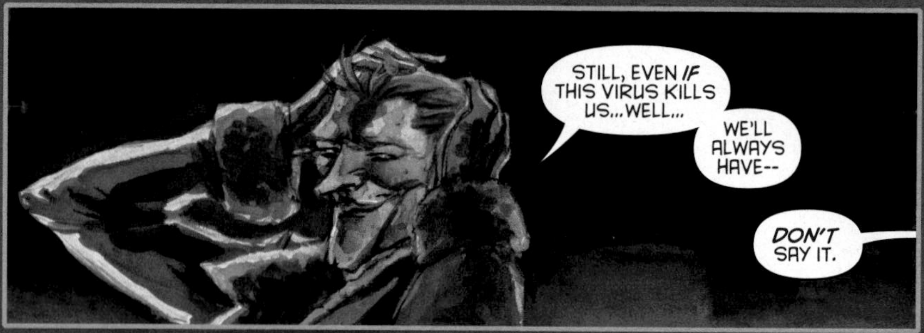
STILL, EVEN *IF* THIS VIRUS KILLS US...WELL...
WE'LL ALWAYS HAVE--
DON'T SAY IT.

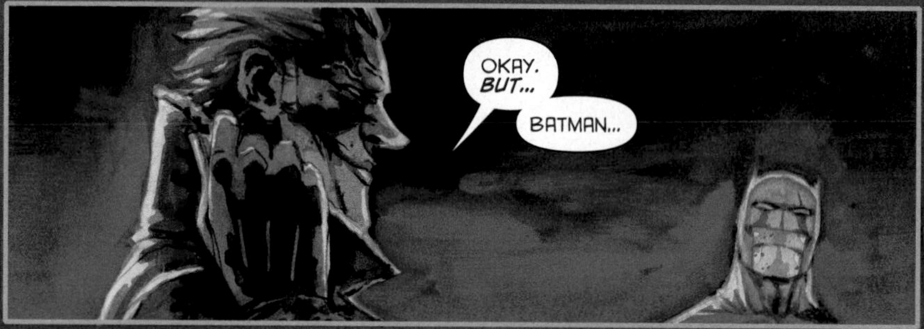
OKAY. *BUT...*
BATMAN...

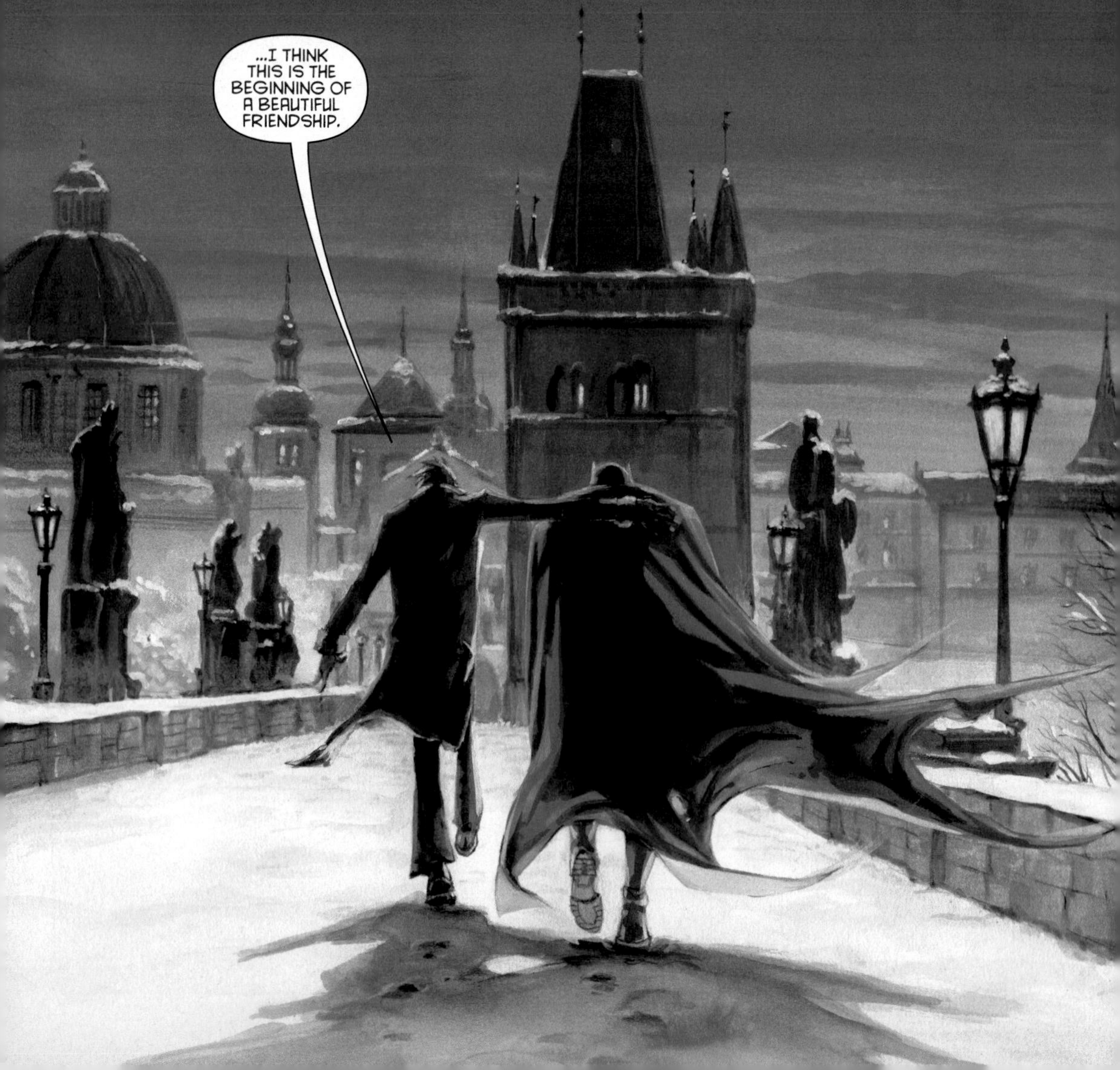
...I THINK THIS IS THE BEGINNING OF A BEAUTIFUL FRIENDSHIP.

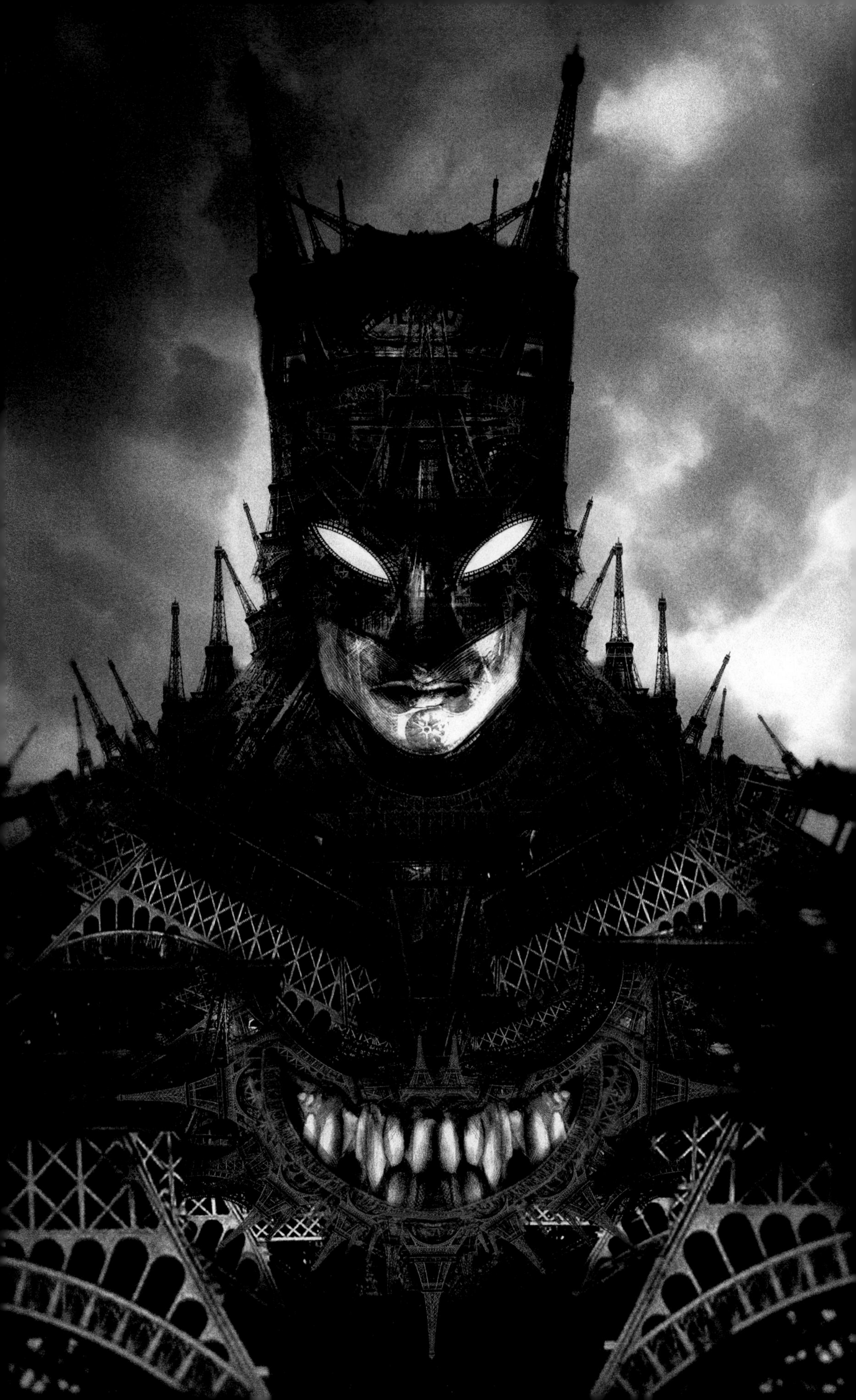

CHAPTER 3 PARIS

Story by Matteo Casali and Brian Azzarello
Layouts by Giuseppe Camuncoli
Art by Diego Latorre
Letters by Pat Brosseau
Cover by Diego Latorre

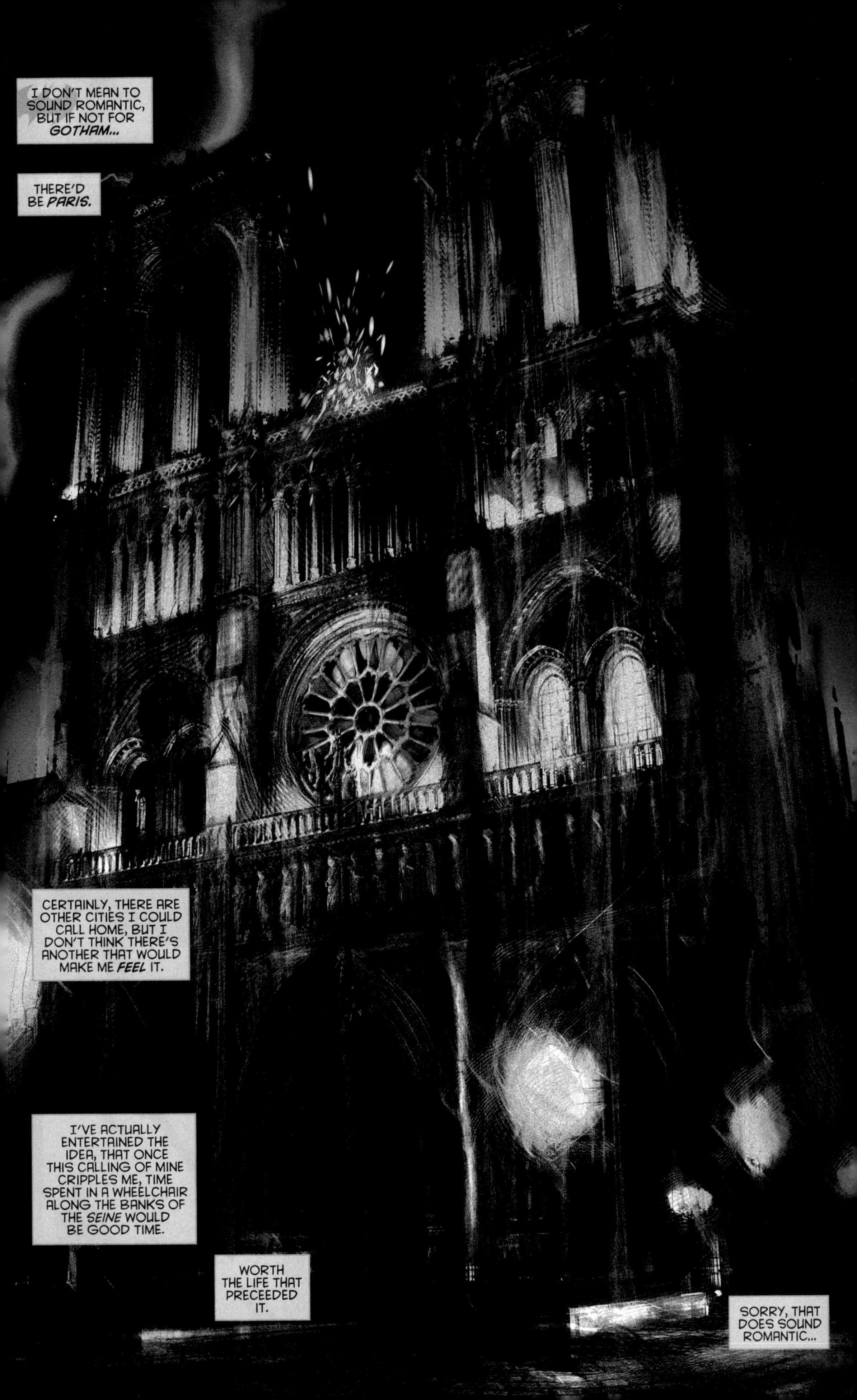
I DON'T MEAN TO SOUND ROMANTIC, BUT IF NOT FOR *GOTHAM*...
THERE'D BE *PARIS.*
CERTAINLY, THERE ARE OTHER CITIES I COULD CALL HOME, BUT I DON'T THINK THERE'S ANOTHER THAT WOULD MAKE ME *FEEL* IT.
I'VE ACTUALLY ENTERTAINED THE IDEA, THAT ONCE THIS CALLING OF MINE CRIPPLES ME, TIME SPENT IN A WHEELCHAIR ALONG THE BANKS OF THE *SEINE* WOULD BE GOOD TIME.
WORTH THE LIFE THAT PRECEEDED IT.
SORRY, THAT DOES SOUND ROMANTIC...

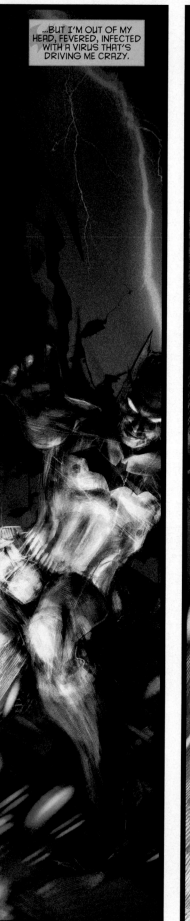

...BUT I'M OUT OF MY HEAD, FEVERED, INFECTED WITH A VIRUS THAT'S DRIVING ME CRAZY.

WHAT IT'S DOING TO JOKER IS YOUR GUESS, NOT MINE. HE CAN'T GET *CRAZIER,* CAN HE?

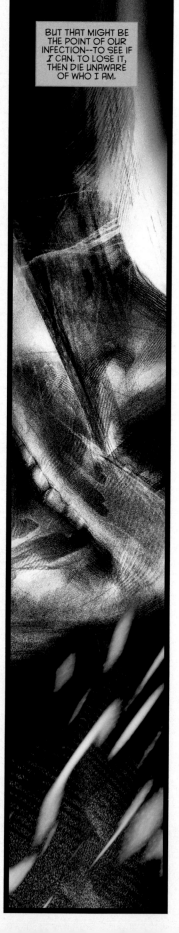

BUT THAT MIGHT BE THE POINT OF OUR INFECTION--TO SEE IF *I* CAN. TO LOSE IT, THEN DIE UNAWARE OF WHO I AM.

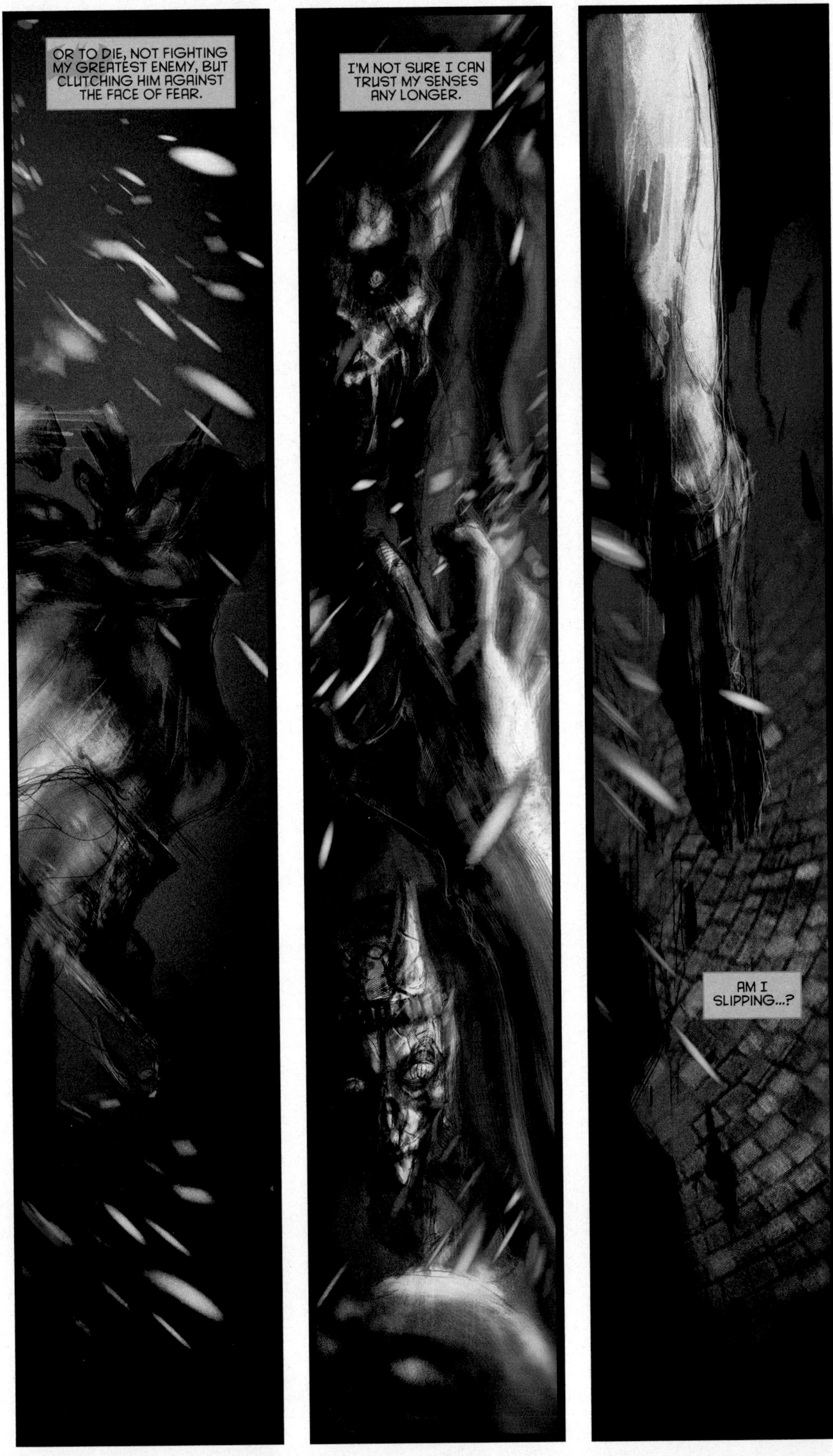
OR TO DIE, NOT FIGHTING MY GREATEST ENEMY, BUT CLUTCHING HIM AGAINST THE FACE OF FEAR.
I'M NOT SURE I CAN TRUST MY SENSES ANY LONGER.
AM I SLIPPING...?

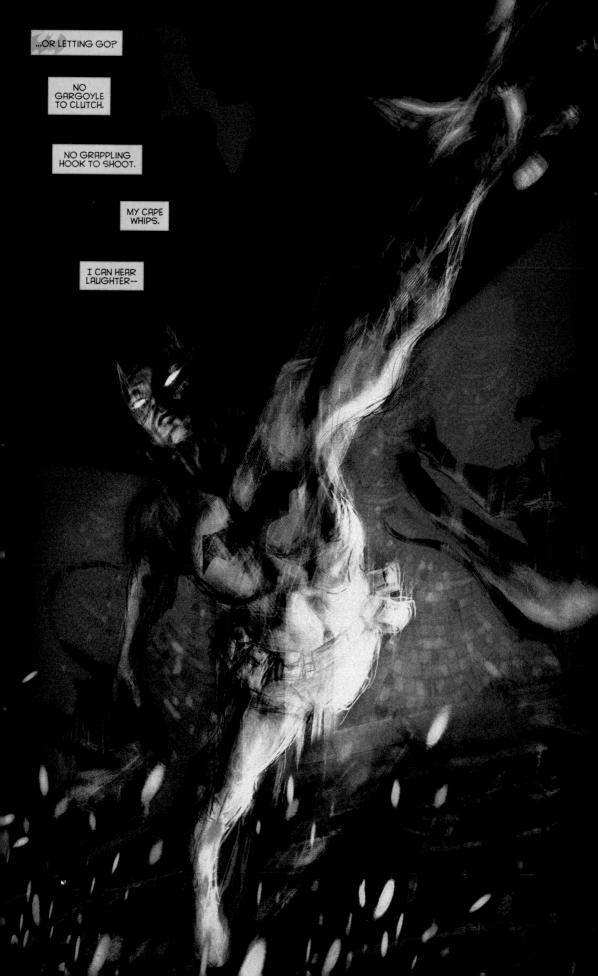

...OR LETTING GO?

NO GARGOYLE TO CLUTCH.

NO GRAPPLING HOOK TO SHOOT.

MY CAPE WHIPS.

I CAN HEAR LAUGHTER--

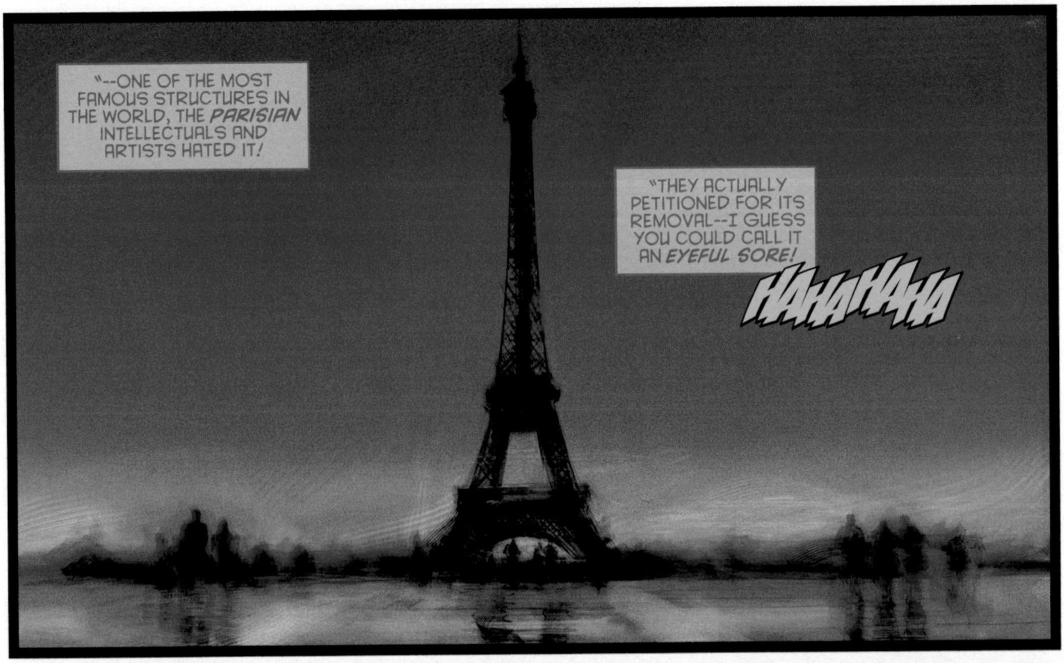
"--ONE OF THE MOST FAMOUS STRUCTURES IN THE WORLD, THE PARISIAN INTELLECTUALS AND ARTISTS HATED IT!
"THEY ACTUALLY PETITIONED FOR ITS REMOVAL--I GUESS YOU COULD CALL IT AN EYEFUL SORE!
HAHAHAHA

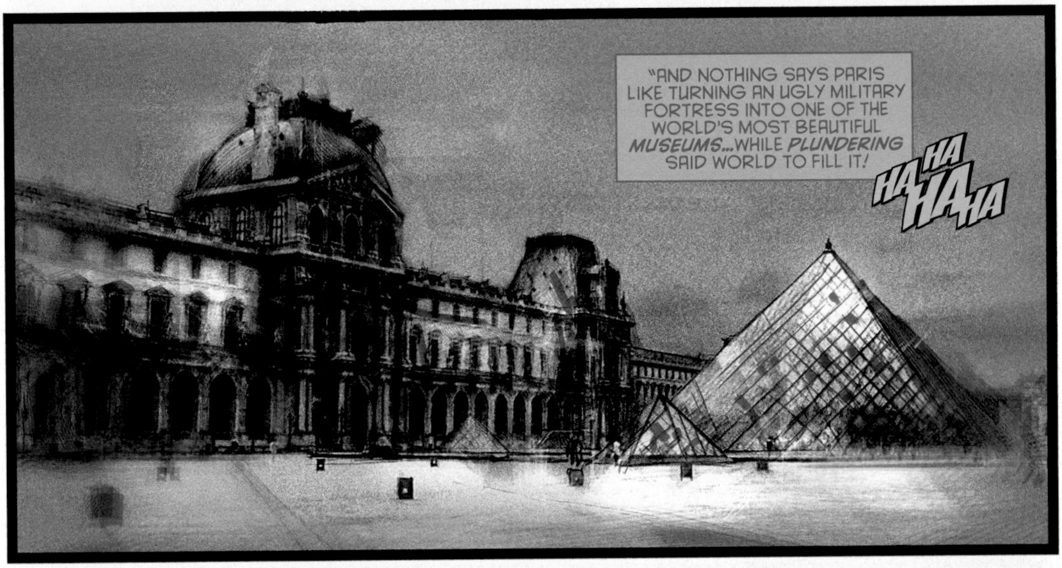
"AND NOTHING SAYS PARIS LIKE TURNING AN UGLY MILITARY FORTRESS INTO ONE OF THE WORLD'S MOST BEAUTIFUL MUSEUMS...WHILE PLUNDERING SAID WORLD TO FILL IT!
HA HA HA HA

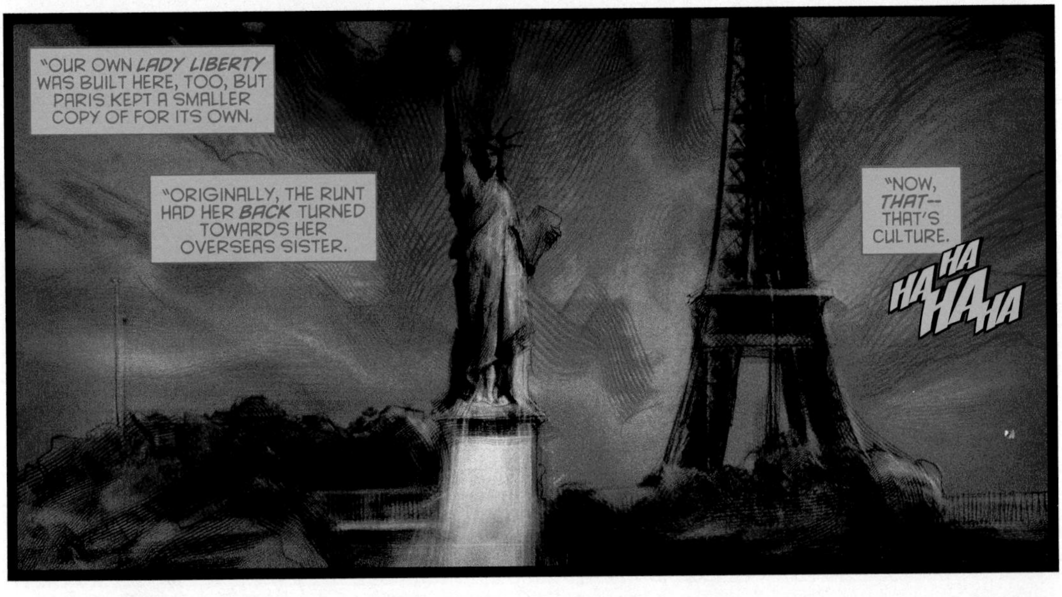
"OUR OWN LADY LIBERTY WAS BUILT HERE, TOO, BUT PARIS KEPT A SMALLER COPY OF FOR ITS OWN.
"ORIGINALLY, THE RUNT HAD HER BACK TURNED TOWARDS HER OVERSEAS SISTER.
"NOW, THAT--THAT'S CULTURE.
HA HA HA HA

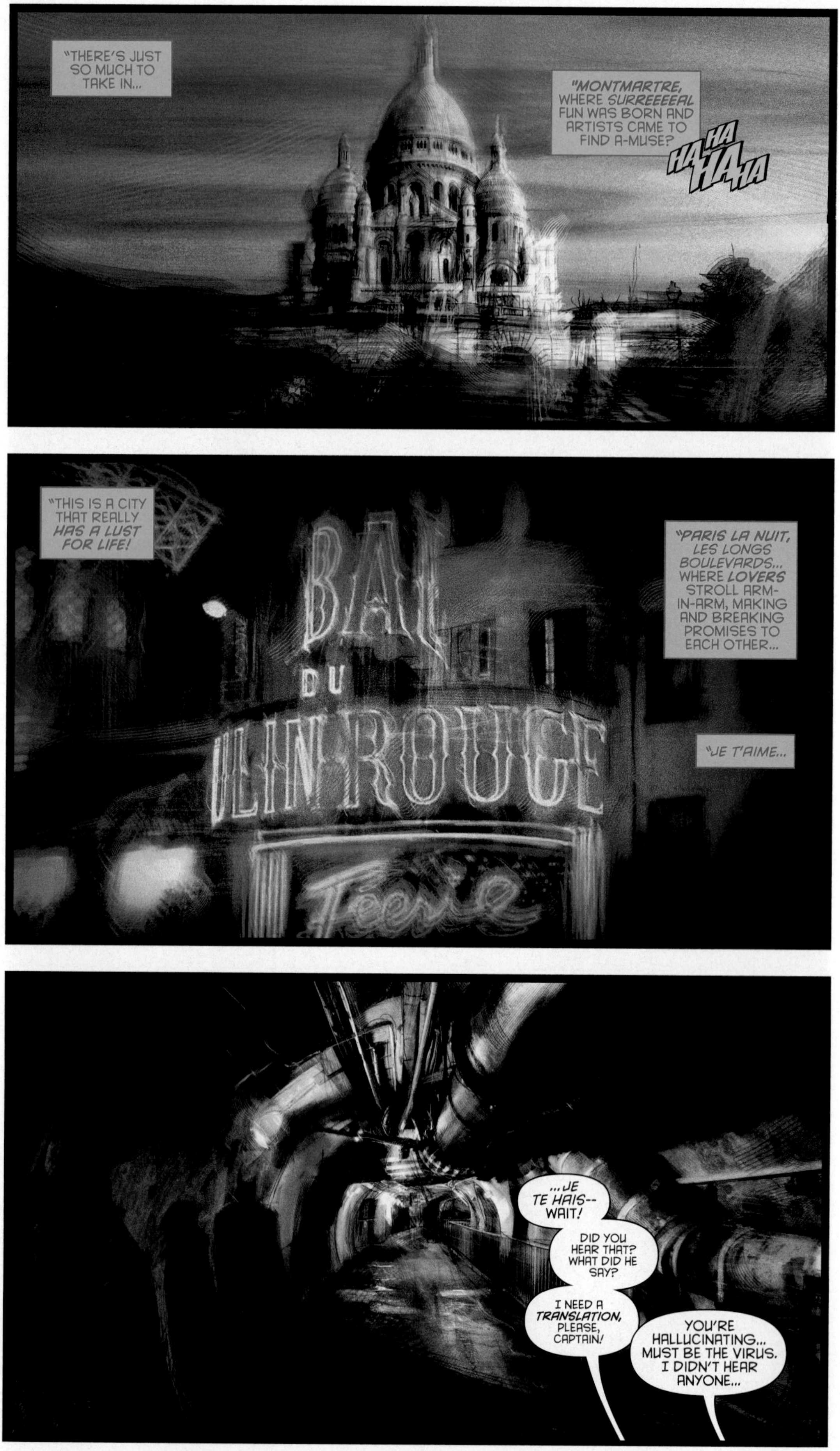
"THERE'S JUST SO MUCH TO TAKE IN...
"MONTMARTRE, WHERE SURREEEEAL FUN WAS BORN AND ARTISTS CAME TO FIND A-MUSE?
HA HA HA HA
"THIS IS A CITY THAT REALLY HAS A LUST FOR LIFE!
"PARIS LA NUIT, LES LONGS BOULEVARDS... WHERE LOVERS STROLL ARM-IN-ARM, MAKING AND BREAKING PROMISES TO EACH OTHER...
"JE T'AIME...
...JE TE HAIS-- WAIT!
DID YOU HEAR THAT? WHAT DID HE SAY?
I NEED A TRANSLATION, PLEASE, CAPTAIN!
YOU'RE HALLUCINATING... MUST BE THE VIRUS. I DIDN'T HEAR ANYONE...

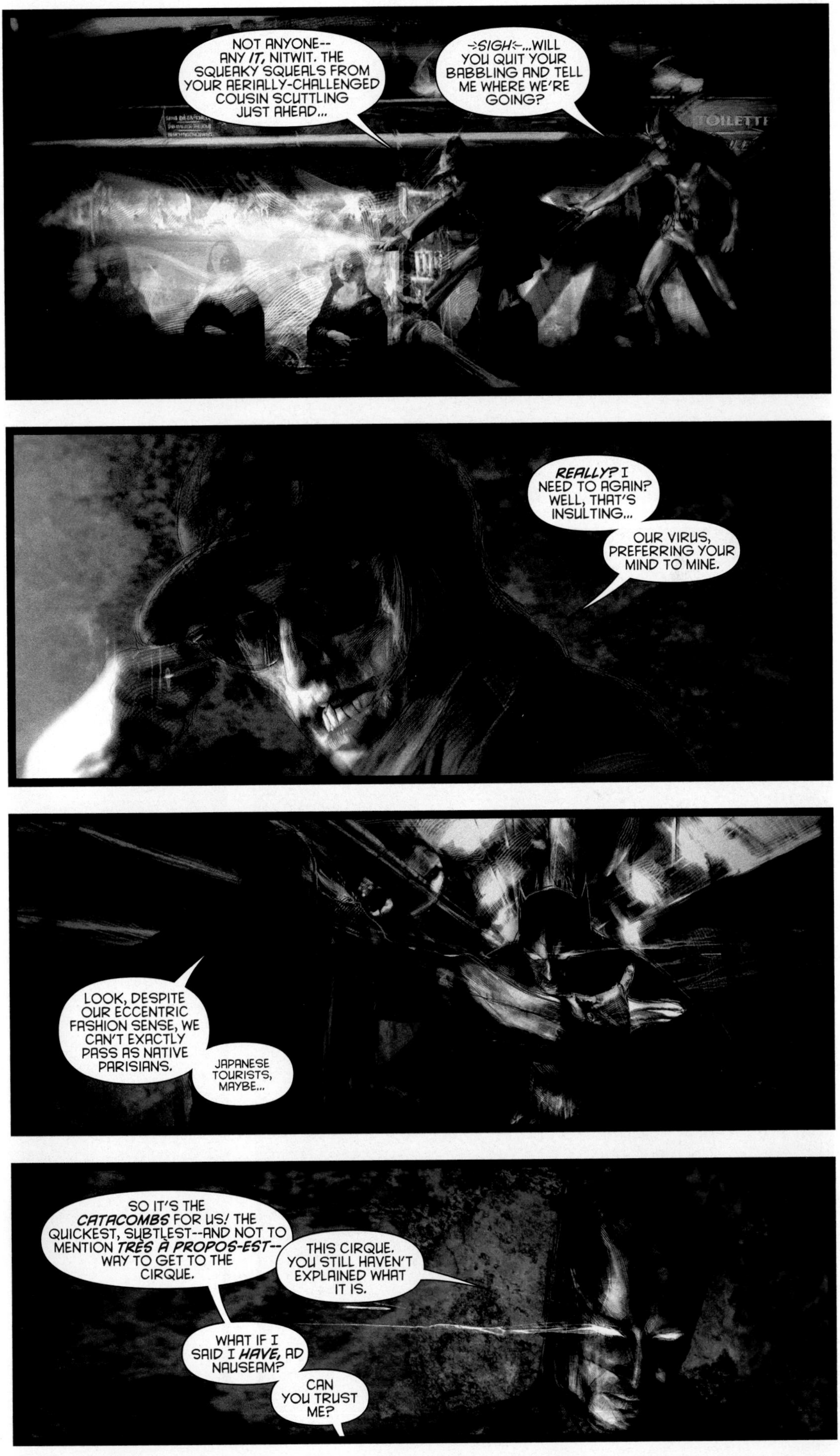
NOT ANYONE-- ANY *IT,* NITWIT. THE SQUEAKY SQUEALS FROM YOUR AERIALLY-CHALLENGED COUSIN SCUTTLING JUST AHEAD...
-SIGH-...WILL YOU QUIT YOUR BABBLING AND TELL ME WHERE WE'RE GOING?
REALLY? I NEED TO AGAIN? WELL, THAT'S INSULTING...
OUR VIRUS, PREFERRING YOUR MIND TO MINE.
LOOK, DESPITE OUR ECCENTRIC FASHION SENSE, WE CAN'T EXACTLY PASS AS NATIVE PARISIANS.
JAPANESE TOURISTS, MAYBE...
SO IT'S THE *CATACOMBS* FOR US! THE QUICKEST, SUBTLEST--AND NOT TO MENTION *TRÈS À PROPOS-EST*-- WAY TO GET TO THE CIRQUE.
THIS CIRQUE. YOU STILL HAVEN'T EXPLAINED WHAT IT IS.
WHAT IF I SAID I *HAVE,* AD NAUSEAM?
CAN YOU TRUST ME?

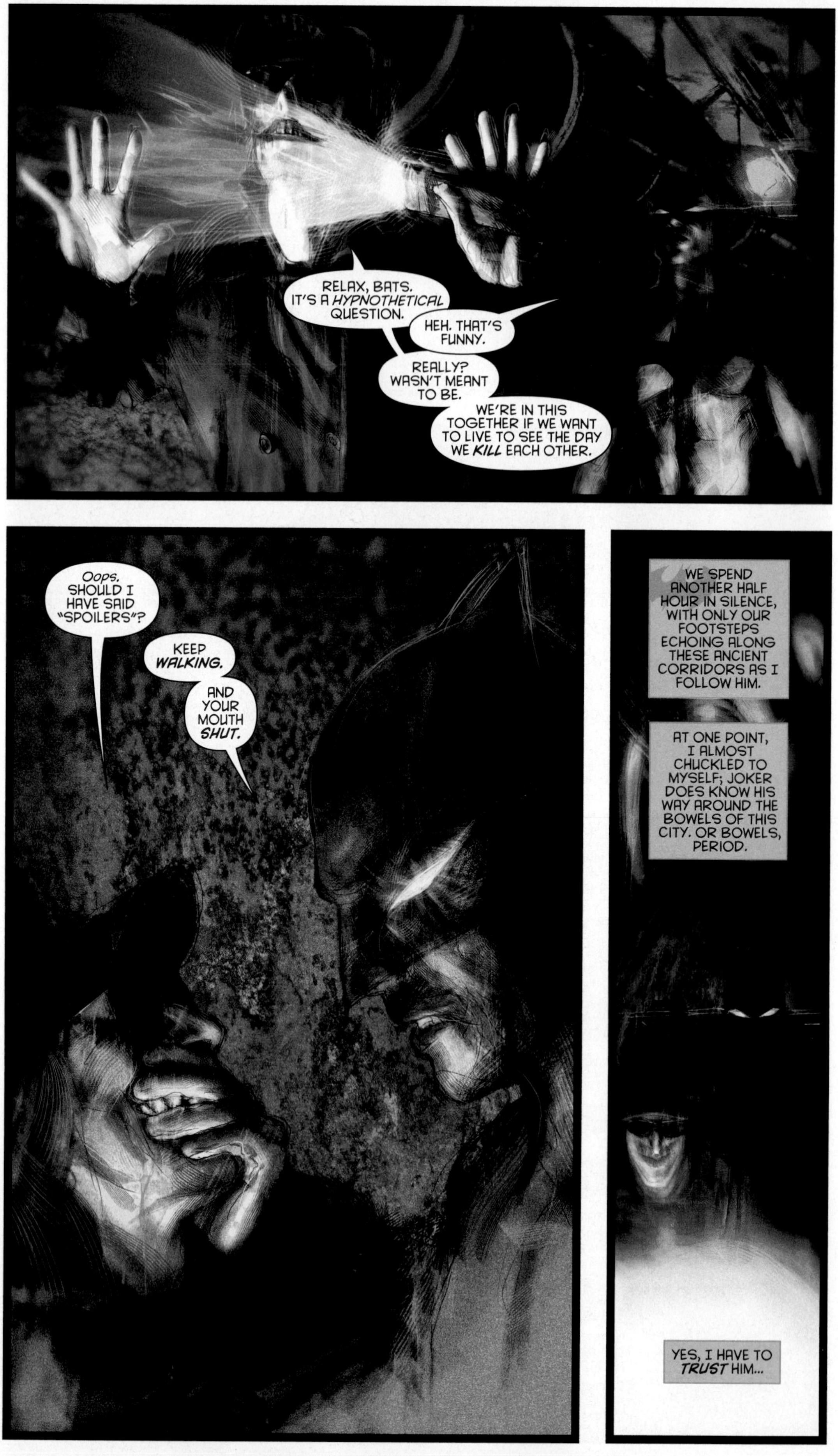
RELAX, BATS. IT'S A *HYPNOTHETICAL* QUESTION.
HEH. THAT'S FUNNY.
REALLY? WASN'T MEANT TO BE.
WE'RE IN THIS TOGETHER IF WE WANT TO LIVE TO SEE THE DAY WE ***KILL*** EACH OTHER.
Oops, SHOULD I HAVE SAID "SPOILERS"?
KEEP ***WALKING.***
AND YOUR MOUTH ***SHUT.***
WE SPEND ANOTHER HALF HOUR IN SILENCE, WITH ONLY OUR FOOTSTEPS ECHOING ALONG THESE ANCIENT CORRIDORS AS I FOLLOW HIM.
AT ONE POINT, I ALMOST CHUCKLED TO MYSELF; JOKER DOES KNOW HIS WAY AROUND THE BOWELS OF THIS CITY. OR BOWELS, PERIOD.
YES, I HAVE TO ***TRUST*** HIM...

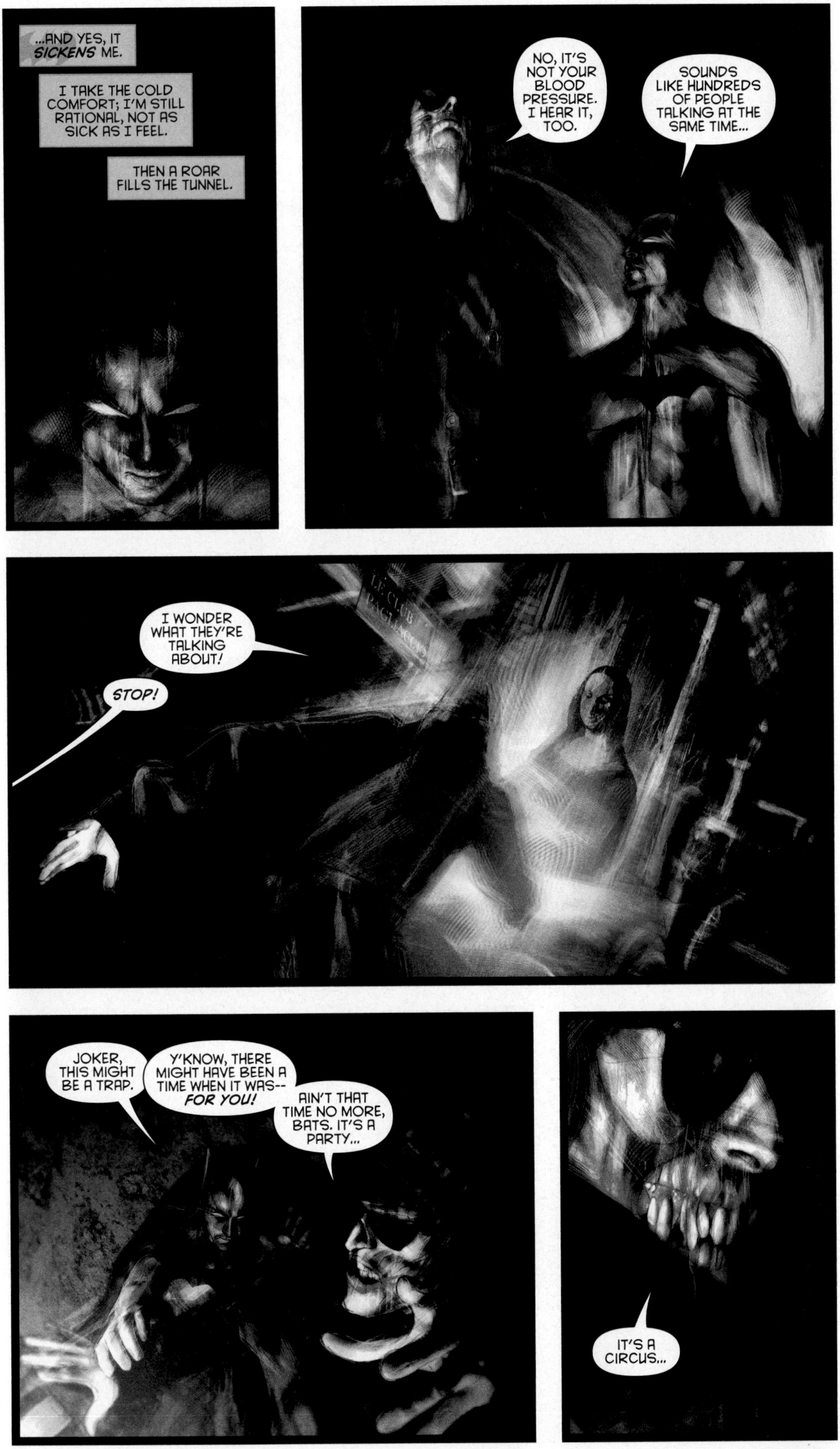
...AND YES, IT SICKENS ME.
I TAKE THE COLD COMFORT; I'M STILL RATIONAL, NOT AS SICK AS I FEEL.
THEN A ROAR FILLS THE TUNNEL.
NO, IT'S NOT YOUR BLOOD PRESSURE. I HEAR IT, TOO.
SOUNDS LIKE HUNDREDS OF PEOPLE TALKING AT THE SAME TIME...
I WONDER WHAT THEY'RE TALKING ABOUT!
STOP!
JOKER, THIS MIGHT BE A TRAP.
Y'KNOW, THERE MIGHT HAVE BEEN A TIME WHEN IT WAS-- FOR YOU!
AIN'T THAT TIME NO MORE, BATS. IT'S A PARTY...
IT'S A CIRCUS...

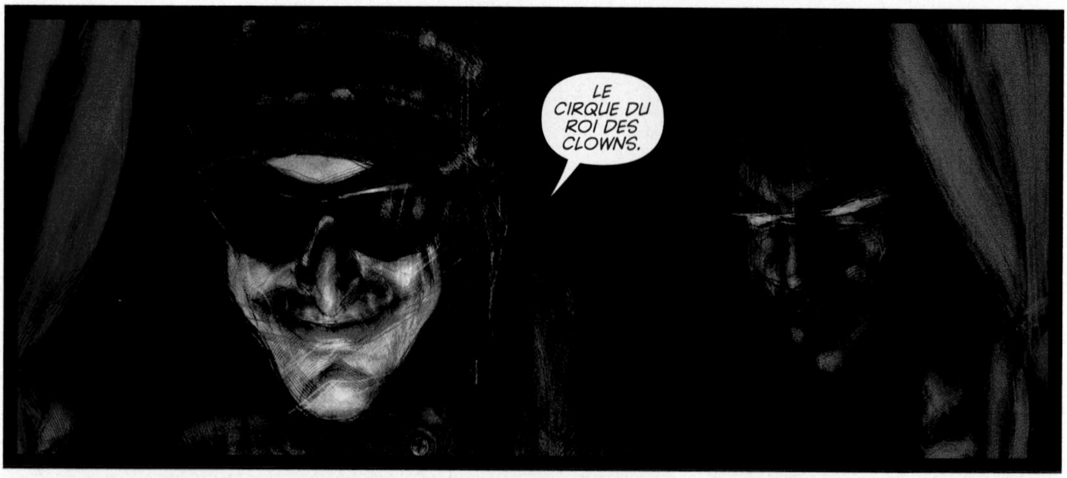
LE CIRQUE DU ROI DES CLOWNS.

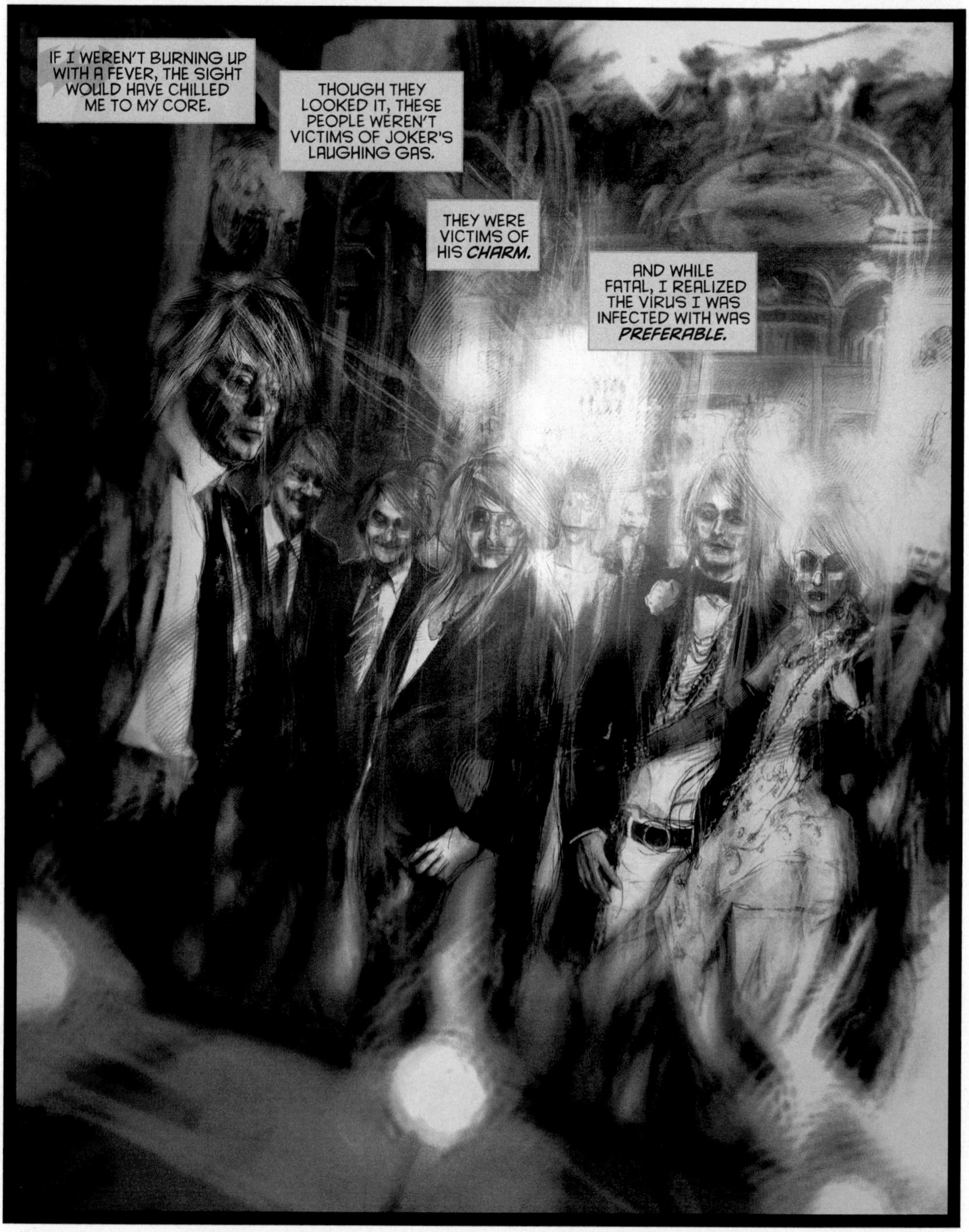
IF I WEREN'T BURNING UP WITH A FEVER, THE SIGHT WOULD HAVE CHILLED ME TO MY CORE.
THOUGH THEY LOOKED IT, THESE PEOPLE WEREN'T VICTIMS OF JOKER'S LAUGHING GAS.
THEY WERE VICTIMS OF HIS *CHARM.*
AND WHILE FATAL, I REALIZED THE VIRUS I WAS INFECTED WITH WAS *PREFERABLE.*

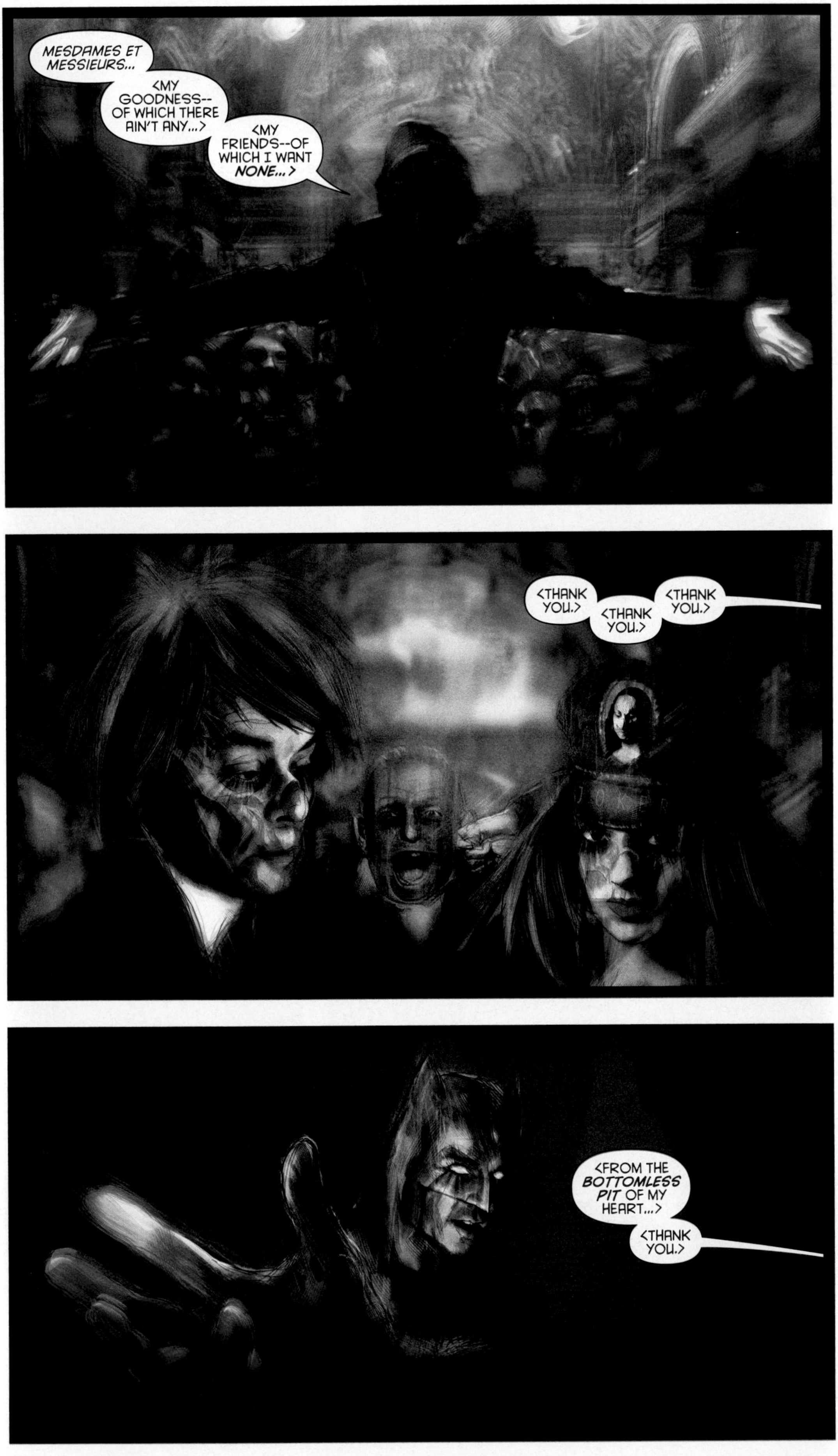
MESDAMES ET MESSIEURS...
<MY GOODNESS--OF WHICH THERE AIN'T ANY...>
<MY FRIENDS--OF WHICH I WANT *NONE...*>
<THANK YOU.>
<THANK YOU.>
<THANK YOU.>
<FROM THE *BOTTOMLESS PIT* OF MY HEART...>
<THANK YOU.>

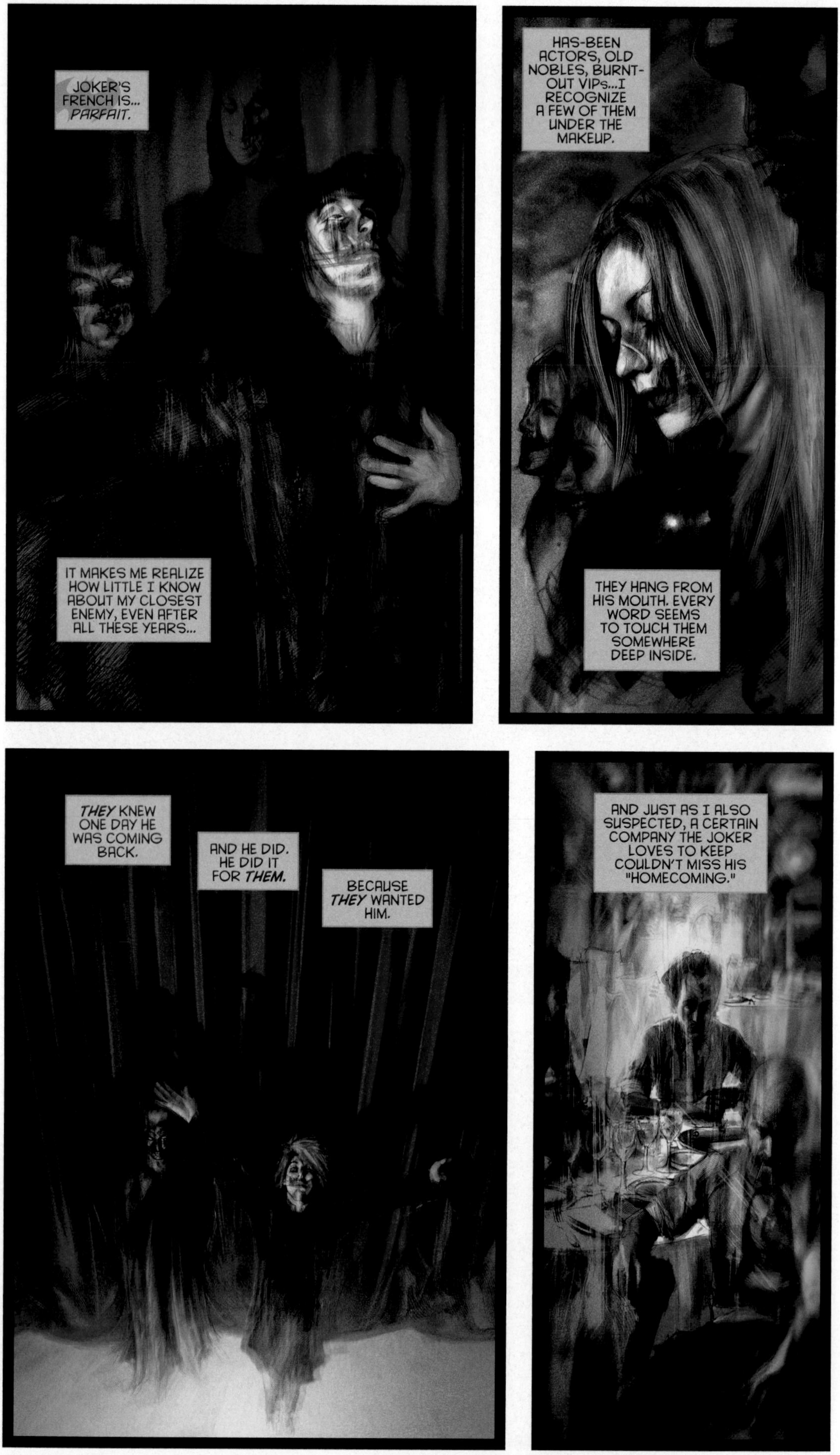
JOKER'S FRENCH IS... *PARFAIT.*
IT MAKES ME REALIZE HOW LITTLE I KNOW ABOUT MY CLOSEST ENEMY, EVEN AFTER ALL THESE YEARS...
HAS-BEEN ACTORS, OLD NOBLES, BURNT-OUT VIPS...I RECOGNIZE A FEW OF THEM UNDER THE MAKEUP.
THEY HANG FROM HIS MOUTH. EVERY WORD SEEMS TO TOUCH THEM SOMEWHERE DEEP INSIDE.
THEY KNEW ONE DAY HE WAS COMING BACK.
AND HE DID. HE DID IT FOR *THEM.*
BECAUSE *THEY* WANTED HIM.
AND JUST AS I ALSO SUSPECTED, A CERTAIN COMPANY THE JOKER LOVES TO KEEP COULDN'T MISS HIS "HOMECOMING."

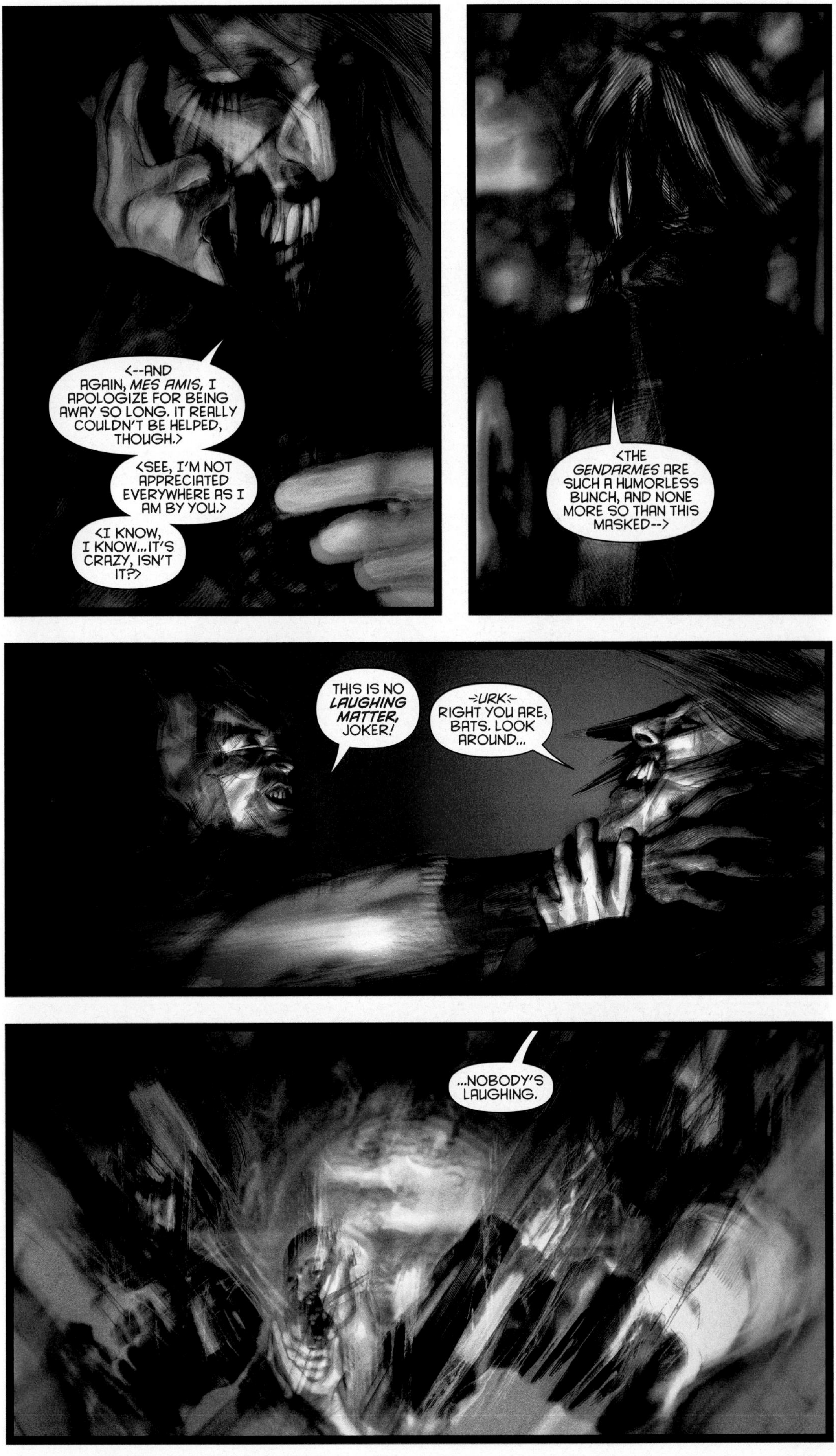
<--AND AGAIN, *MES AMIS,* I APOLOGIZE FOR BEING AWAY SO LONG. IT REALLY COULDN'T BE HELPED, THOUGH.>
<SEE, I'M NOT APPRECIATED EVERYWHERE AS I AM BY YOU.>
<I KNOW, I KNOW...IT'S CRAZY, ISN'T IT?>
<THE *GENDARMES* ARE SUCH A HUMORLESS BUNCH, AND NONE MORE SO THAN THIS MASKED-->
THIS IS NO ***LAUGHING MATTER,*** JOKER!
-*URK*- RIGHT YOU ARE, BATS. LOOK AROUND...
...NOBODY'S LAUGHING.

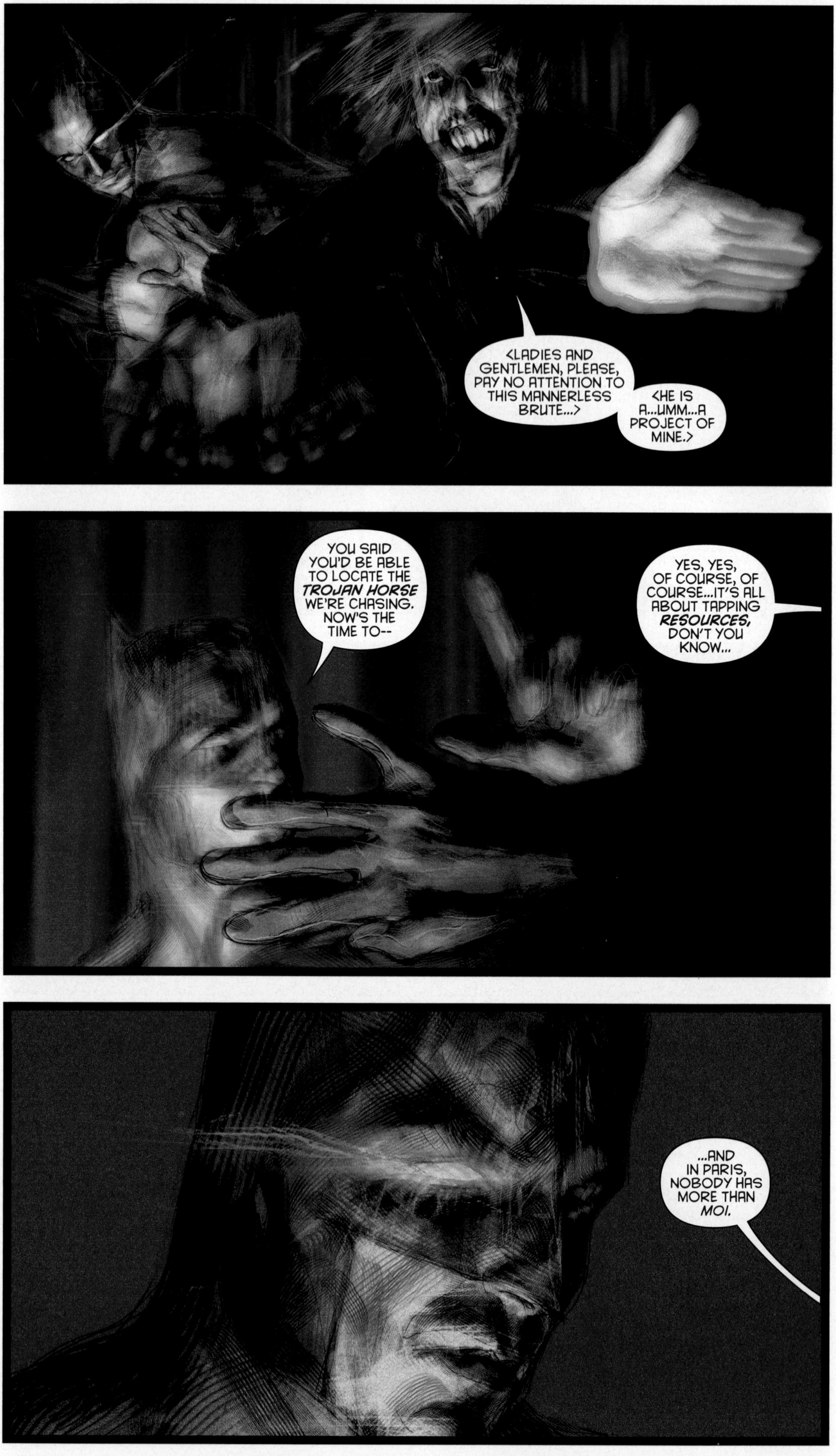
<LADIES AND GENTLEMEN, PLEASE, PAY NO ATTENTION TO THIS MANNERLESS BRUTE...>
<HE IS A...UMM...A PROJECT OF MINE.>
YOU SAID YOU'D BE ABLE TO LOCATE THE *TROJAN HORSE* WE'RE CHASING. NOW'S THE TIME TO--
YES, YES, OF COURSE, OF COURSE...IT'S ALL ABOUT TAPPING *RESOURCES,* DON'T YOU KNOW...
...AND IN PARIS, NOBODY HAS MORE THAN *MOI.*

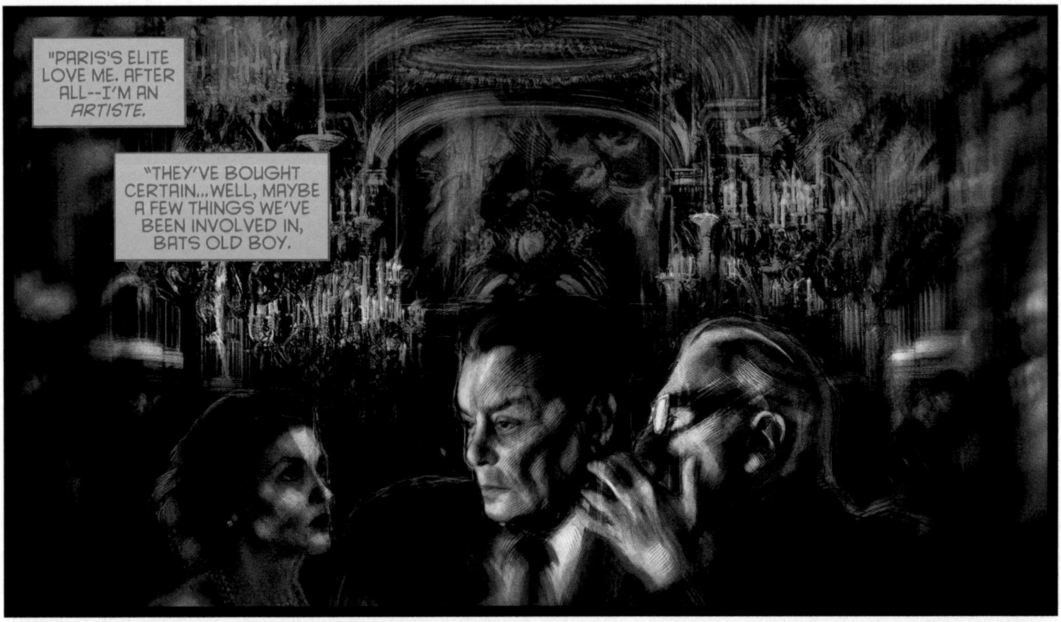
"PARIS'S ELITE LOVE ME. AFTER ALL--I'M AN *ARTISTE.*
"THEY'VE BOUGHT CERTAIN...WELL, MAYBE A FEW THINGS WE'VE BEEN INVOLVED IN, BATS OLD BOY.

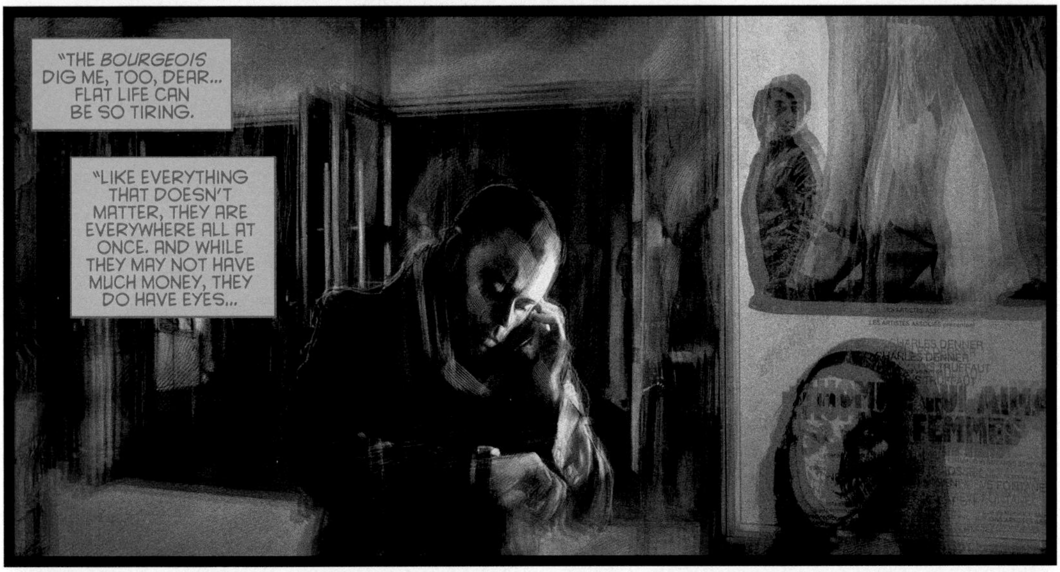
"THE *BOURGEOIS* DIG ME, TOO, DEAR... FLAT LIFE CAN BE SO TIRING.
"LIKE EVERYTHING THAT DOESN'T MATTER, THEY ARE EVERYWHERE ALL AT ONCE. AND WHILE THEY MAY NOT HAVE MUCH MONEY, THEY DO HAVE EYES...

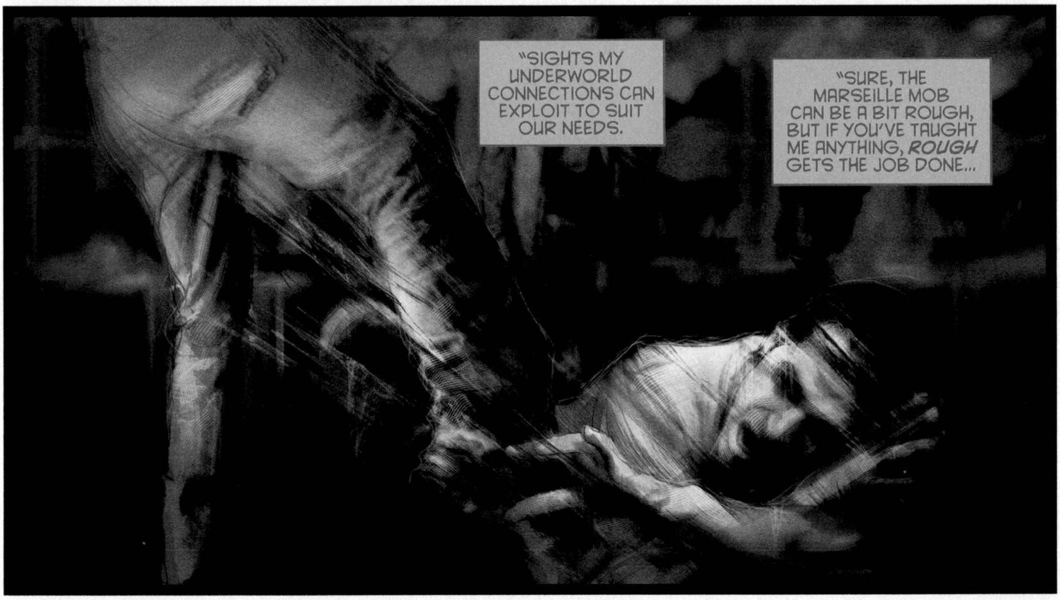
"SIGHTS MY UNDERWORLD CONNECTIONS CAN EXPLOIT TO SUIT OUR NEEDS.
"SURE, THE MARSEILLE MOB CAN BE A BIT ROUGH, BUT IF YOU'VE TAUGHT ME ANYTHING, *ROUGH* GETS THE JOB DONE...

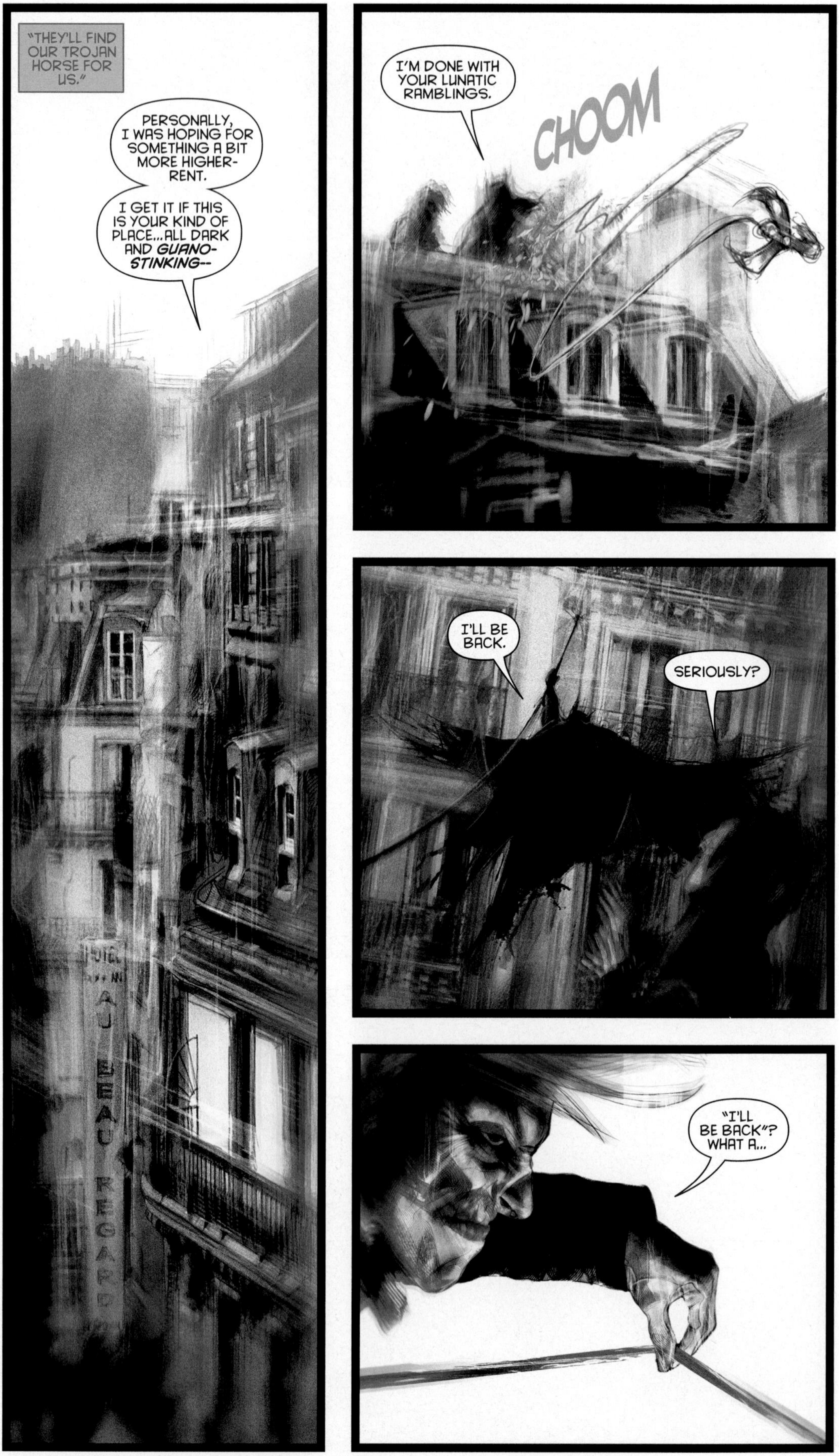
"THEY'LL FIND OUR TROJAN HORSE FOR US."
PERSONALLY, I WAS HOPING FOR SOMETHING A BIT MORE HIGHER-RENT.
I GET IT IF THIS IS YOUR KIND OF PLACE...ALL DARK AND GUANO-STINKING--
I'M DONE WITH YOUR LUNATIC RAMBLINGS.
CHOOM
I'LL BE BACK.
SERIOUSLY?
"I'LL BE BACK"? WHAT A...

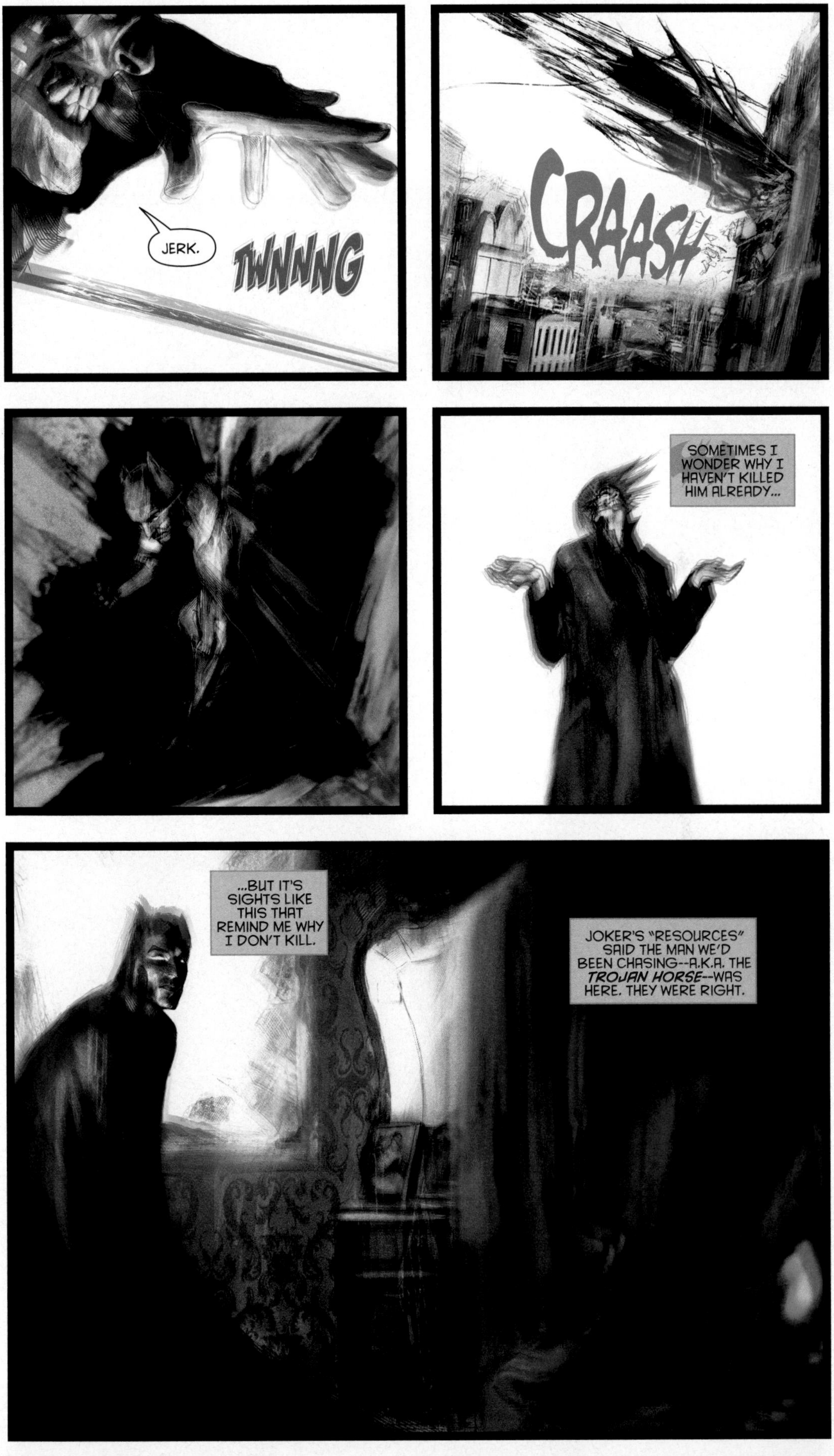
JERK.
TWNNNG
CRAASH
SOMETIMES I WONDER WHY I HAVEN'T KILLED HIM ALREADY...
...BUT IT'S SIGHTS LIKE THIS THAT REMIND ME WHY I DON'T KILL.
JOKER'S "RESOURCES" SAID THE MAN WE'D BEEN CHASING--A.K.A. THE TROJAN HORSE--WAS HERE. THEY WERE RIGHT.

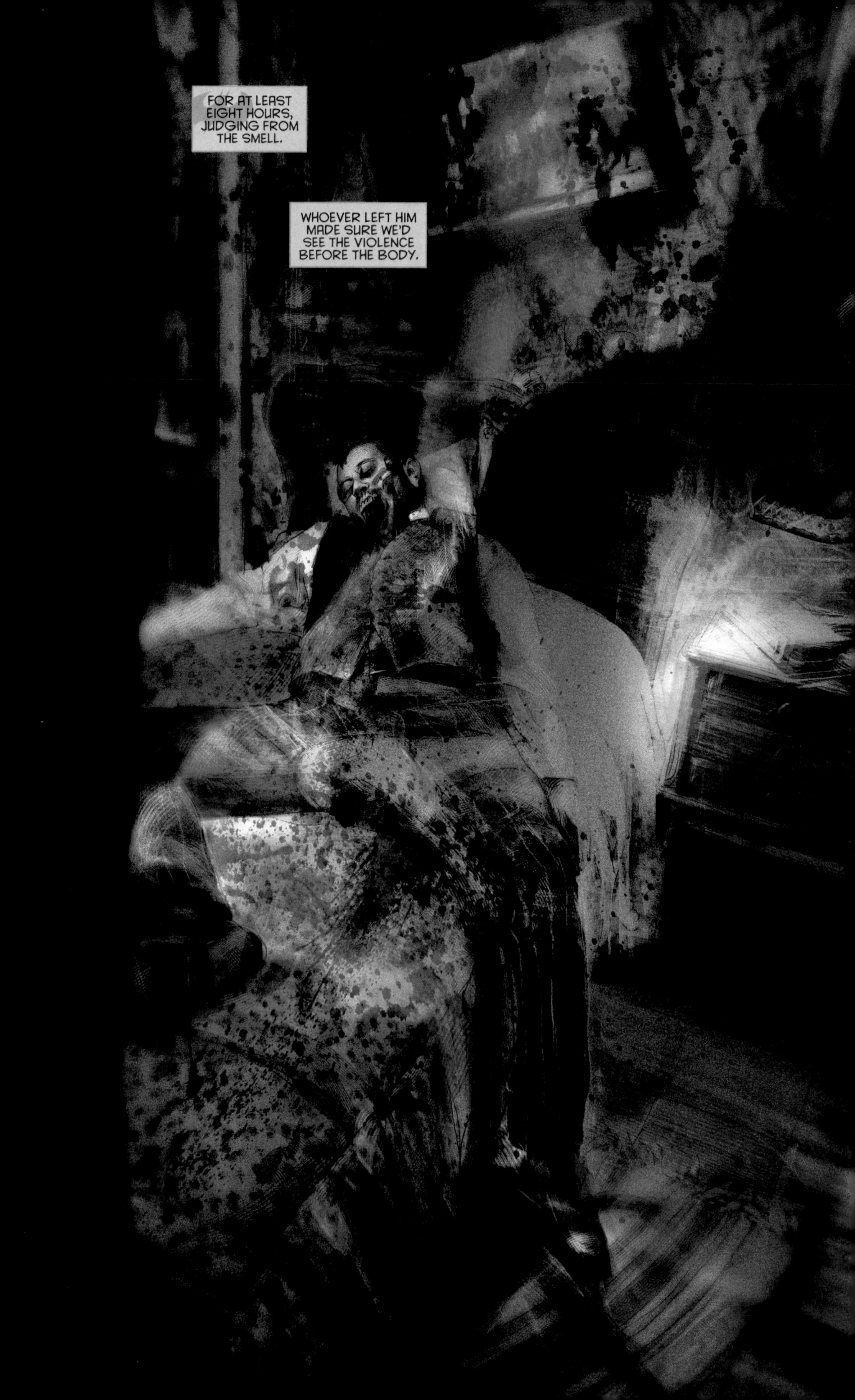
FOR AT LEAST EIGHT HOURS, JUDGING FROM THE SMELL.
WHOEVER LEFT HIM MADE SURE WE'D SEE THE VIOLENCE BEFORE THE BODY.

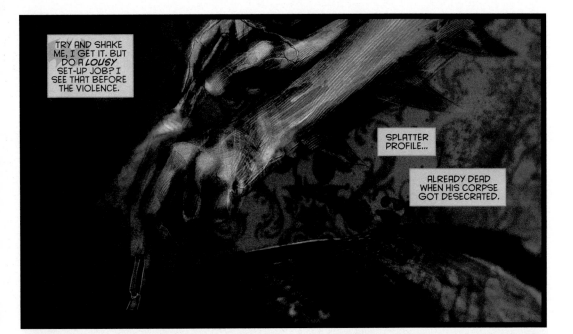

TRY AND SHAKE ME, I GET IT. BUT DO A *LOUSY* SET-UP JOB? I SEE THAT BEFORE THE VIOLENCE.

SPLATTER PROFILE...

ALREADY DEAD WHEN HIS CORPSE GOT DESECRATED.

WHAT LOOKS BAD, IS A RUSE...

HE WAS SHOT. TWICE. AND NOT HERE.

JUST OBVIOUS ENOUGH TO MEAN I WAS SUPPOSED TO--

DONNG DONNG DONNG DONNG DONNG DONNG

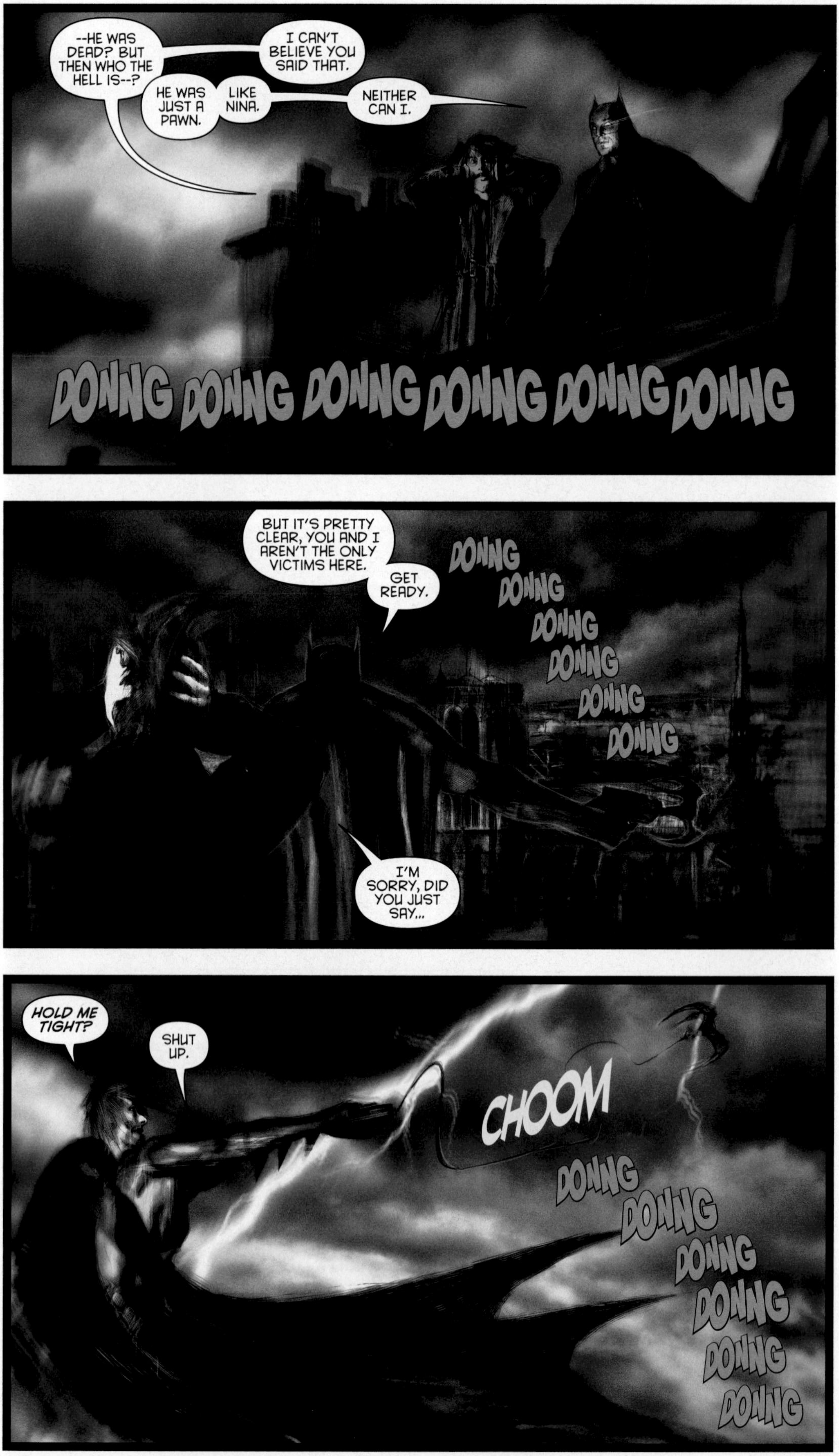
--HE WAS DEAD? BUT THEN WHO THE HELL IS--?
I CAN'T BELIEVE YOU SAID THAT.
HE WAS JUST A PAWN.
LIKE NINA.
NEITHER CAN I.
DONNG DONNG DONNG DONNG DONNG DONNG
BUT IT'S PRETTY CLEAR, YOU AND I AREN'T THE ONLY VICTIMS HERE.
GET READY.
DONNG DONNG DONNG DONNG DONNG DONNG
I'M SORRY, DID YOU JUST SAY...
HOLD ME TIGHT?
SHUT UP.
CHOOM
DONNG DONNG DONNG DONNG DONNG DONNG

GETTING TO THE ROOF WAS HARDER THAN IT SHOULD HAVE BEEN.

BUT THEN, I HAVE MY MONKEY ON MY BACK.

HEH.

DONNG DONNG DONNG DONNG DONNG DONNG

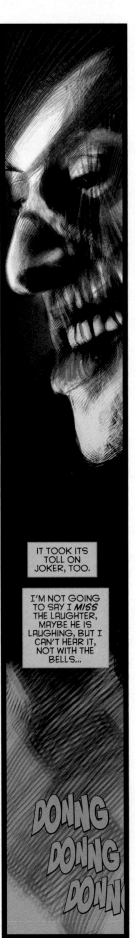

IT TOOK ITS TOLL ON JOKER, TOO.

I'M NOT GOING TO SAY I *MISS* THE LAUGHTER, MAYBE HE IS LAUGHING, BUT I CAN'T HEAR IT, NOT WITH THE BELLS...

DONNG DONNG DONN

...OR THE NIGHTMARE.

YOU MADE IT?! *BRAVO!* HOW FORTUNATE THAT THE VIRUS HAS NOT FINISHED YOU YET.

THOUGH I CONFESS, I THOUGHT ONE OF YOU WOULD BE DEAD BY NOW.

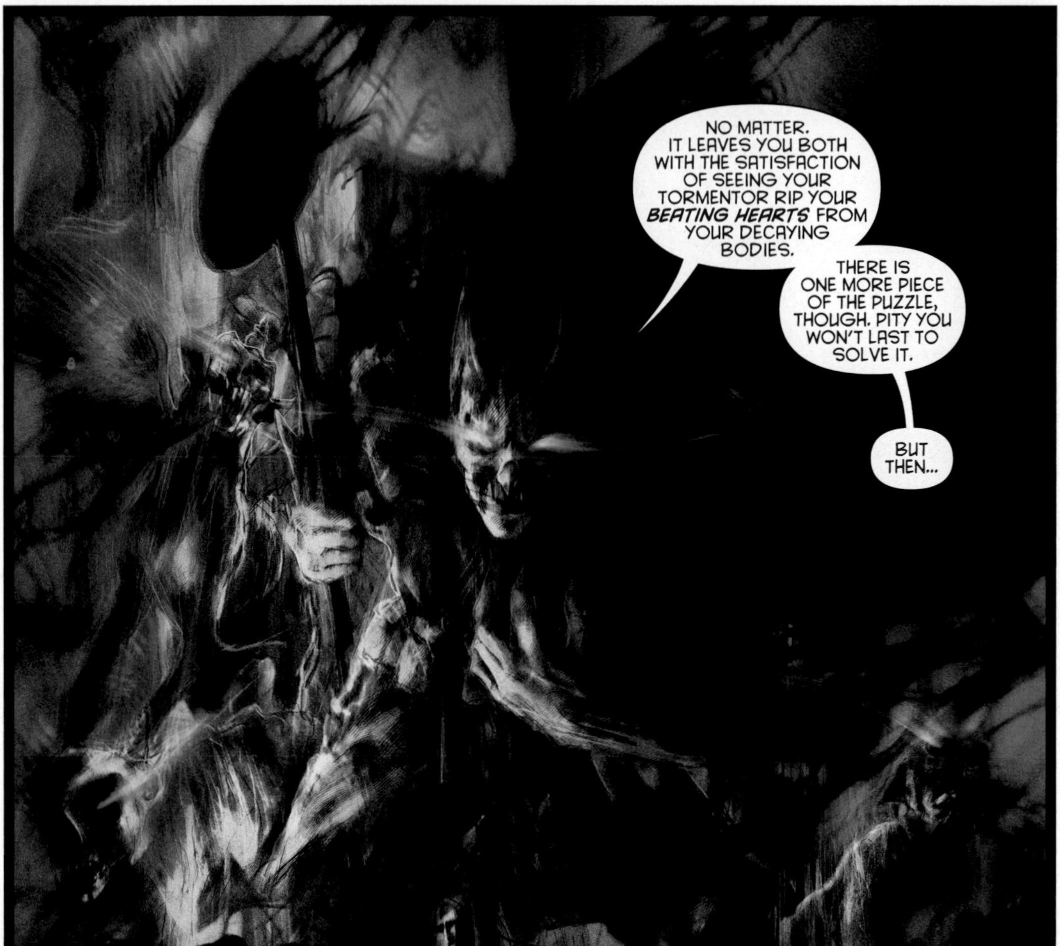
NO MATTER. IT LEAVES YOU BOTH WITH THE SATISFACTION OF SEEING YOUR TORMENTOR RIP YOUR *BEATING HEARTS* FROM YOUR DECAYING BODIES.
THERE IS ONE MORE PIECE OF THE PUZZLE, THOUGH. PITY YOU WON'T LAST TO SOLVE IT.
BUT THEN...

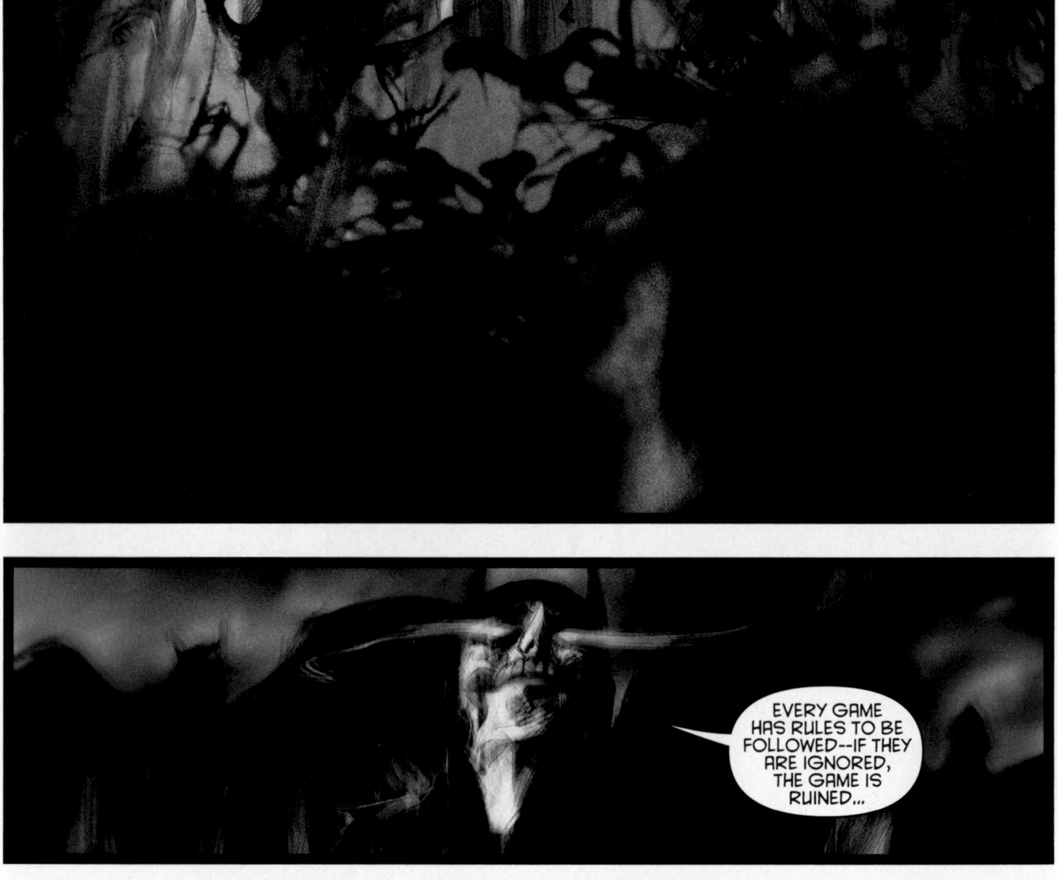
EVERY GAME HAS RULES TO BE FOLLOWED--IF THEY ARE IGNORED, THE GAME IS RUINED...

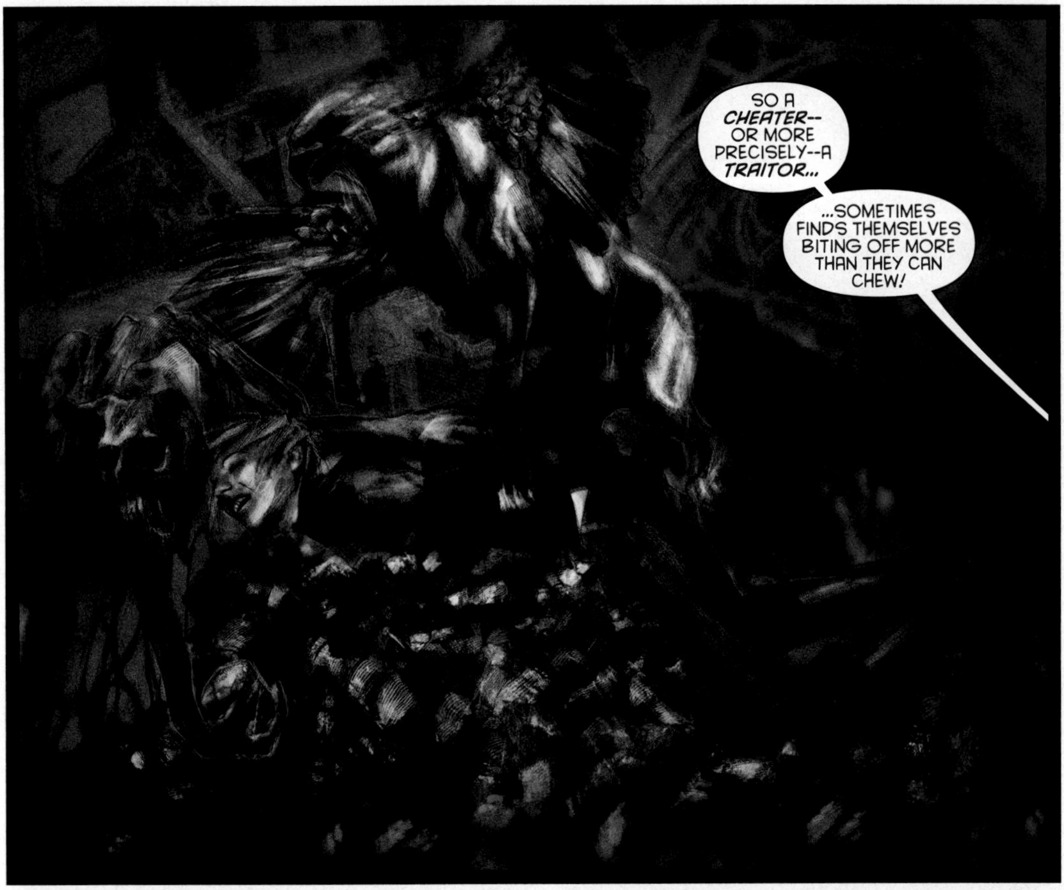
SO A *CHEATER*-- OR MORE PRECISELY--A *TRAITOR*...
...SOMETIMES FINDS THEMSELVES BITING OFF MORE THAN THEY CAN CHEW!

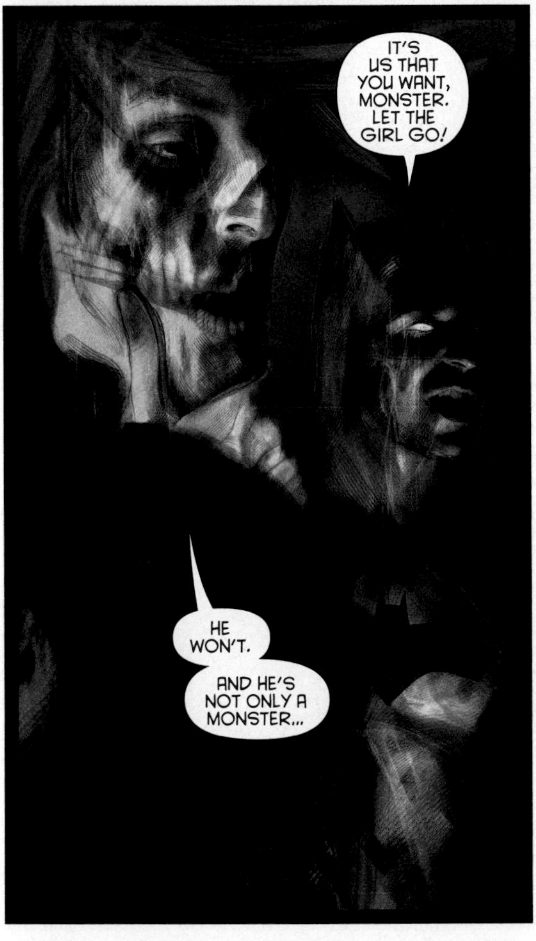
IT'S US THAT YOU WANT, MONSTER. LET THE GIRL GO!
HE WON'T.
AND HE'S NOT ONLY A MONSTER...

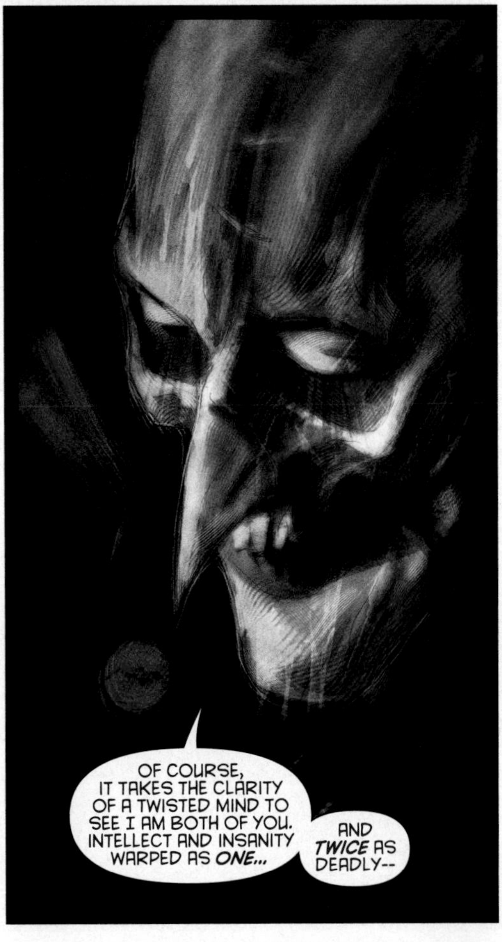
OF COURSE, IT TAKES THE CLARITY OF A TWISTED MIND TO SEE I AM BOTH OF YOU. INTELLECT AND INSANITY WARPED AS *ONE*...
AND *TWICE* AS DEADLY--

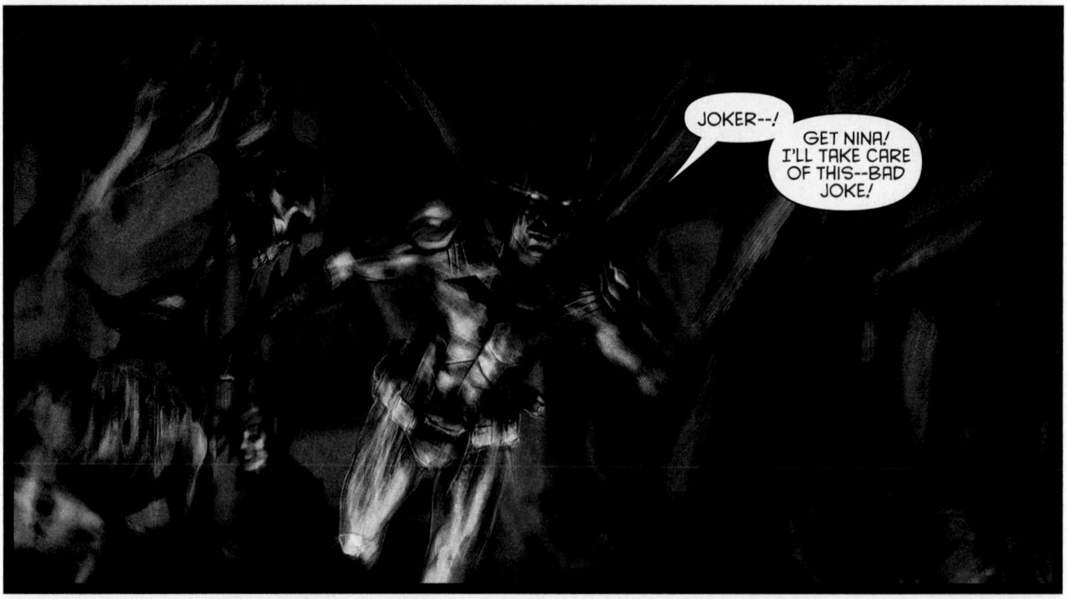
JOKER--!
GET NINA! I'LL TAKE CARE OF THIS--BAD JOKE!

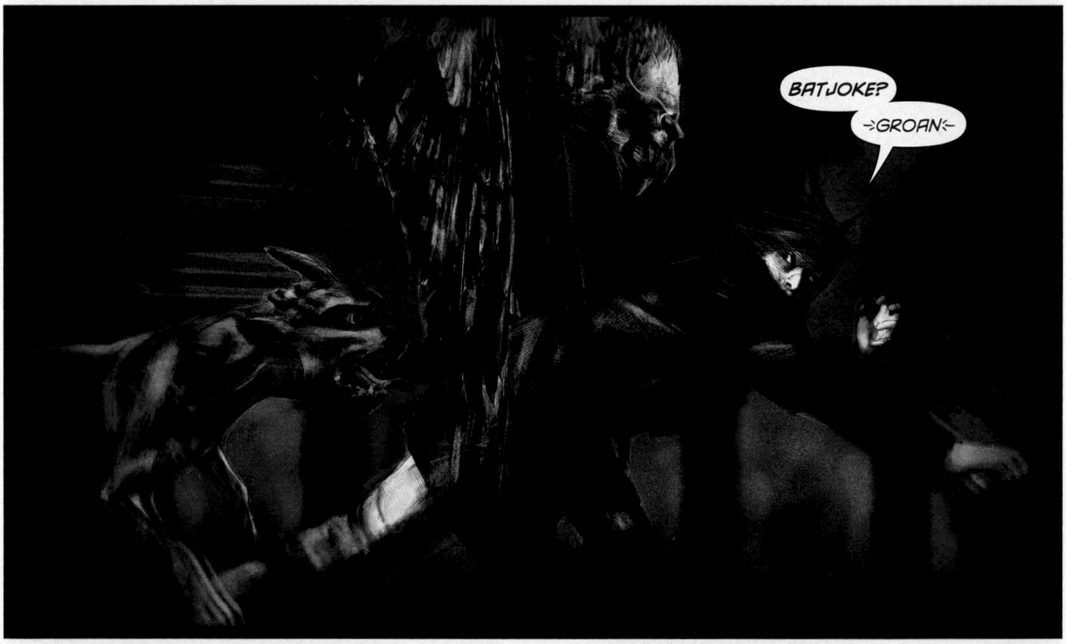
BATJOKE?
-GROAN-

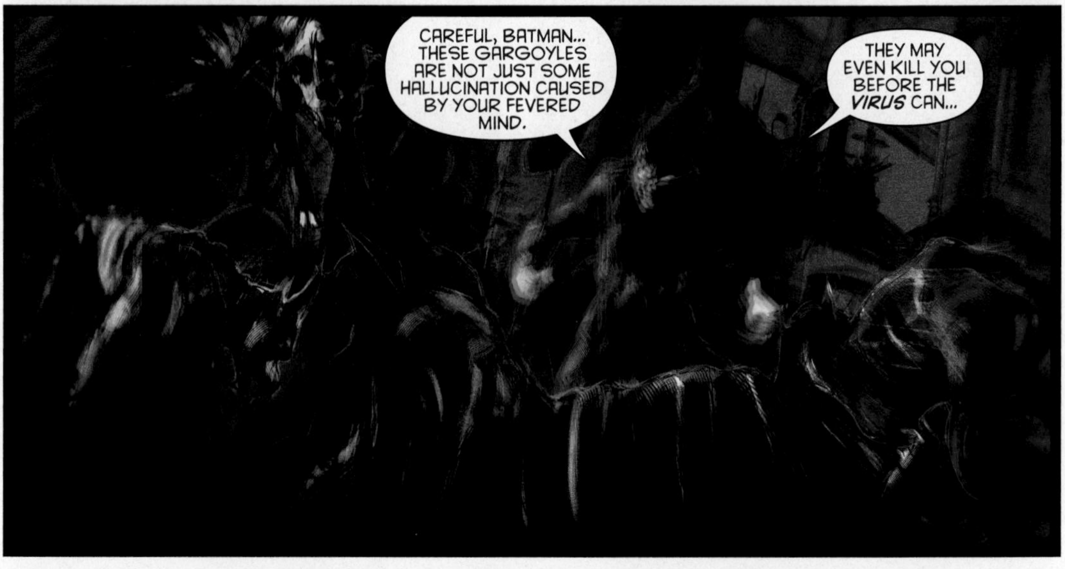
CAREFUL, BATMAN... THESE GARGOYLES ARE NOT JUST SOME HALLUCINATION CAUSED BY YOUR FEVERED MIND.
THEY MAY EVEN KILL YOU BEFORE THE *VIRUS* CAN...

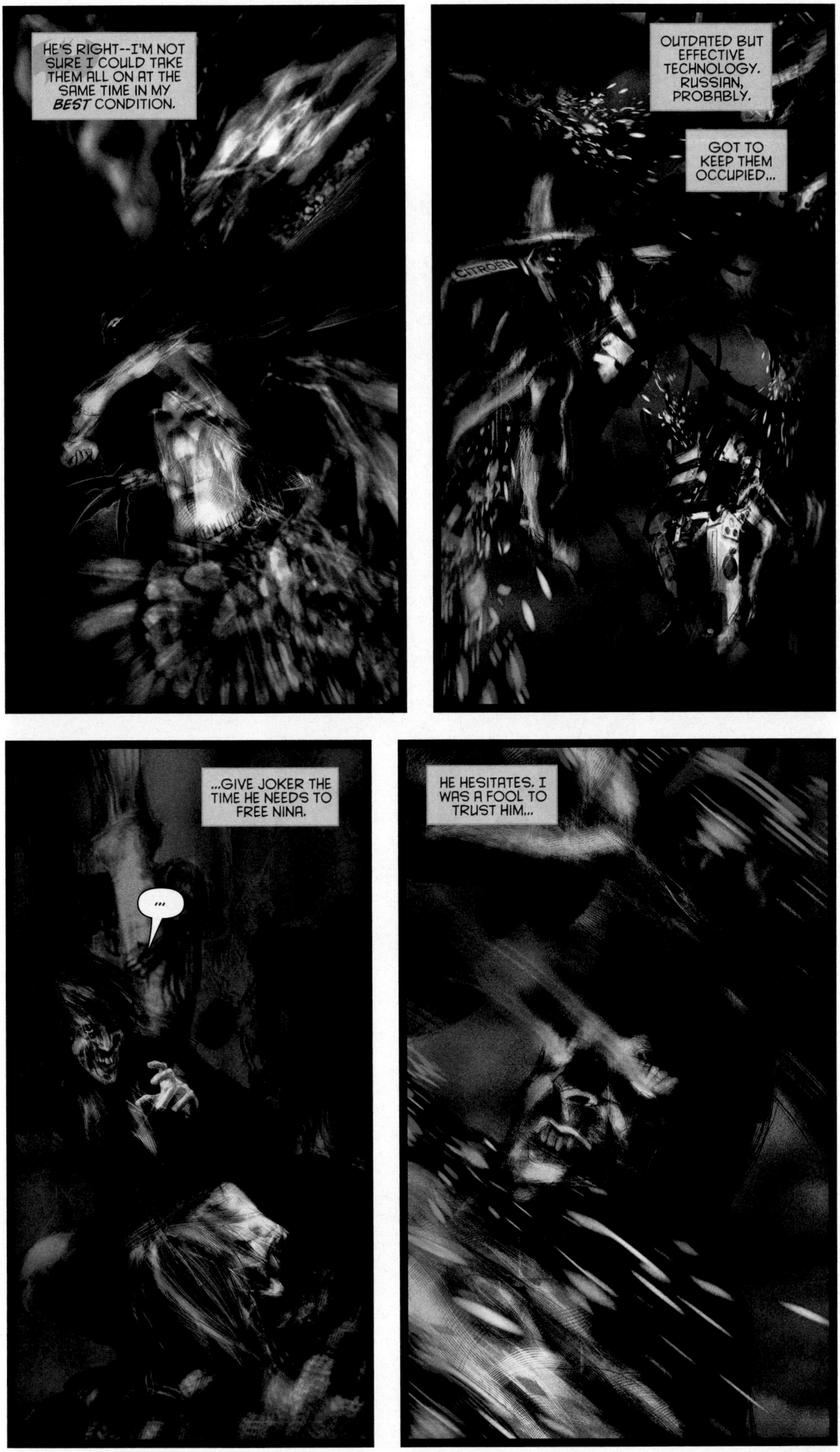
HE'S RIGHT--I'M NOT SURE I COULD TAKE THEM ALL ON AT THE SAME TIME IN MY *BEST* CONDITION.
OUTDATED BUT EFFECTIVE TECHNOLOGY. RUSSIAN, PROBABLY.
GOT TO KEEP THEM OCCUPIED...
CITROËN
...GIVE JOKER THE TIME HE NEEDS TO FREE NINA.
...
HE HESITATES. I WAS A FOOL TO TRUST HIM...

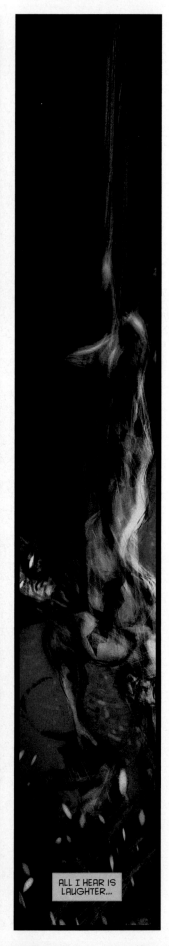

AM I SLIPPING... OR LETTING GO?

CLUTCHING MADNESS OR STRAWS IN THE FACE OF FEAR?

I CAN FEEL THE BELLS TOLL, BUT I CAN'T HEAR THEM.

ALL I HEAR IS LAUGHTER...

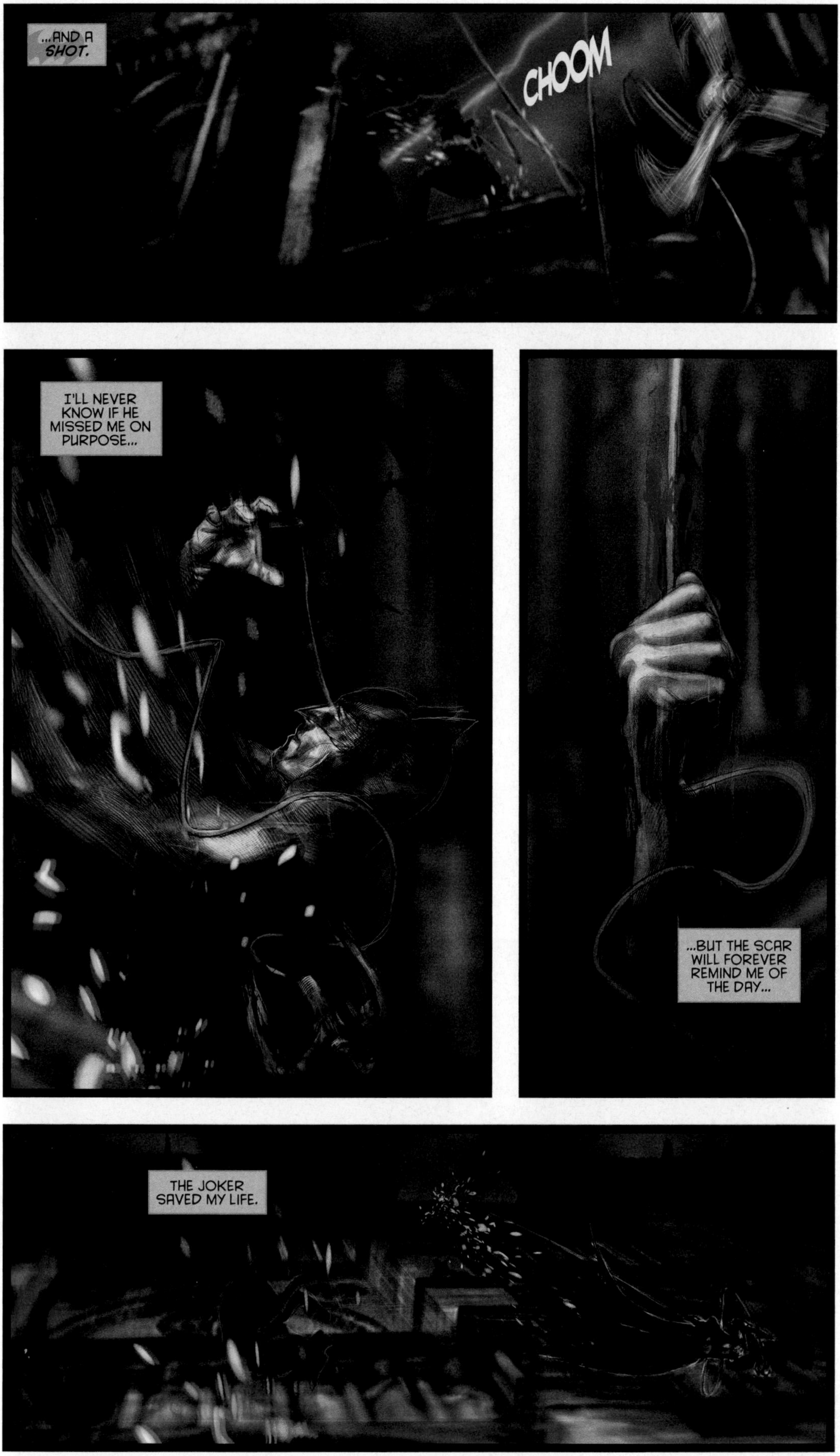
...AND A SHOT.
CHOOM
I'LL NEVER KNOW IF HE MISSED ME ON PURPOSE...
...BUT THE SCAR WILL FOREVER REMIND ME OF THE DAY...
THE JOKER SAVED MY LIFE.

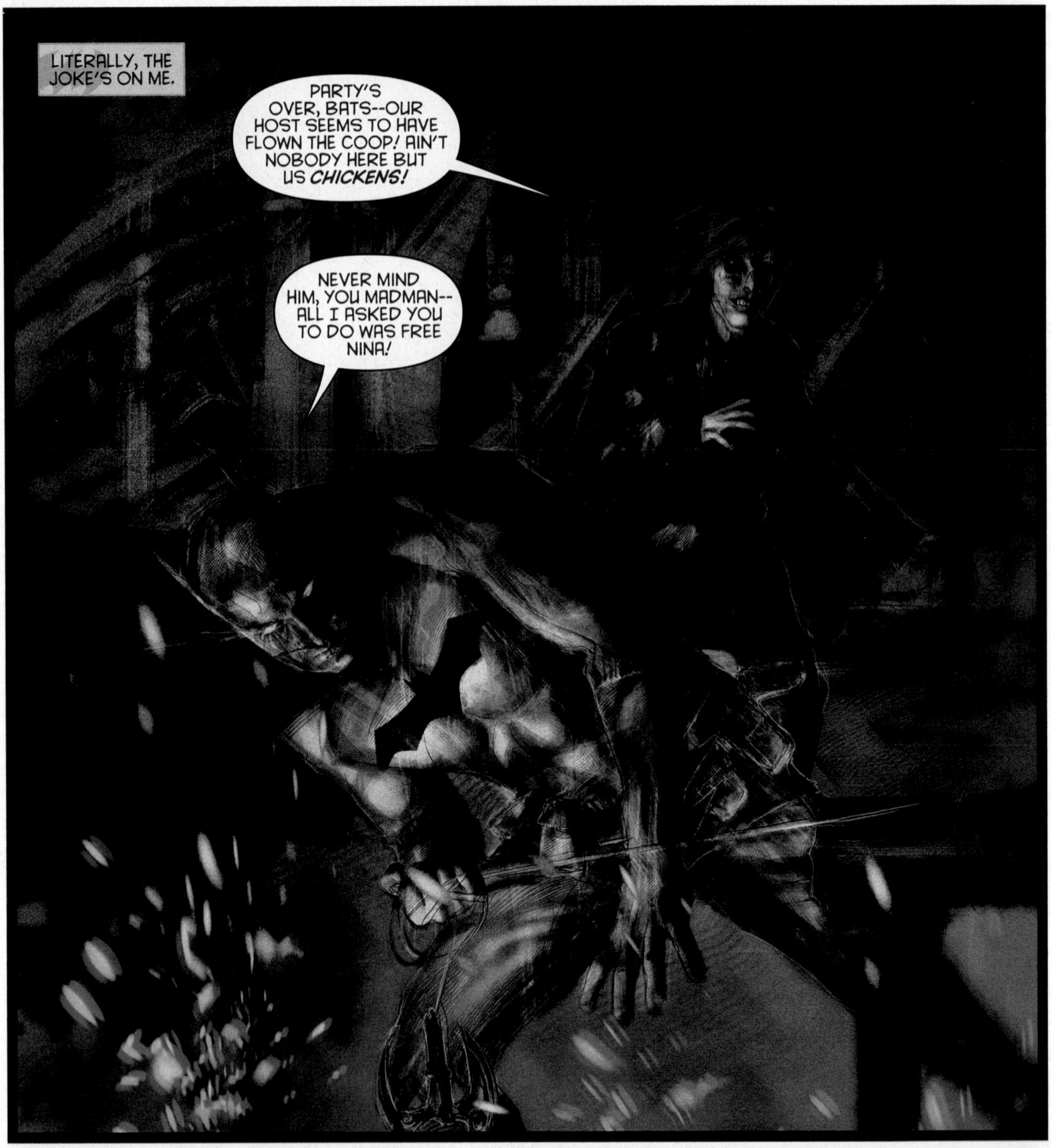
LITERALLY, THE JOKE'S ON ME.
PARTY'S OVER, BATS--OUR HOST SEEMS TO HAVE FLOWN THE COOP! AIN'T NOBODY HERE BUT US CHICKENS!
NEVER MIND HIM, YOU MADMAN--ALL I ASKED YOU TO DO WAS FREE NINA!
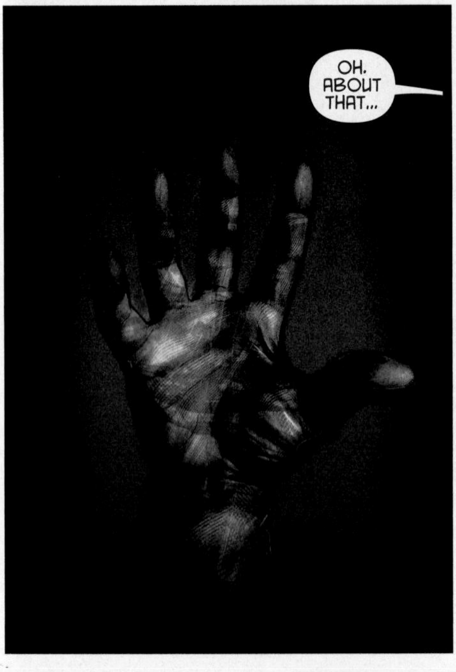
OH. ABOUT THAT...
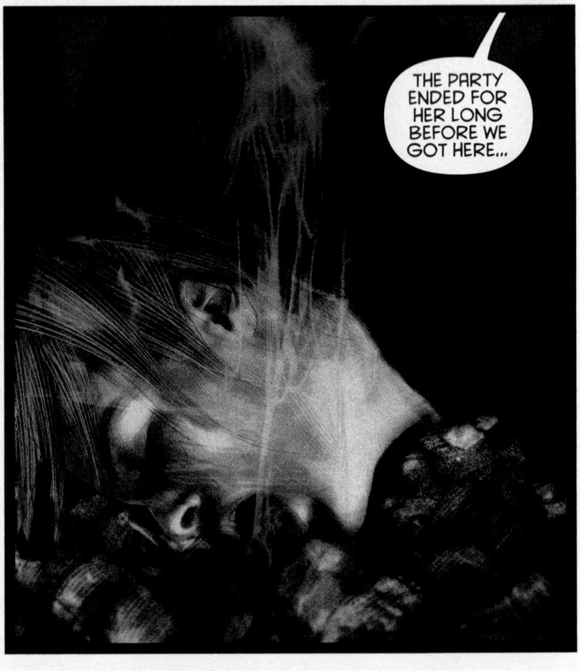
THE PARTY ENDED FOR HER LONG BEFORE WE GOT HERE...

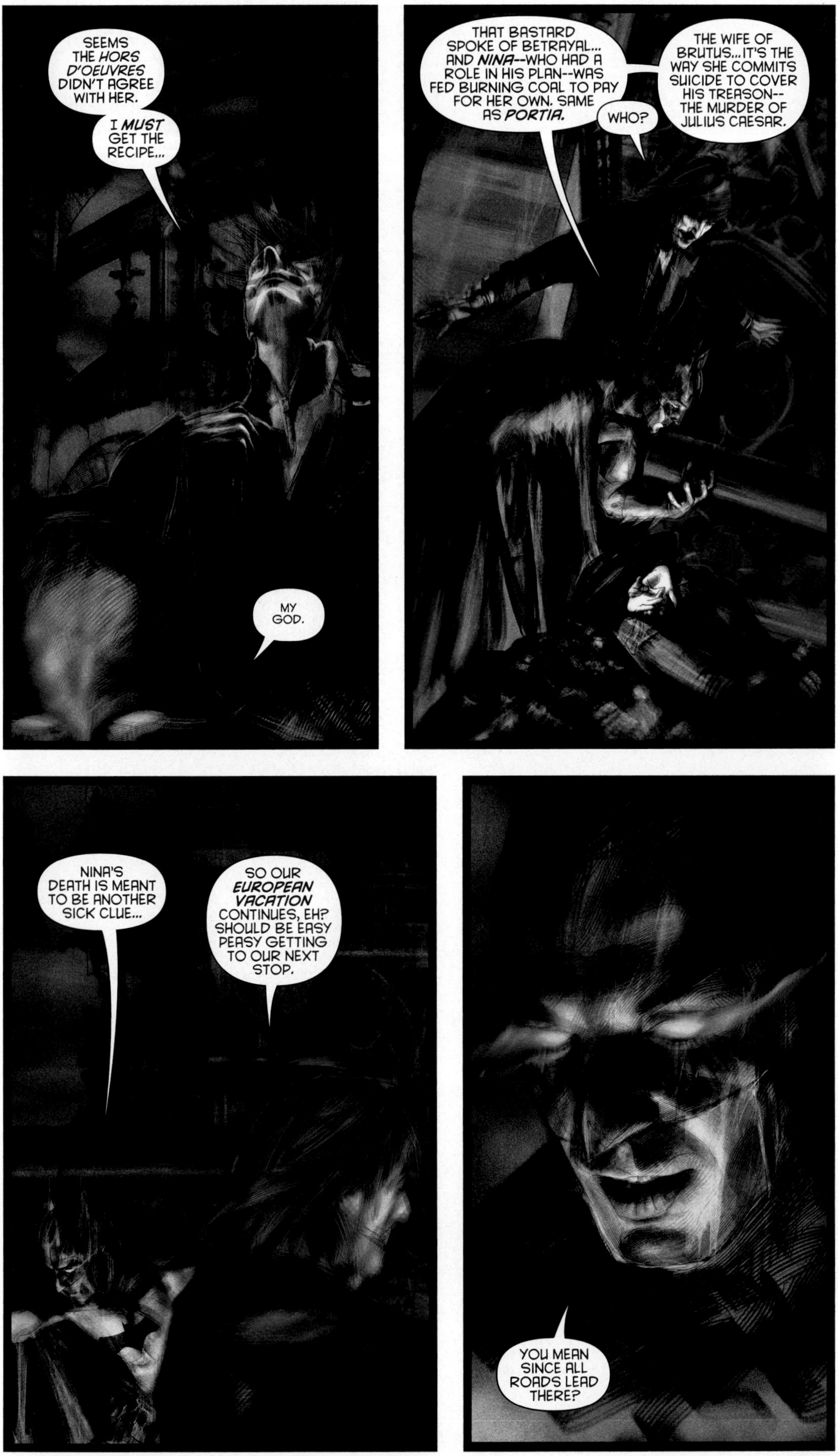
SEEMS THE *HORS D'OEUVRES* DIDN'T AGREE WITH HER.
I *MUST* GET THE RECIPE...
MY GOD.
THAT BASTARD SPOKE OF BETRAYAL... AND *NINA*--WHO HAD A ROLE IN HIS PLAN--WAS FED BURNING COAL TO PAY FOR HER OWN. SAME AS *PORTIA.*
WHO?
THE WIFE OF BRUTUS...IT'S THE WAY SHE COMMITS SUICIDE TO COVER HIS TREASON--THE MURDER OF JULIUS CAESAR.
NINA'S DEATH IS MEANT TO BE ANOTHER SICK CLUE...
SO OUR *EUROPEAN VACATION* CONTINUES, EH? SHOULD BE EASY PEASY GETTING TO OUR NEXT STOP.
YOU MEAN SINCE ALL ROADS LEAD THERE?

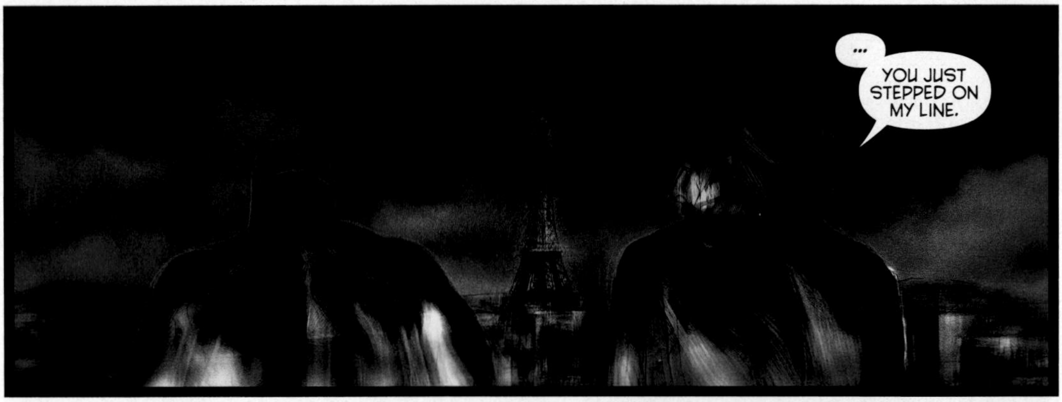
...
YOU JUST STEPPED ON MY LINE.

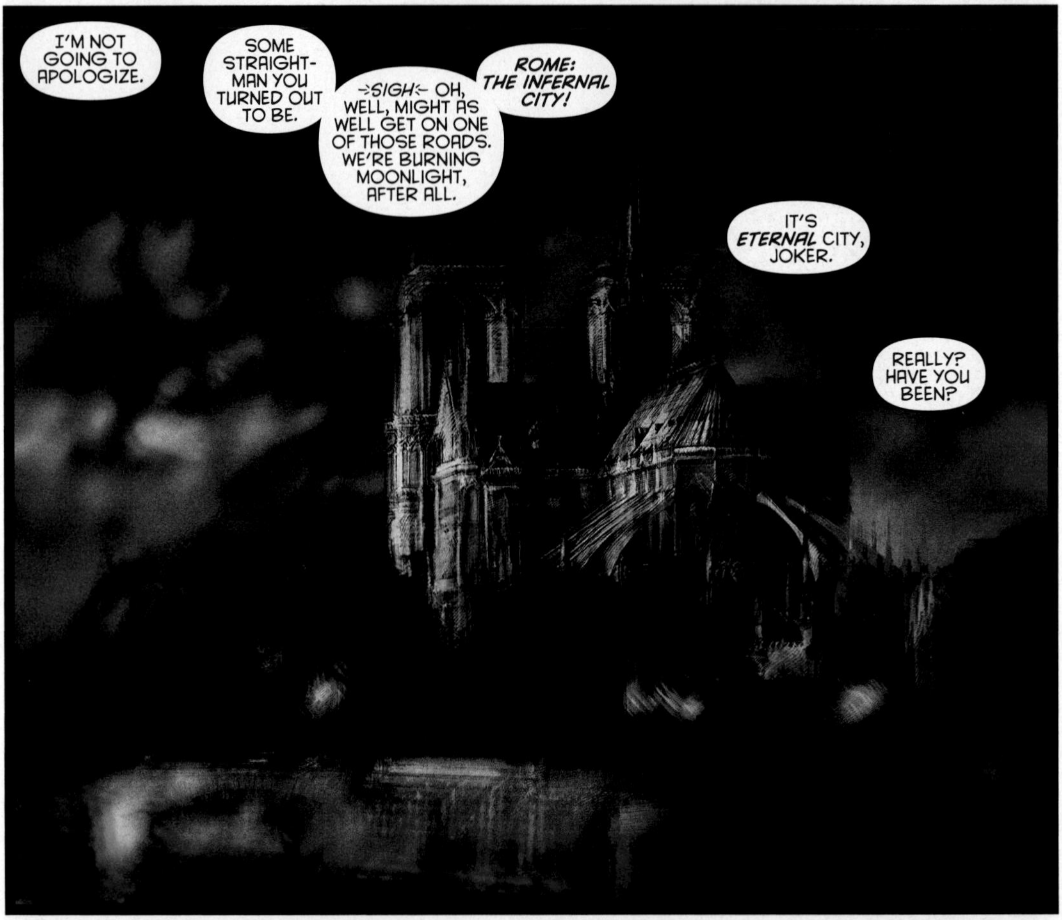
I'M NOT GOING TO APOLOGIZE.
SOME STRAIGHT-MAN YOU TURNED OUT TO BE.
ROME: THE INFERNAL CITY!
⇒SIGH⇐ OH, WELL, MIGHT AS WELL GET ON ONE OF THOSE ROADS. WE'RE BURNING MOONLIGHT, AFTER ALL.
IT'S ETERNAL CITY, JOKER.
REALLY? HAVE YOU BEEN?

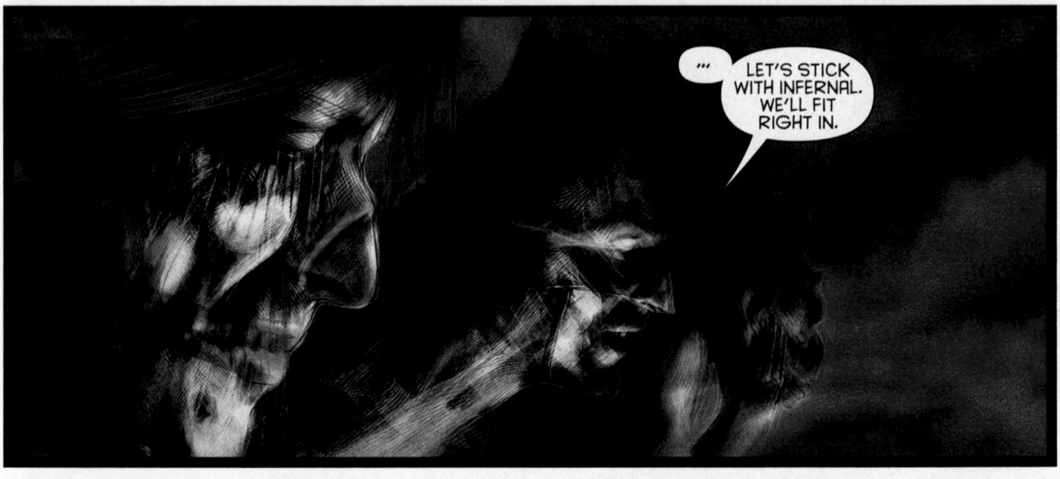
...
LET'S STICK WITH INFERNAL. WE'LL FIT RIGHT IN.

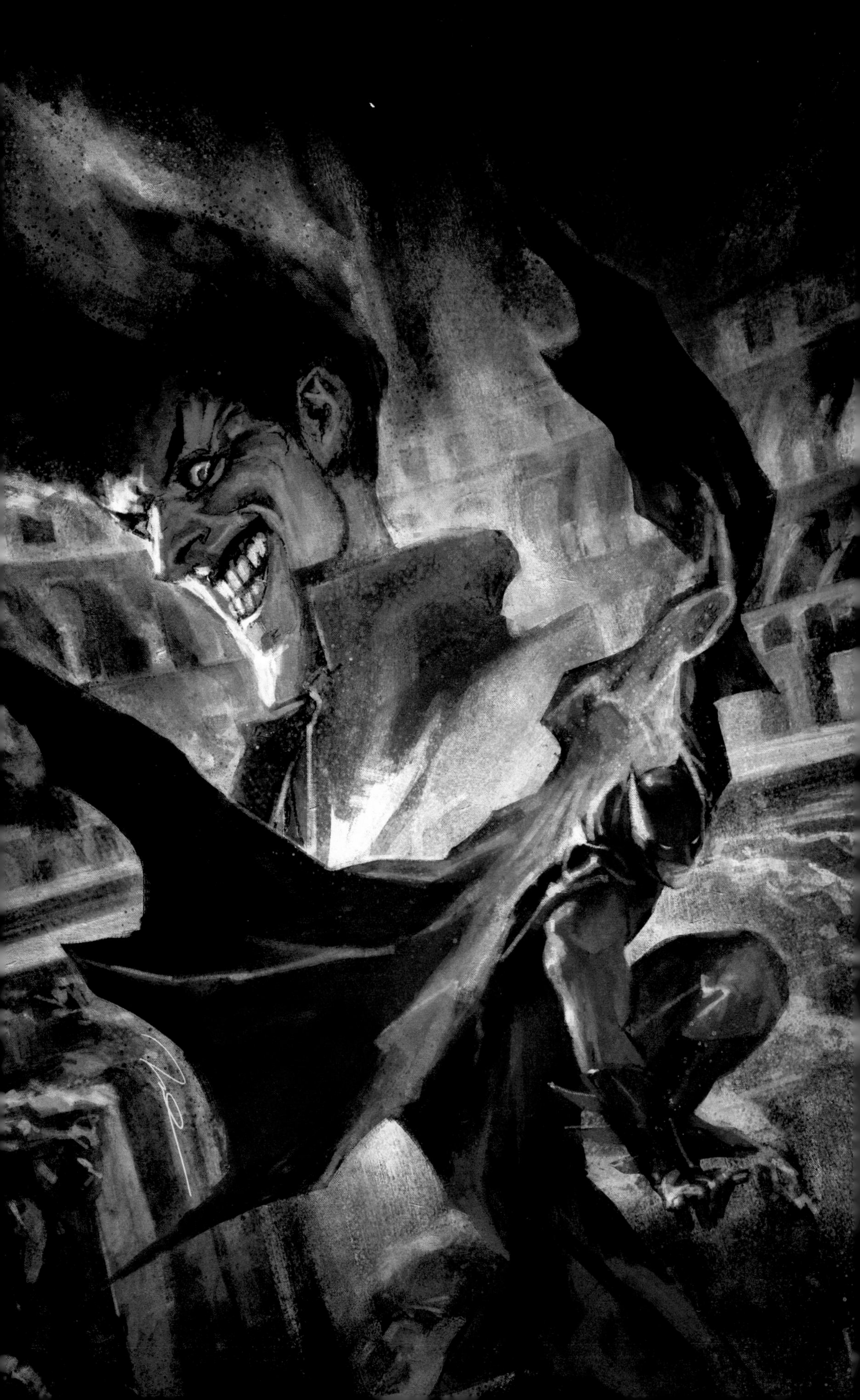

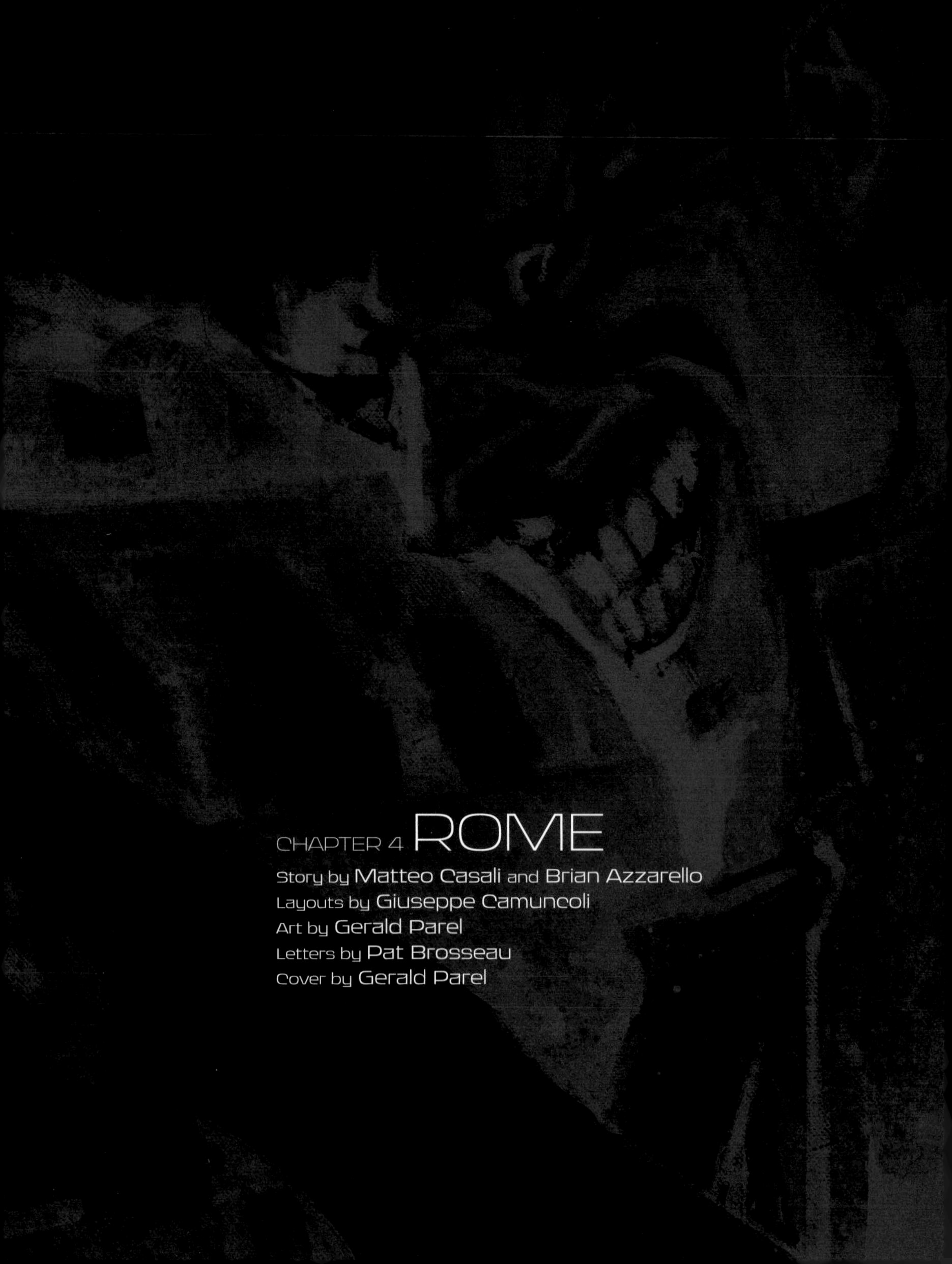

CHAPTER 4 ROME

Story by Matteo Casali and Brian Azzarello
Layouts by Giuseppe Camuncoli
Art by Gerald Parel
Letters by Pat Brosseau
Cover by Gerald Parel

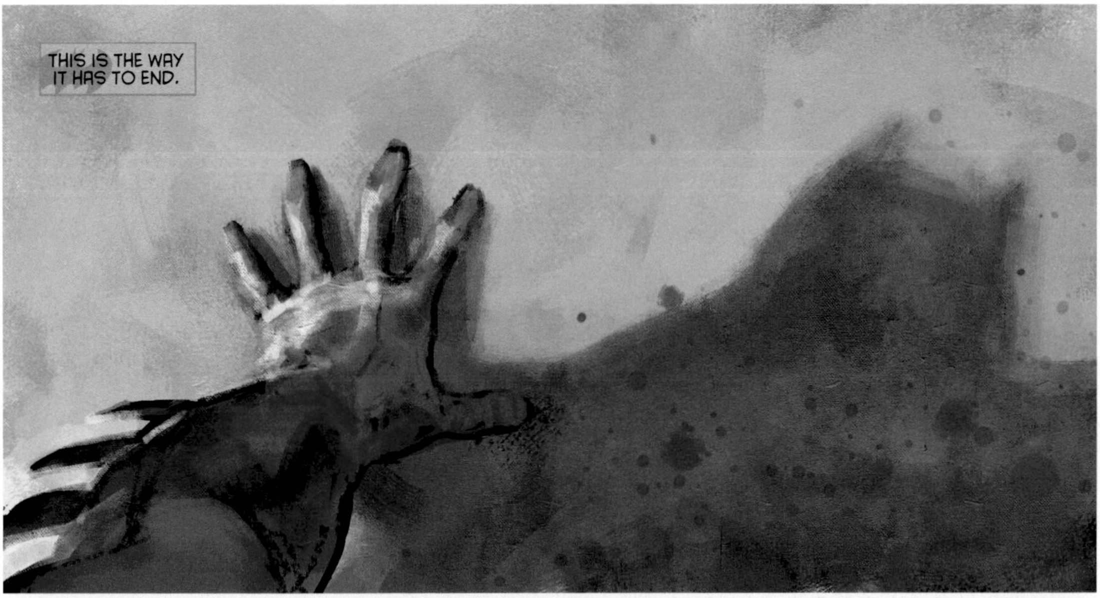
THIS IS THE WAY IT HAS TO END.

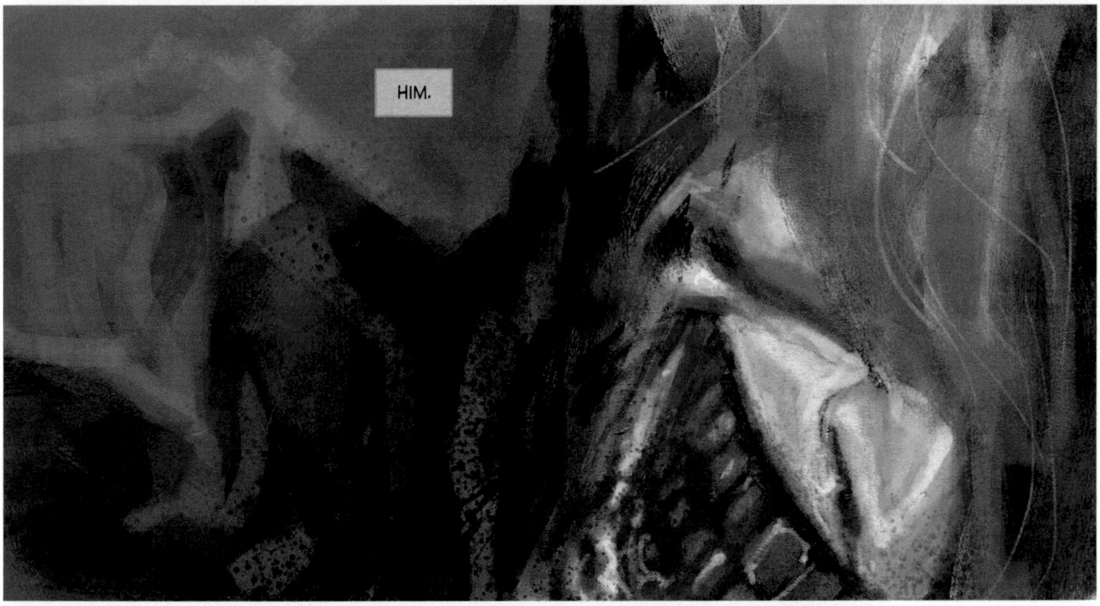
HIM.

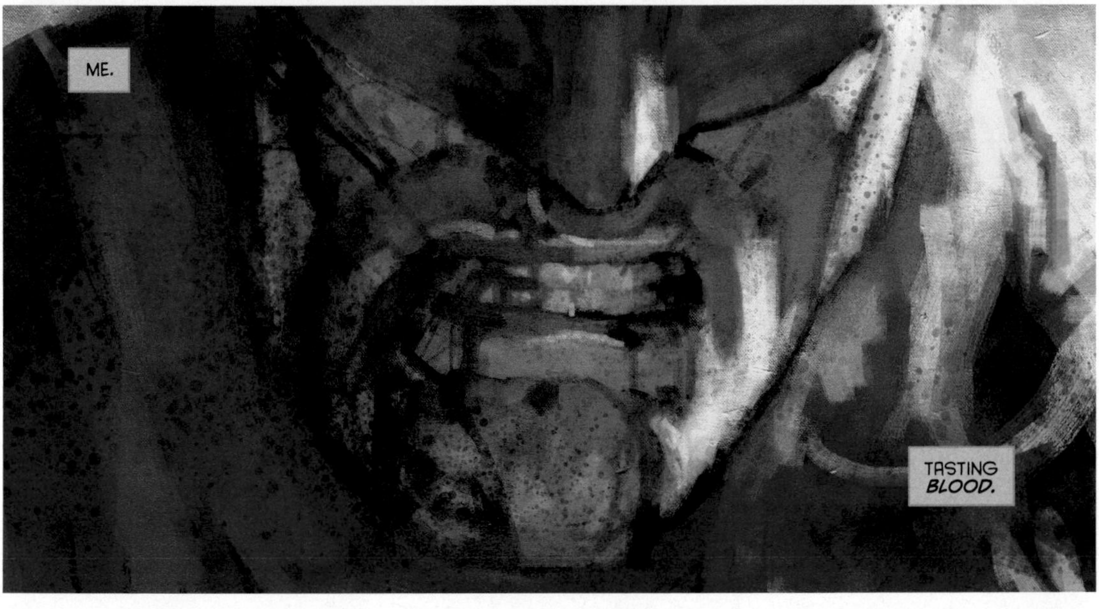
ME.
TASTING *BLOOD.*

INFECTED AND BROKEN, WE'VE TAKEN A BEATING.
BOTH OF US.
I STEEL MYSELF FOR WHAT I'M ABOUT TO DO.
HE STILL LAUGHS. I'M NOT SURE IF IT'S IN THE FACE OF DEATH...
OR IF HIS *IS* THE FACE OF DEATH.

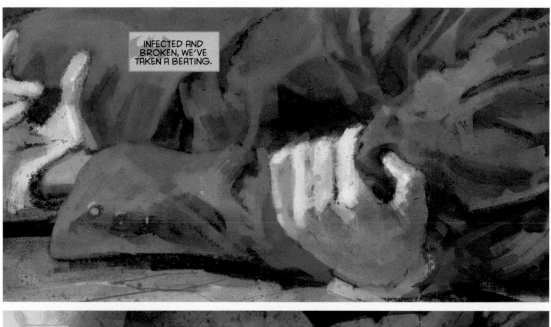

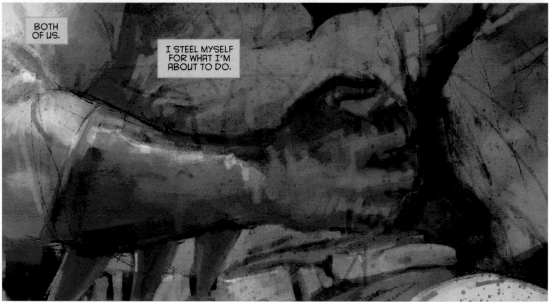

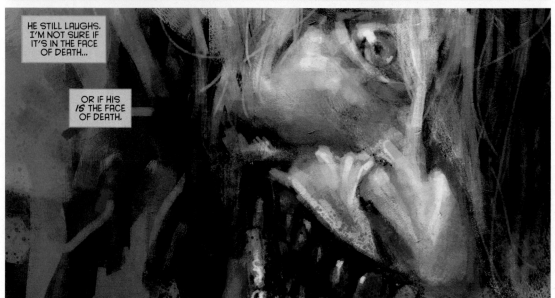

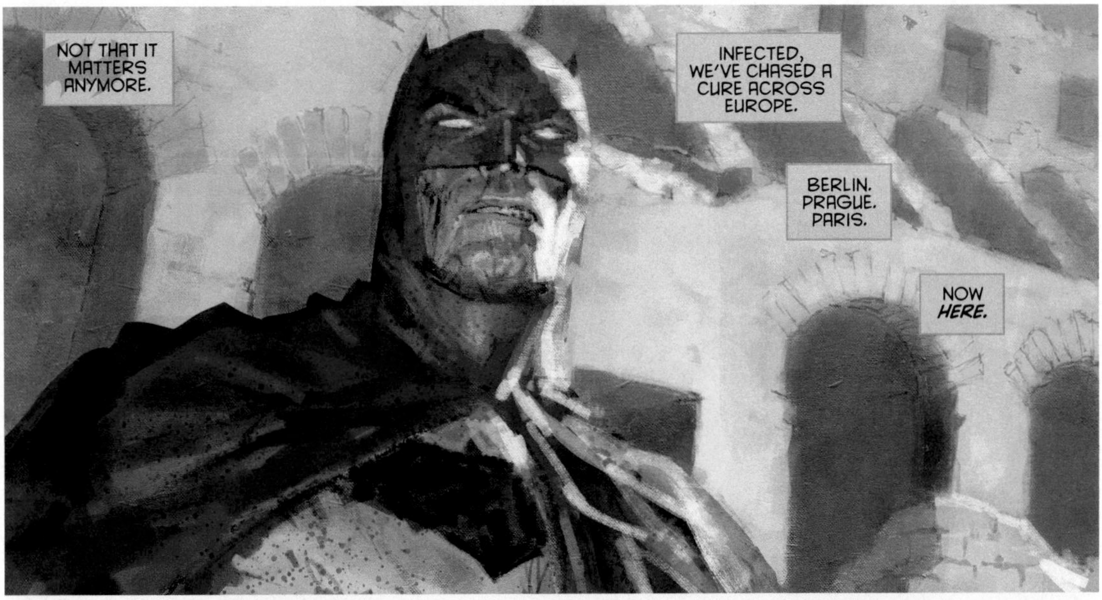
NOT THAT IT MATTERS ANYMORE.
INFECTED, WE'VE CHASED A CURE ACROSS EUROPE.
BERLIN. PRAGUE. PARIS.
NOW *HERE.*

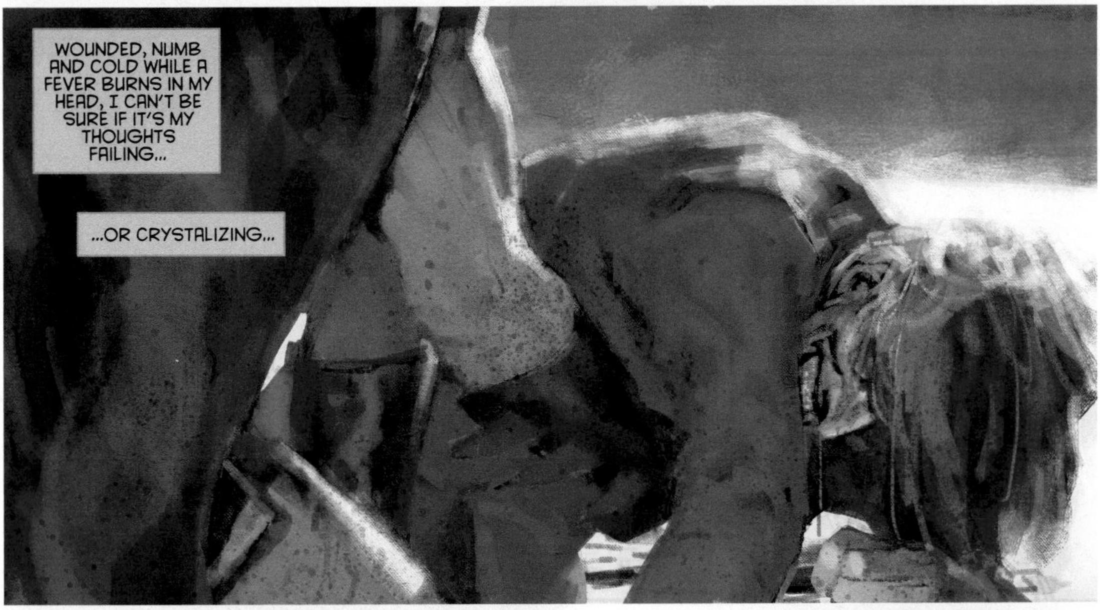
WOUNDED, NUMB AND COLD WHILE A FEVER BURNS IN MY HEAD, I CAN'T BE SURE IF IT'S MY THOUGHTS FAILING...
...OR CRYSTALIZING...

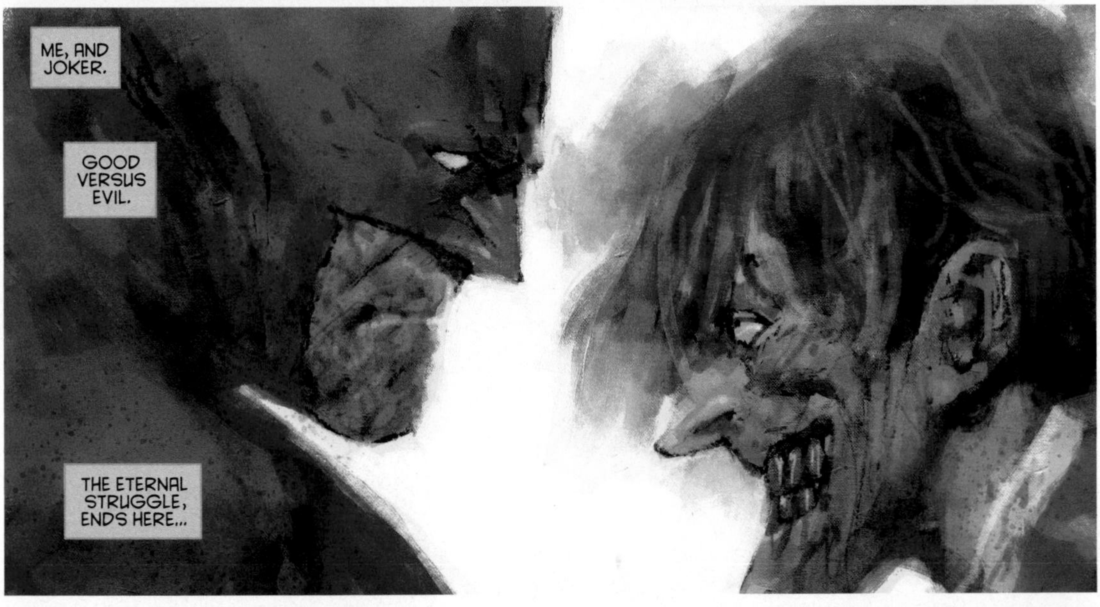
ME, AND JOKER.
GOOD VERSUS EVIL.
THE ETERNAL STRUGGLE, ENDS HERE...

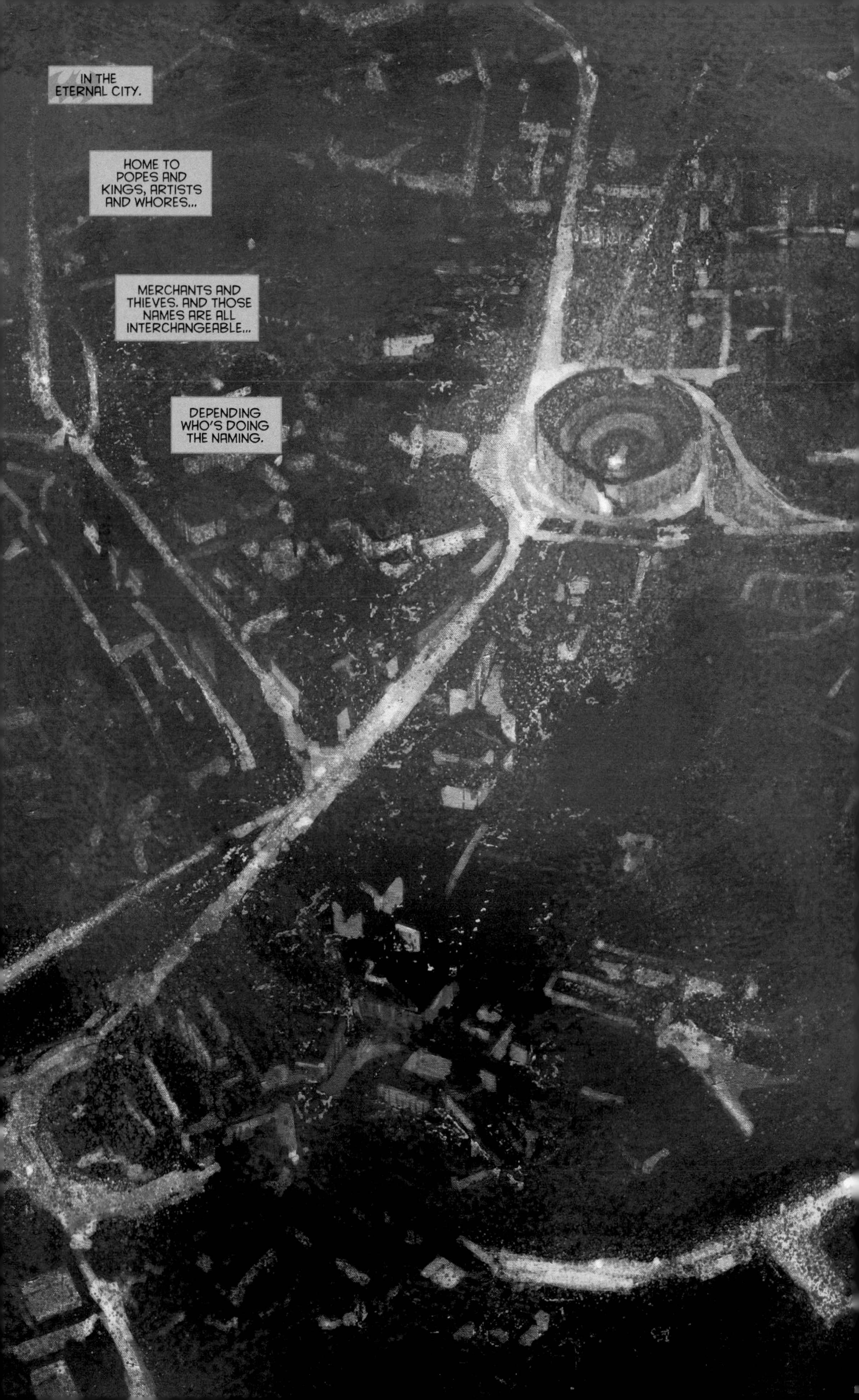
IN THE ETERNAL CITY.
HOME TO POPES AND KINGS, ARTISTS AND WHORES...
MERCHANTS AND THIEVES. AND THOSE NAMES ARE ALL INTERCHANGEABLE...
DEPENDING WHO'S DOING THE NAMING.

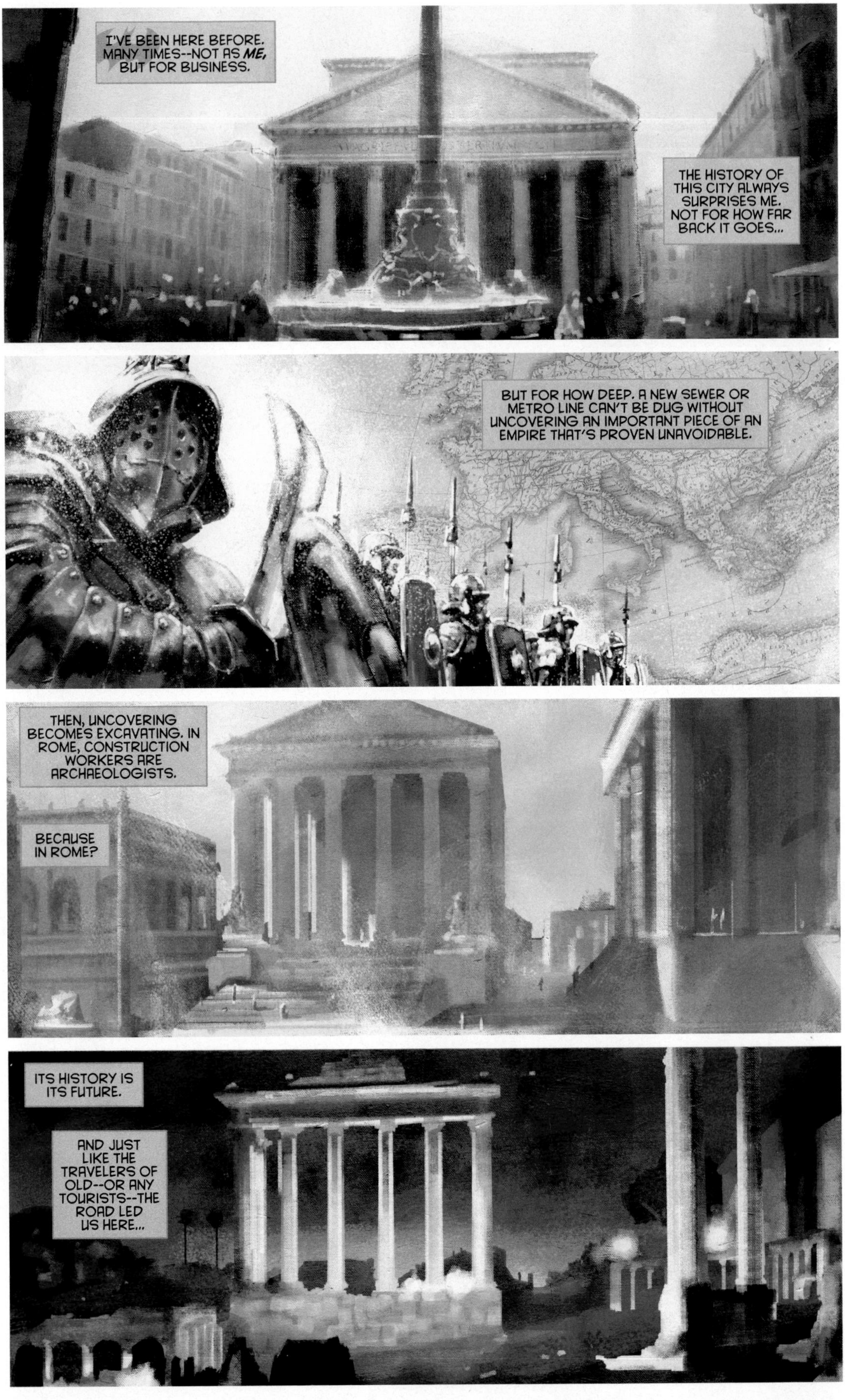
I'VE BEEN HERE BEFORE. MANY TIMES--NOT AS *ME,* BUT FOR BUSINESS.
THE HISTORY OF THIS CITY ALWAYS SURPRISES ME. NOT FOR HOW FAR BACK IT GOES...
BUT FOR HOW DEEP. A NEW SEWER OR METRO LINE CAN'T BE DUG WITHOUT UNCOVERING AN IMPORTANT PIECE OF AN EMPIRE THAT'S PROVEN UNAVOIDABLE.
THEN, UNCOVERING BECOMES EXCAVATING. IN ROME, CONSTRUCTION WORKERS ARE ARCHAEOLOGISTS.
BECAUSE IN ROME?
ITS HISTORY IS ITS FUTURE.
AND JUST LIKE THE TRAVELERS OF OLD--OR ANY TOURISTS--THE ROAD LED US HERE...

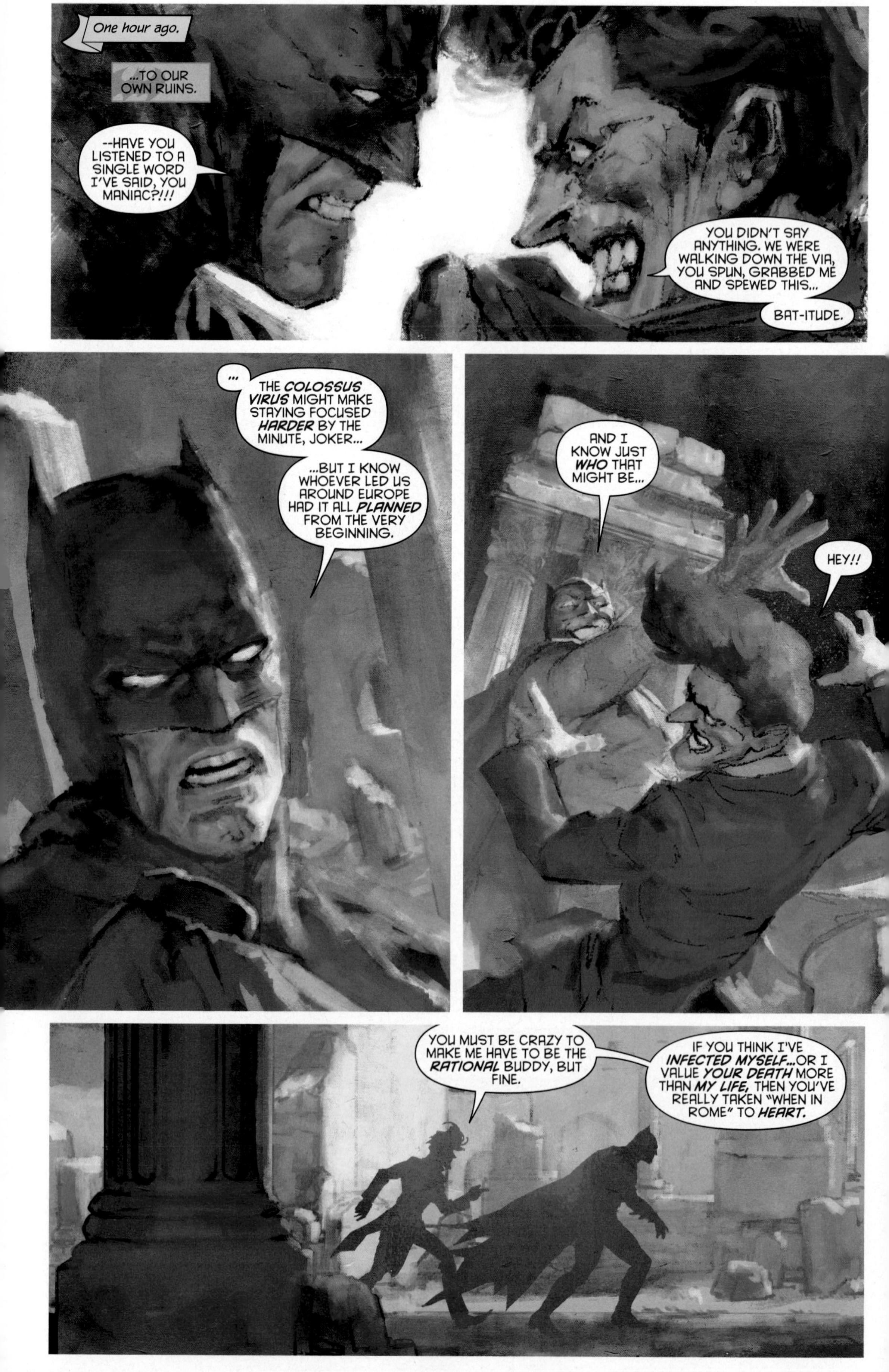
One hour ago.
...TO OUR OWN RUINS.
--HAVE YOU LISTENED TO A SINGLE WORD I'VE SAID, YOU MANIAC?!!!
YOU DIDN'T SAY ANYTHING. WE WERE WALKING DOWN THE VIA, YOU SPUN, GRABBED ME AND SPEWED THIS...
BAT-ITUDE.
...
THE COLOSSUS VIRUS MIGHT MAKE STAYING FOCUSED HARDER BY THE MINUTE, JOKER...
...BUT I KNOW WHOEVER LED US AROUND EUROPE HAD IT ALL PLANNED FROM THE VERY BEGINNING.
AND I KNOW JUST WHO THAT MIGHT BE...
HEY!!
YOU MUST BE CRAZY TO MAKE ME HAVE TO BE THE RATIONAL BUDDY, BUT FINE.
IF YOU THINK I'VE INFECTED MYSELF...OR I VALUE YOUR DEATH MORE THAN MY LIFE, THEN YOU'VE REALLY TAKEN "WHEN IN ROME" TO HEART.

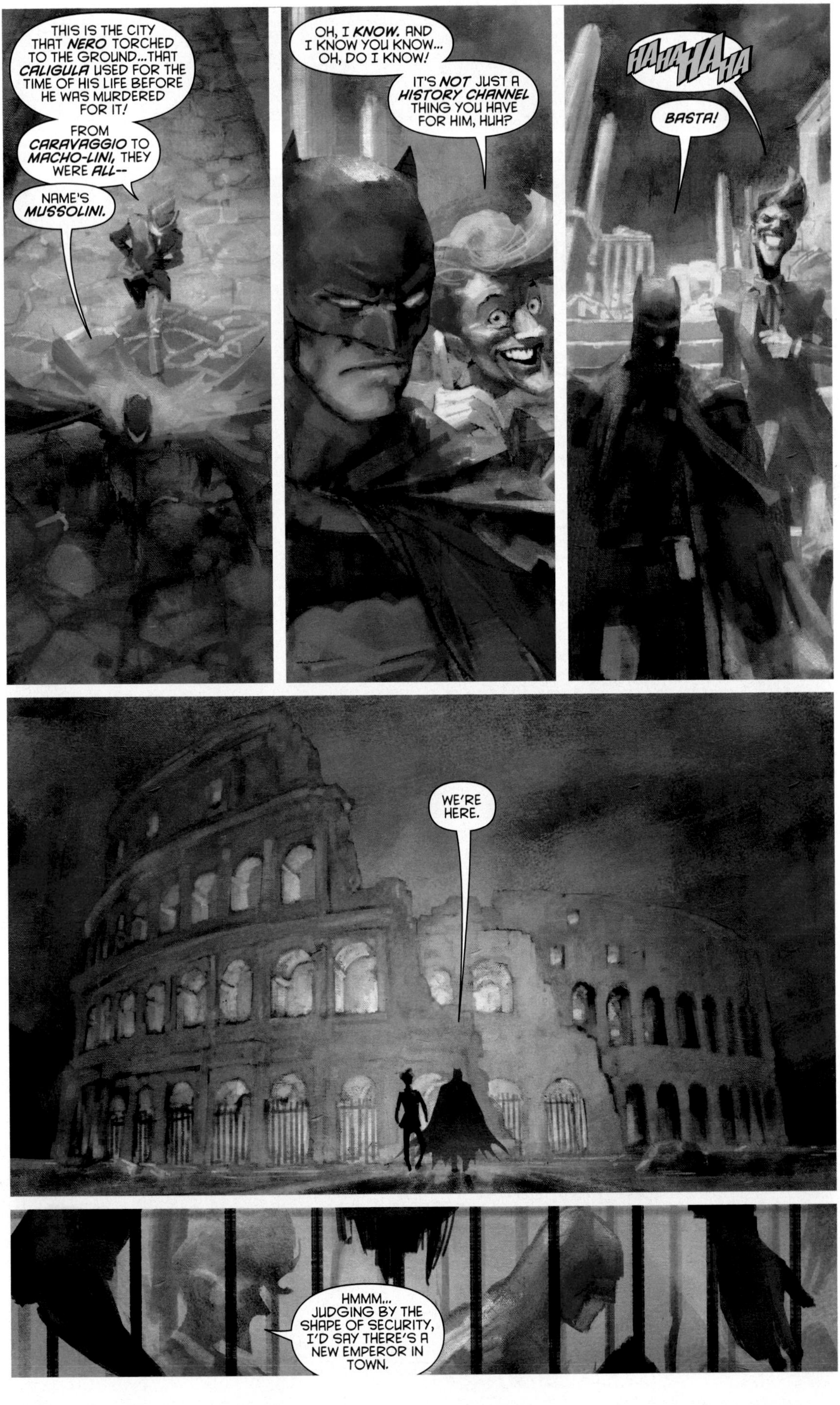
THIS IS THE CITY THAT NERO TORCHED TO THE GROUND...THAT CALIGULA USED FOR THE TIME OF HIS LIFE BEFORE HE WAS MURDERED FOR IT!
FROM CARAVAGGIO TO MACHO-LINI, THEY WERE ALL--
NAME'S MUSSOLINI.
OH, I KNOW. AND I KNOW YOU KNOW... OH, DO I KNOW!
IT'S NOT JUST A HISTORY CHANNEL THING YOU HAVE FOR HIM, HUH?
HAHAHAHA
BASTA!
WE'RE HERE.
HMMM... JUDGING BY THE SHAPE OF SECURITY, I'D SAY THERE'S A NEW EMPEROR IN TOWN.

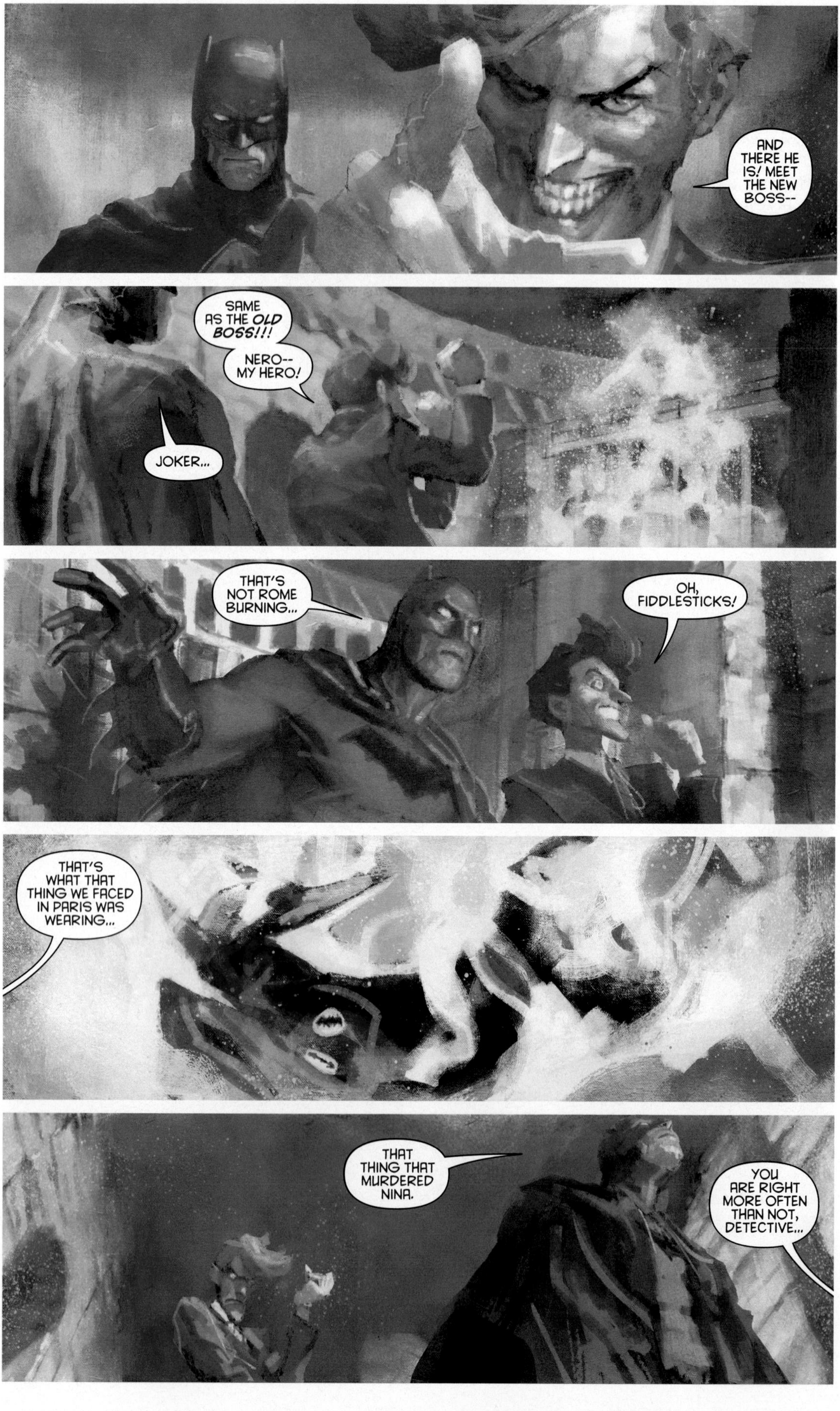
AND THERE HE IS! MEET THE NEW BOSS--
SAME AS THE OLD BOSS!!!
NERO-- MY HERO!
JOKER...
THAT'S NOT ROME BURNING...
OH, FIDDLESTICKS!
THAT'S WHAT THAT THING WE FACED IN PARIS WAS WEARING...
THAT THING THAT MURDERED NINA.
YOU ARE RIGHT MORE OFTEN THAN NOT, DETECTIVE...

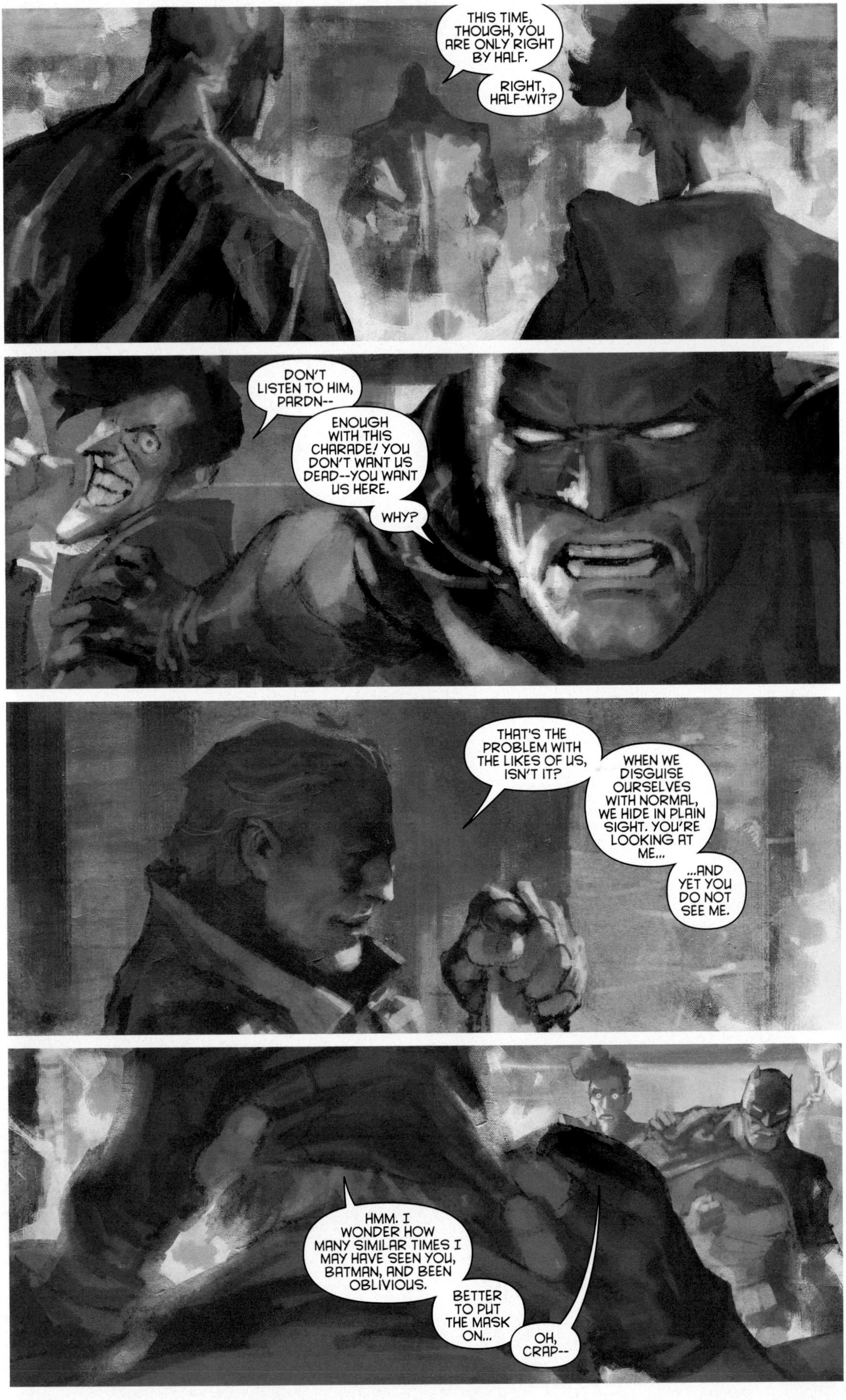
THIS TIME, THOUGH, YOU ARE ONLY RIGHT BY HALF.
RIGHT, HALF-WIT?
DON'T LISTEN TO HIM, PARDN--
ENOUGH WITH THIS CHARADE! YOU DON'T WANT US DEAD--YOU WANT US HERE.
WHY?
THAT'S THE PROBLEM WITH THE LIKES OF US, ISN'T IT?
WHEN WE DISGUISE OURSELVES WITH NORMAL, WE HIDE IN PLAIN SIGHT. YOU'RE LOOKING AT ME...
...AND YET YOU DO NOT SEE ME.
HMM. I WONDER HOW MANY SIMILAR TIMES I MAY HAVE SEEN YOU, BATMAN, AND BEEN OBLIVIOUS.
BETTER TO PUT THE MASK ON...
OH, CRAP--

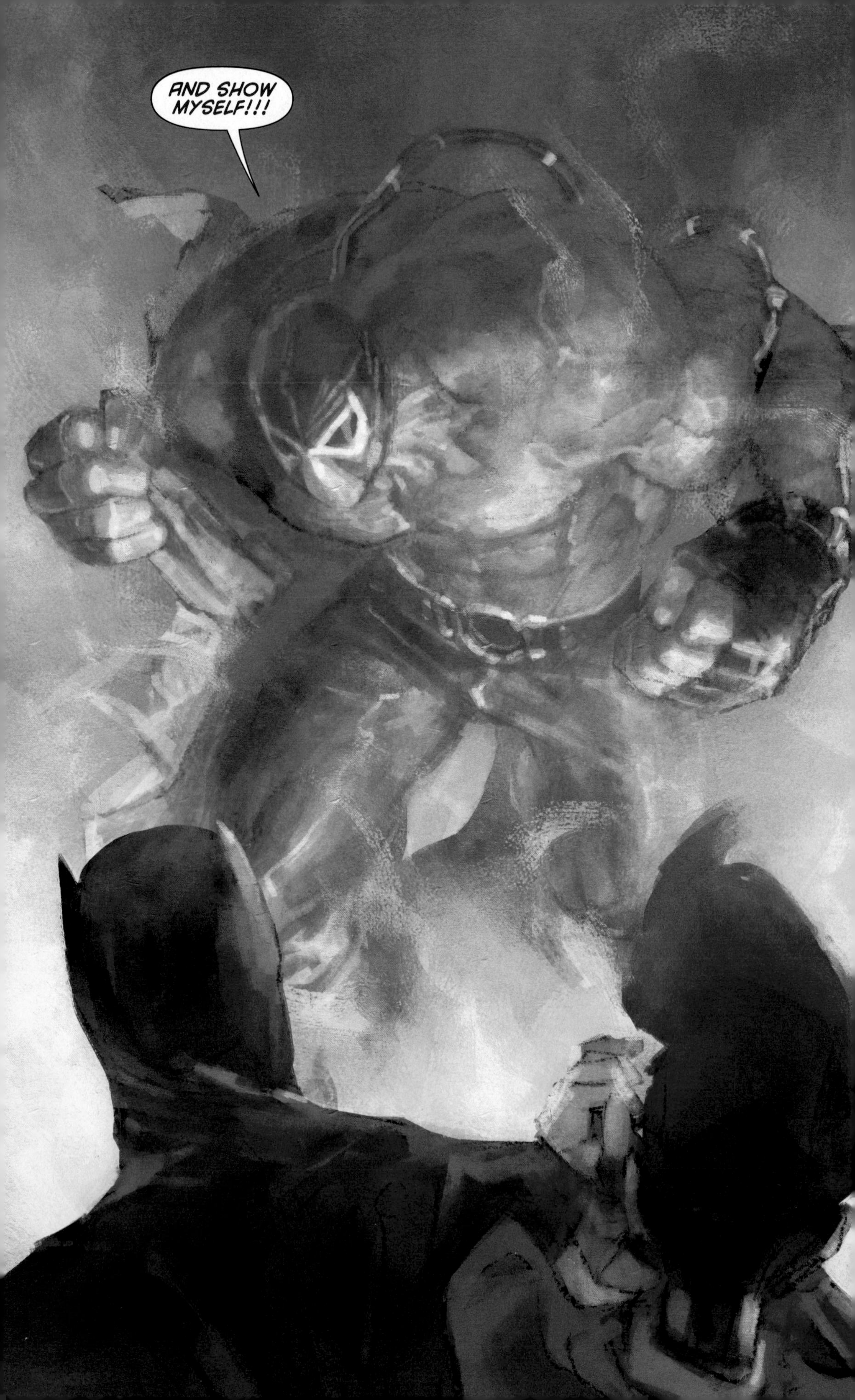
AND SHOW MYSELF!!!

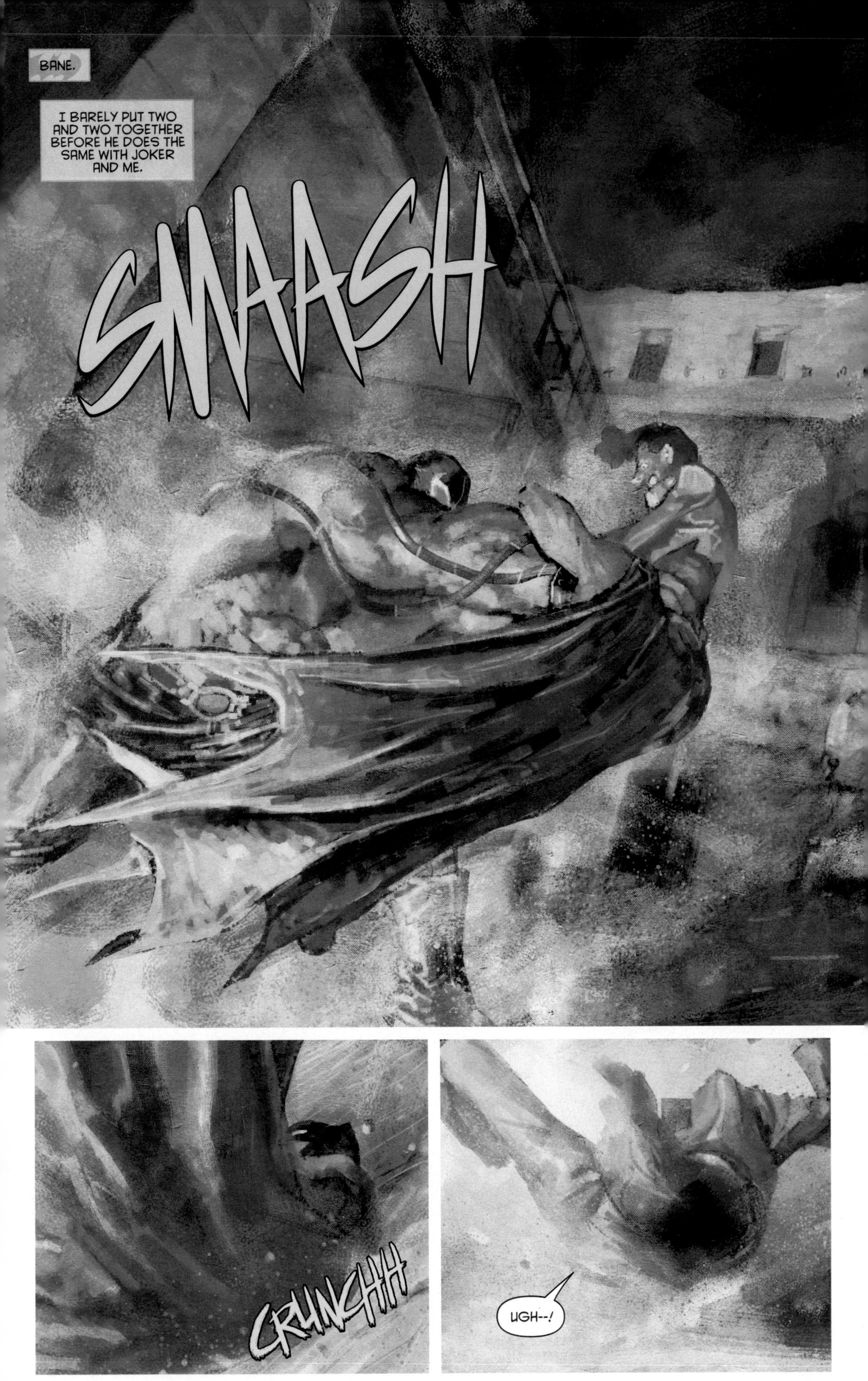
BANE.
I BARELY PUT TWO AND TWO TOGETHER BEFORE HE DOES THE SAME WITH JOKER AND ME.
SMAASH
CRUNCHH
UGH--!

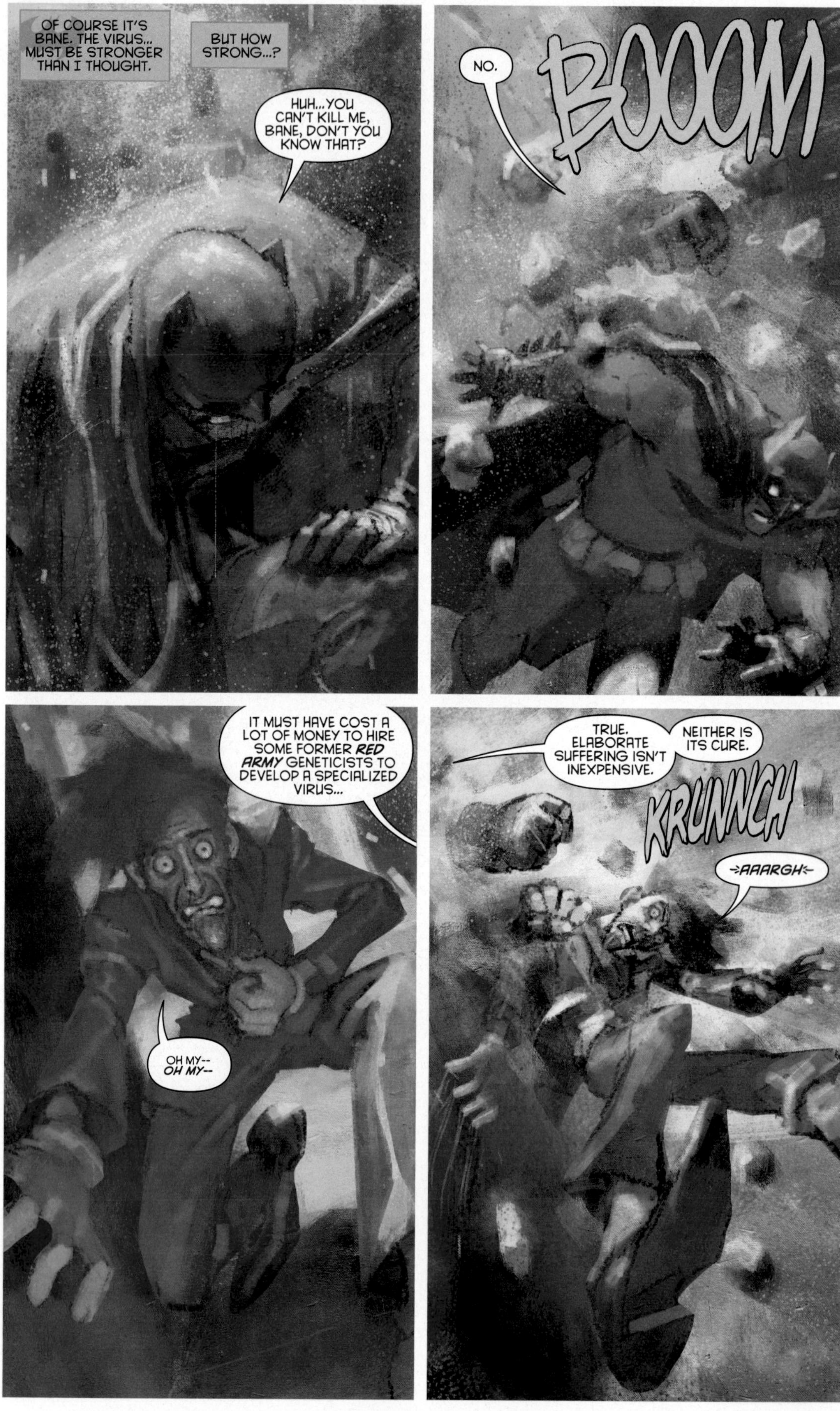
OF COURSE IT'S BANE. THE VIRUS... MUST BE STRONGER THAN I THOUGHT.
BUT HOW STRONG...?
HUH...YOU CAN'T KILL ME, BANE, DON'T YOU KNOW THAT?
NO.
BOOOM
IT MUST HAVE COST A LOT OF MONEY TO HIRE SOME FORMER *RED ARMY* GENETICISTS TO DEVELOP A SPECIALIZED VIRUS...
OH MY-- *OH MY--*
TRUE. ELABORATE SUFFERING ISN'T INEXPENSIVE.
NEITHER IS ITS CURE.
KRUNNCH
AAARGH

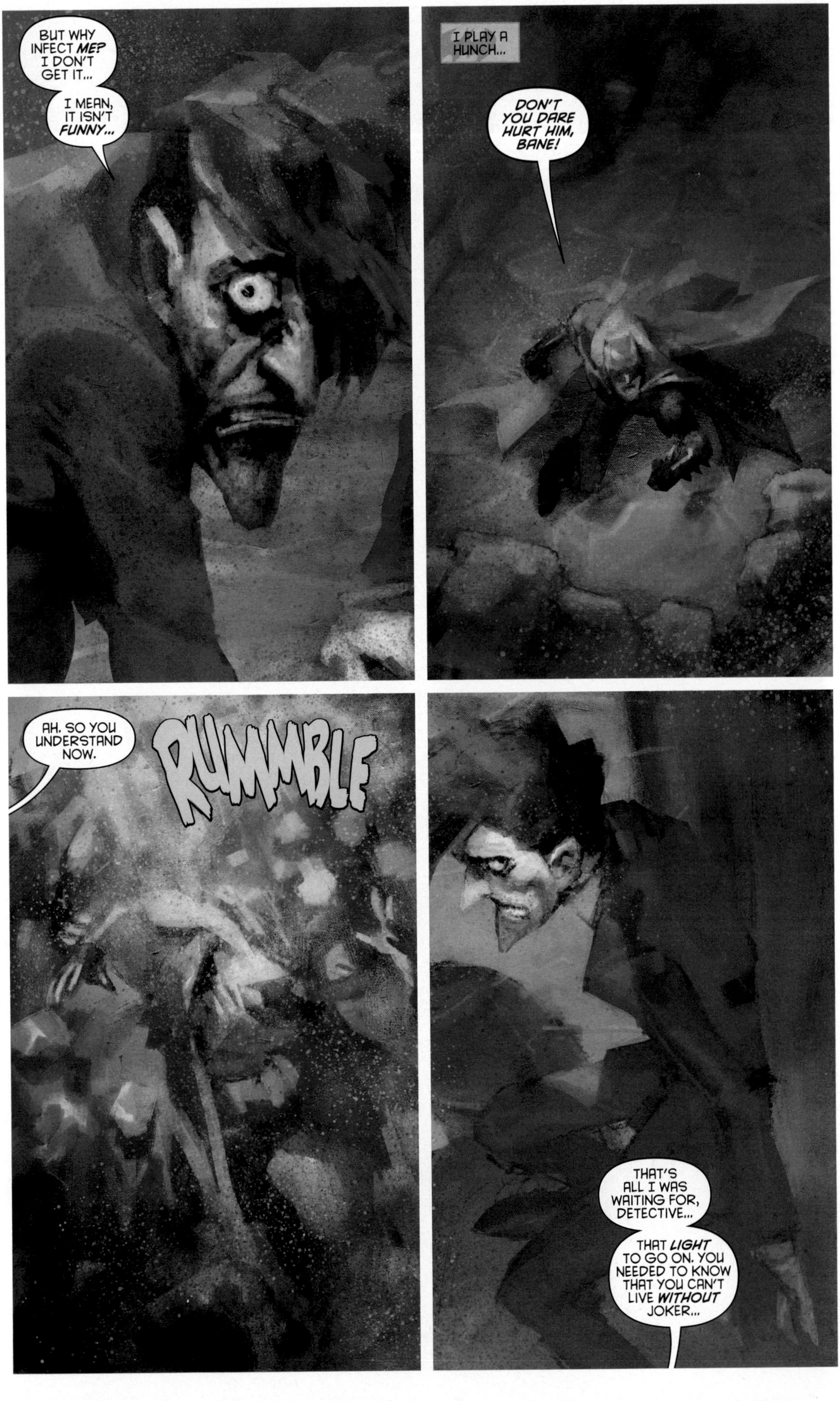
BUT WHY INFECT ME? I DON'T GET IT...
I MEAN, IT ISN'T FUNNY...
I PLAY A HUNCH...
DON'T YOU DARE HURT HIM, BANE!
AH. SO YOU UNDERSTAND NOW.
RUMMBLE
THAT'S ALL I WAS WAITING FOR, DETECTIVE...
THAT LIGHT TO GO ON. YOU NEEDED TO KNOW THAT YOU CAN'T LIVE WITHOUT JOKER...

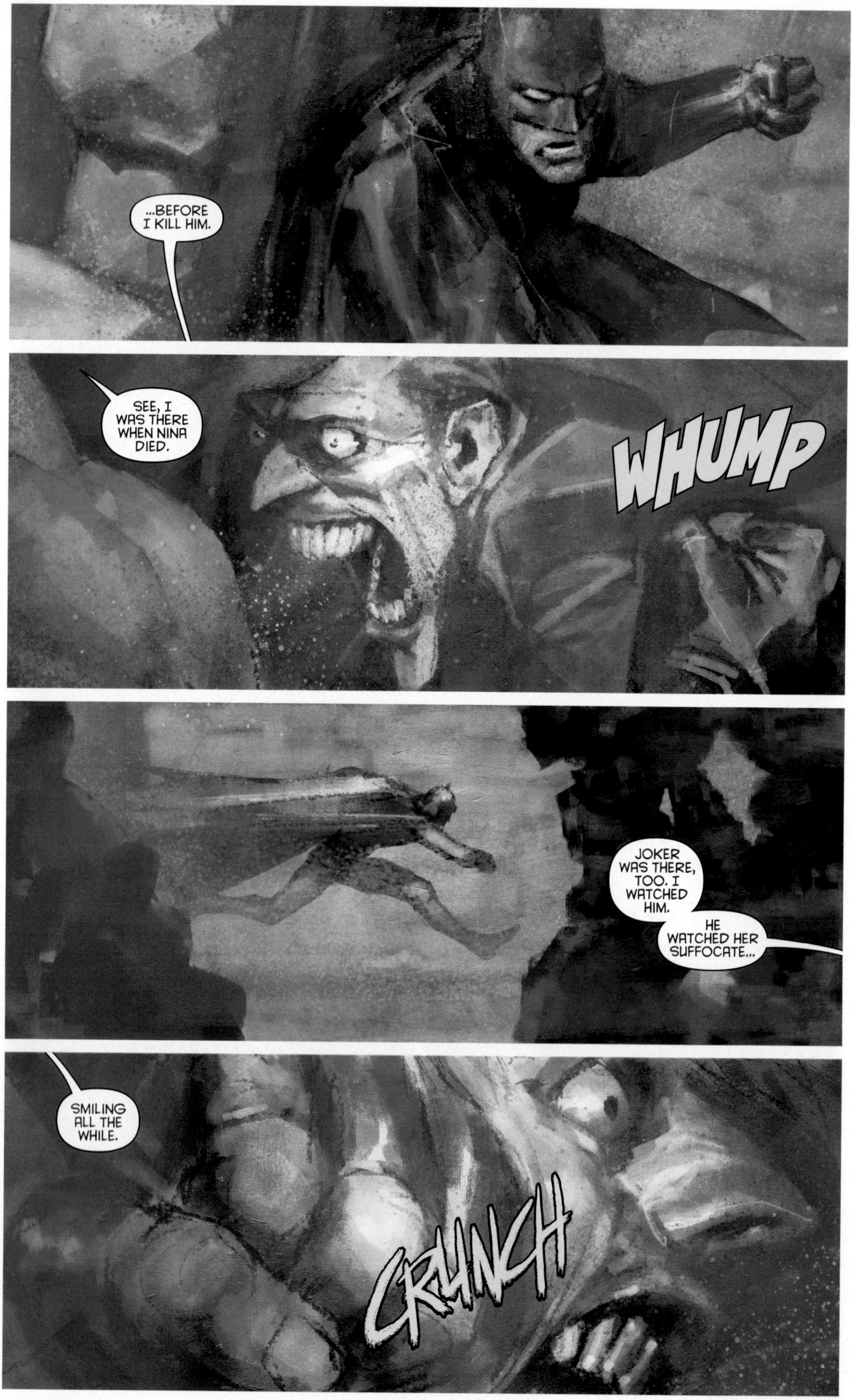
...BEFORE I KILL HIM.
SEE, I WAS THERE WHEN NINA DIED.
WHUMP
JOKER WAS THERE, TOO. I WATCHED HIM.
HE WATCHED HER SUFFOCATE...
SMILING ALL THE WHILE.
CRUNCH

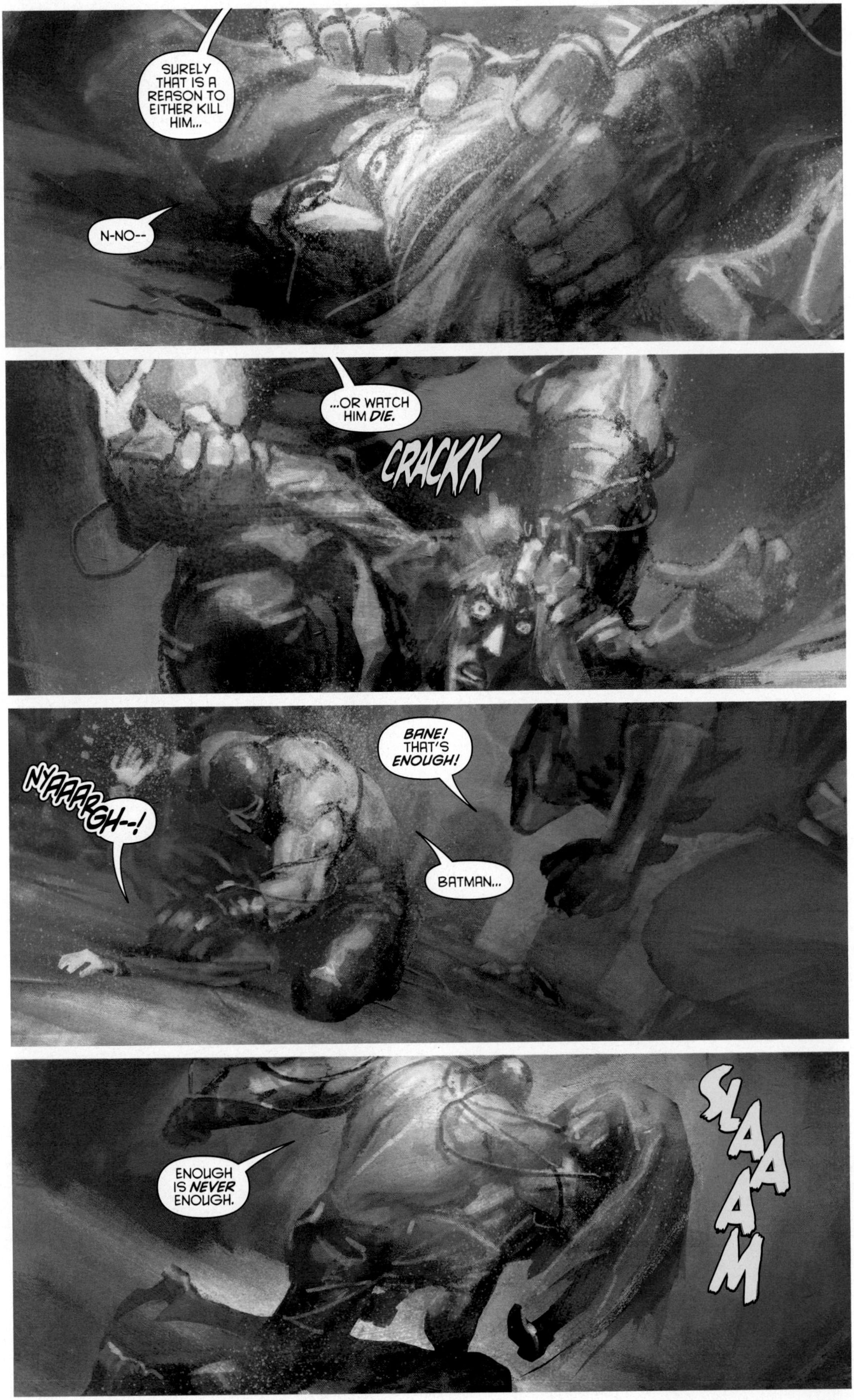

SURELY THAT IS A REASON TO EITHER KILL HIM...
N-NO--
...OR WATCH HIM *DIE.*
CRACKK
BANE! THAT'S *ENOUGH!*
NYAAARGH--!
BATMAN...
ENOUGH IS *NEVER* ENOUGH.
SLAAAAM

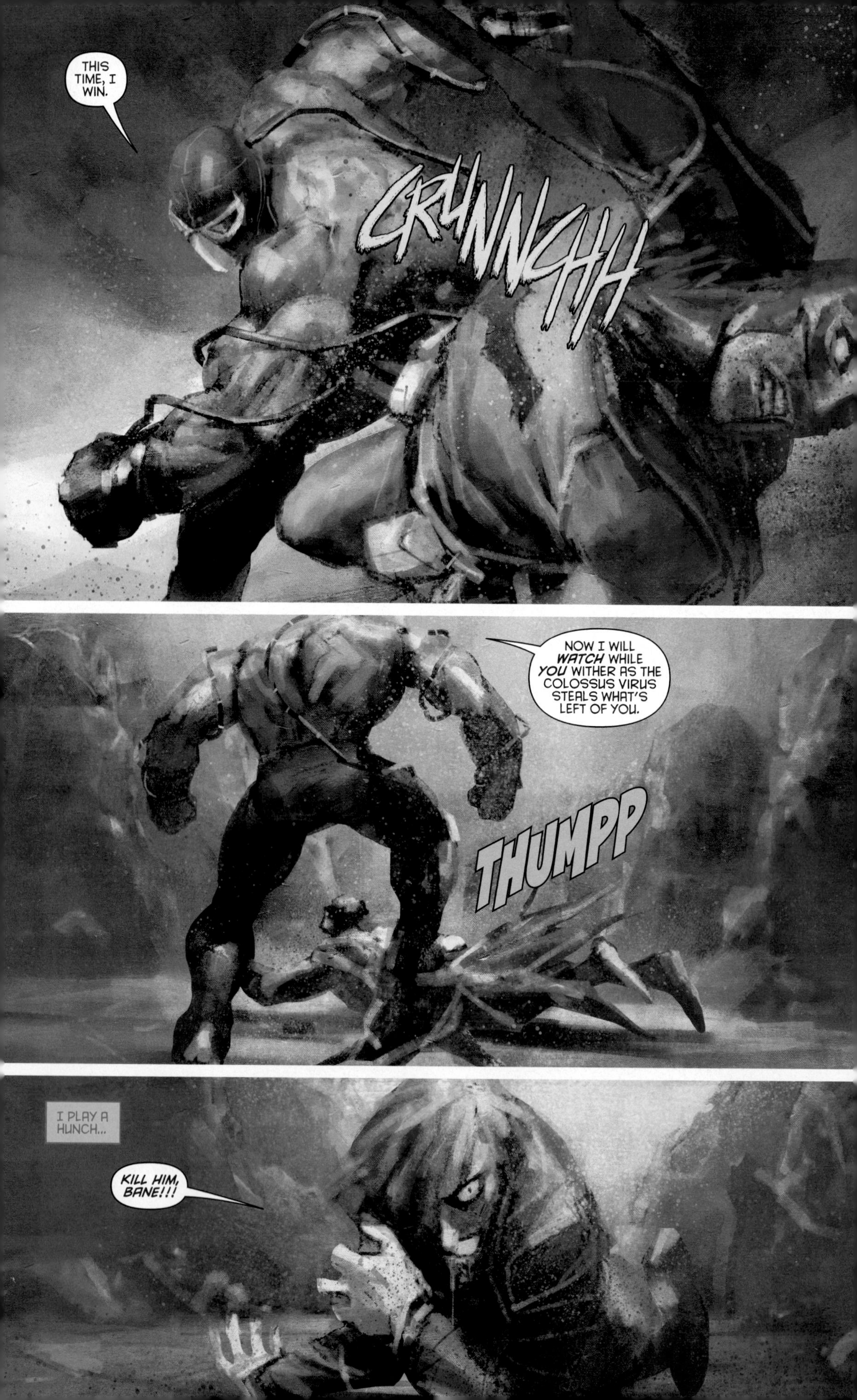
THIS TIME, I WIN.
CRUNNCHH
NOW I WILL WATCH WHILE YOU WITHER AS THE COLOSSUS VIRUS STEALS WHAT'S LEFT OF YOU.
THUMPP
I PLAY A HUNCH...
KILL HIM, BANE!!!

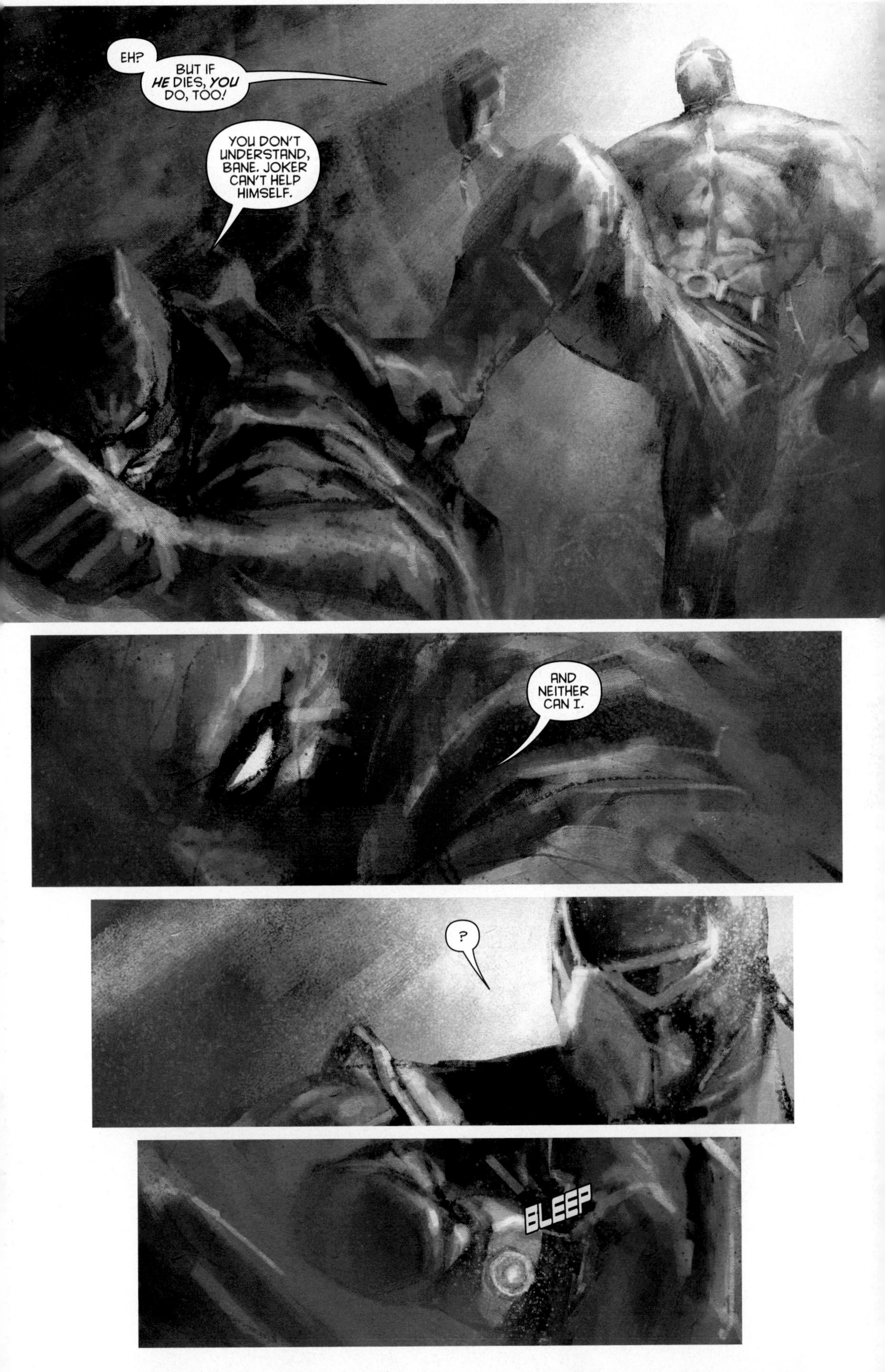
EH?
BUT IF *HE* DIES, *YOU* DO, TOO!
YOU DON'T UNDERSTAND, BANE. JOKER CAN'T HELP HIMSELF.
AND NEITHER CAN I.
?
BLEEP

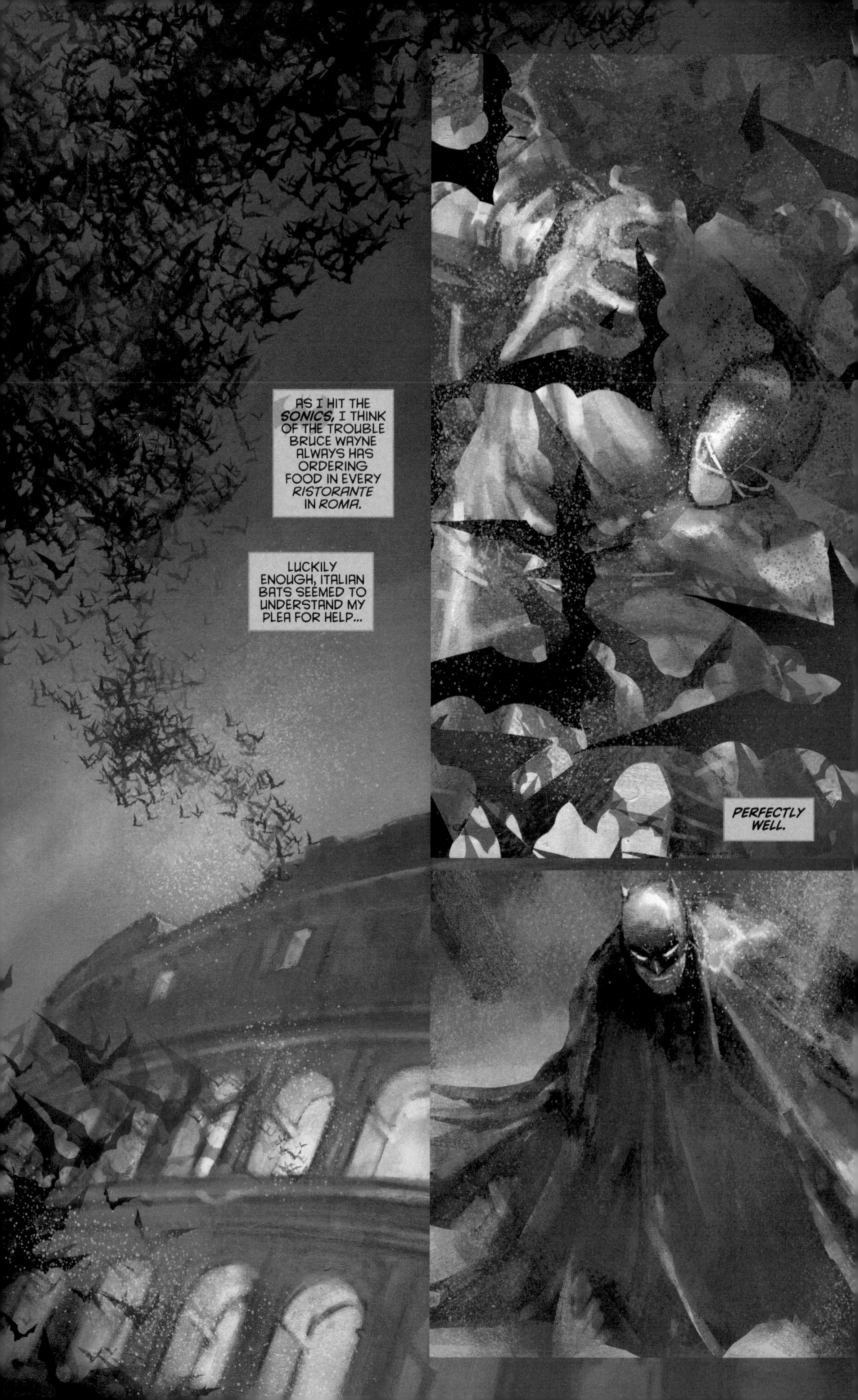
AS I HIT THE *SONICS,* I THINK OF THE TROUBLE BRUCE WAYNE ALWAYS HAS ORDERING FOOD IN EVERY *RISTORANTE* IN *ROMA.*
LUCKILY ENOUGH, ITALIAN BATS SEEMED TO UNDERSTAND MY PLEA FOR HELP...
PERFECTLY WELL.

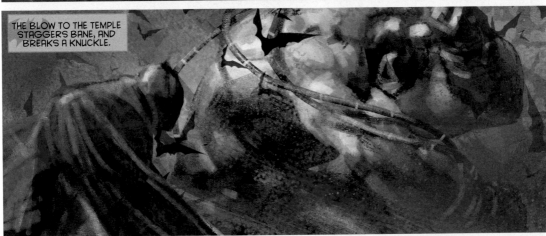

THE BLOW TO THE TEMPLE STAGGERS BANE, AND BREAKS A KNUCKLE.

LUCKILY, I HAVE NINE MORE.

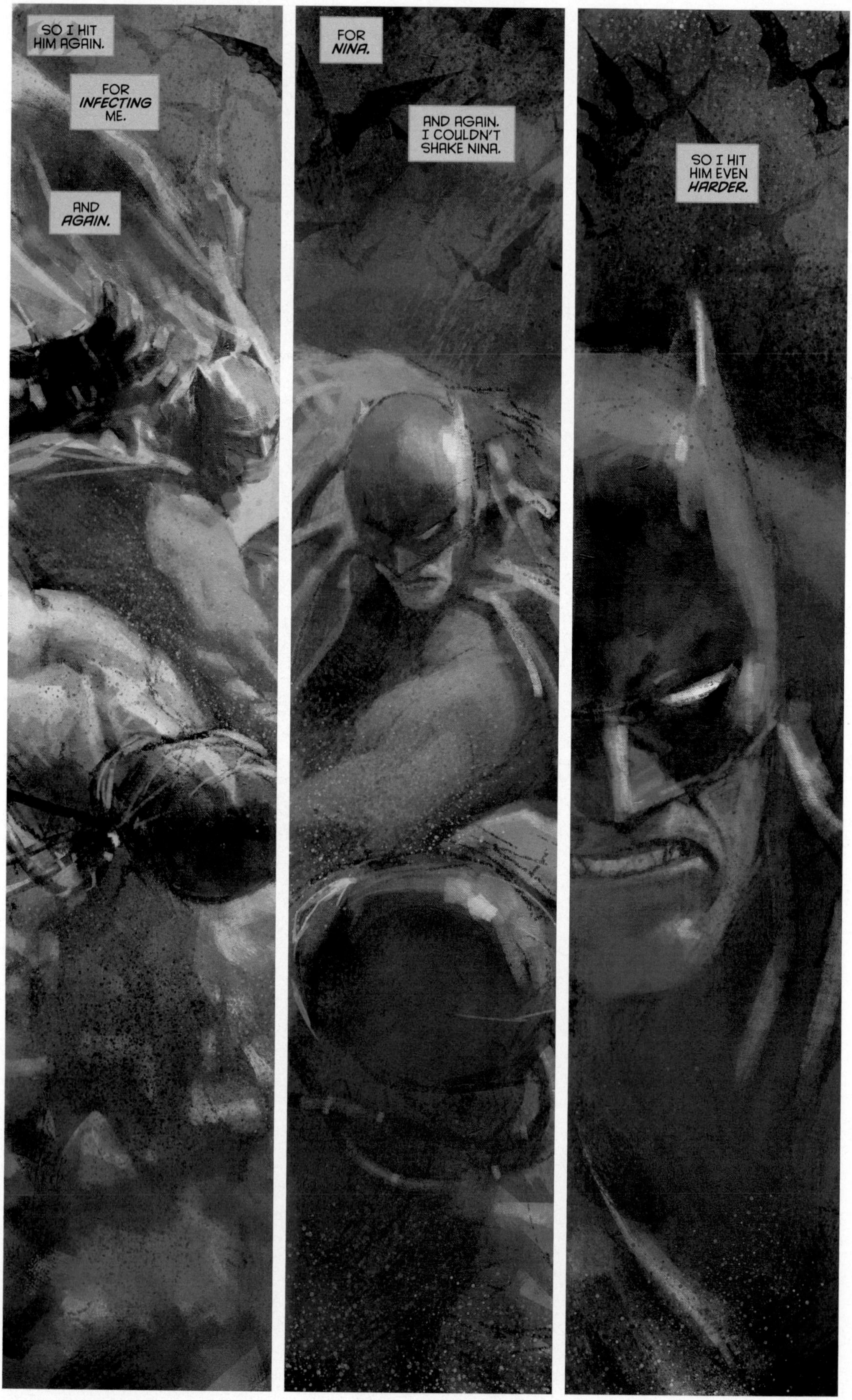
SO I HIT HIM AGAIN.
FOR *INFECTING* ME.
AND *AGAIN.*
FOR *NINA.*
AND AGAIN. I COULDN'T SHAKE NINA.
SO I HIT HIM EVEN *HARDER.*

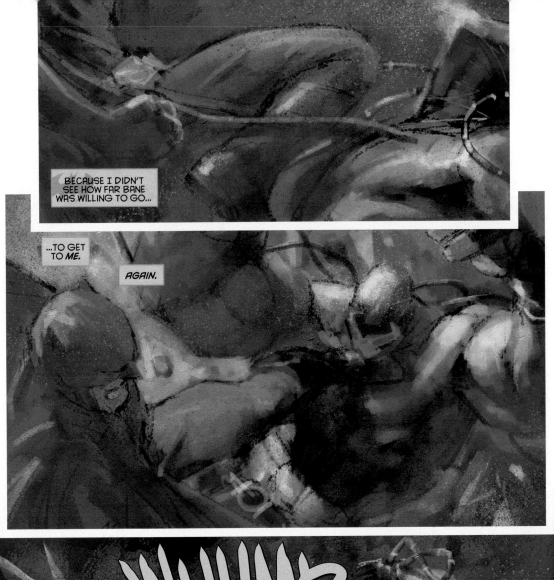

BECAUSE I DIDN'T SEE HOW FAR BANE WAS WILLING TO GO...

...TO GET TO *ME.*

AGAIN.

WHUMP

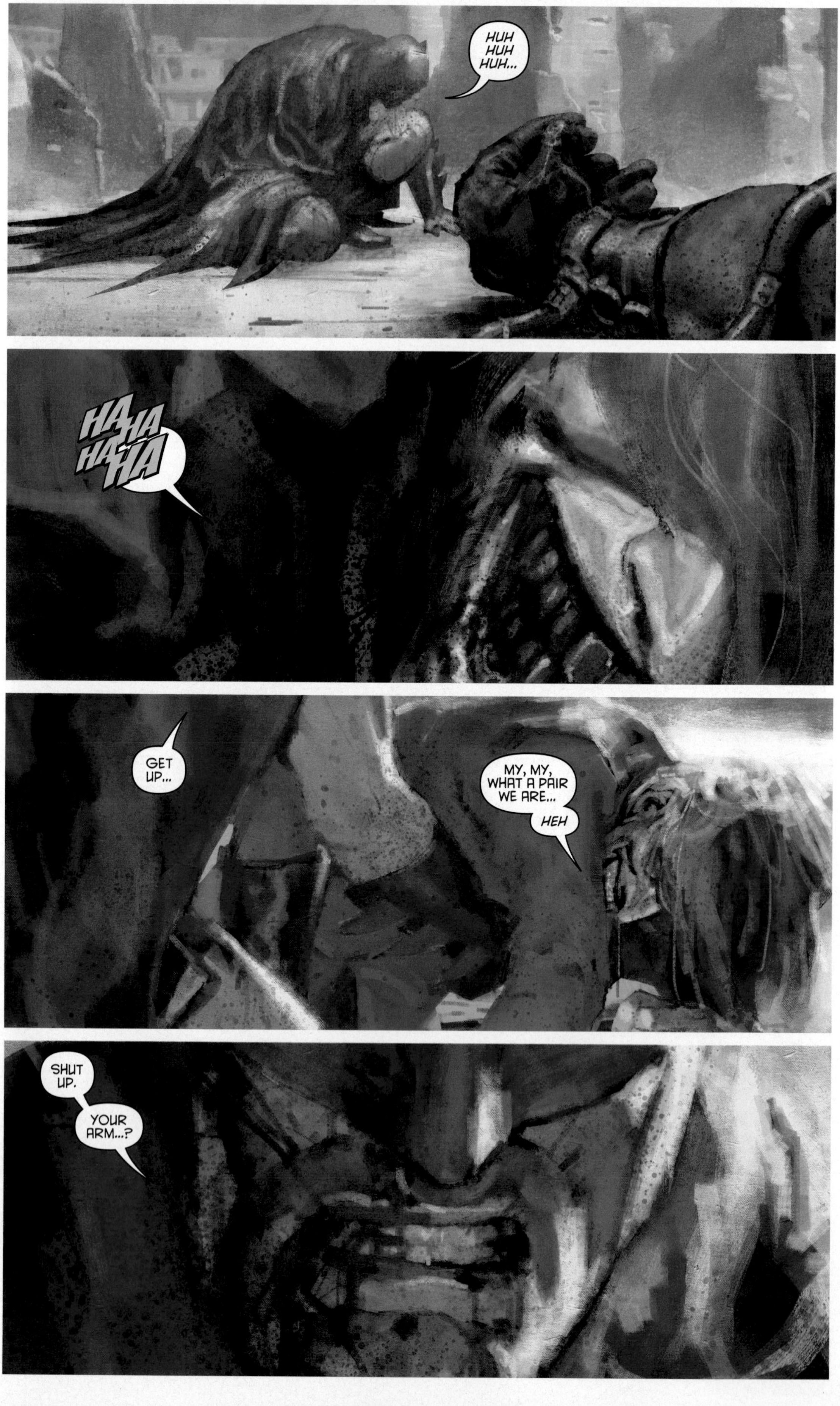
HUH HUH HUH...
HAHA HAHA
GET UP...
MY, MY, WHAT A PAIR WE ARE...
HEH
SHUT UP.
YOUR ARM...?

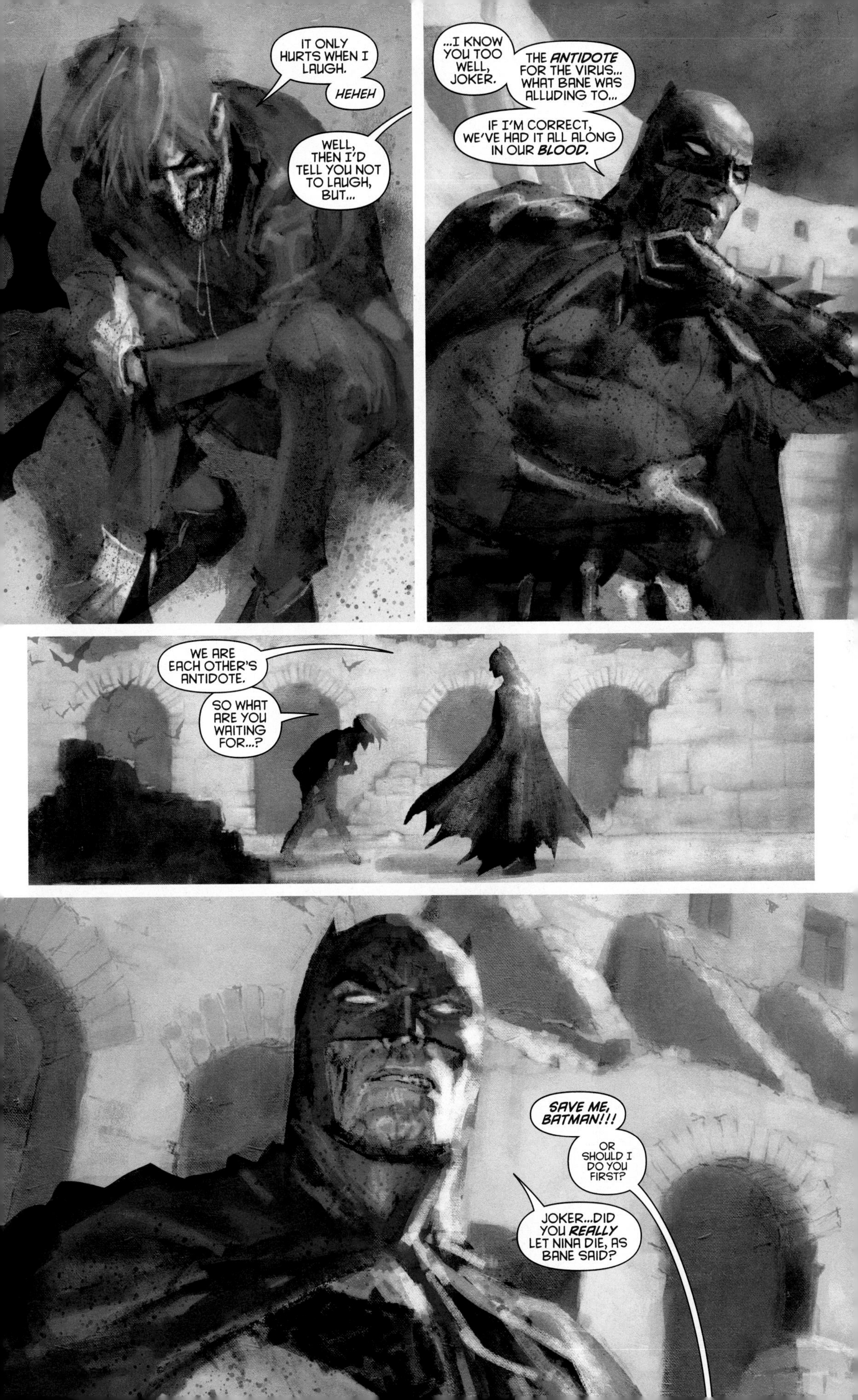
IT ONLY HURTS WHEN I LAUGH.
HEHEH
WELL, THEN I'D TELL YOU NOT TO LAUGH, BUT...
...I KNOW YOU TOO WELL, JOKER.
THE ANTIDOTE FOR THE VIRUS... WHAT BANE WAS ALLUDING TO...
IF I'M CORRECT, WE'VE HAD IT ALL ALONG IN OUR BLOOD.
WE ARE EACH OTHER'S ANTIDOTE.
SO WHAT ARE YOU WAITING FOR...?
SAVE ME, BATMAN!!!
OR SHOULD I DO YOU FIRST?
JOKER...DID YOU REALLY LET NINA DIE, AS BANE SAID?

I AM UTTERLY *SHOCKED.* I MEAN...

"YOU JUST SAID YOU *KNOW ME.*

"RIGHT...?

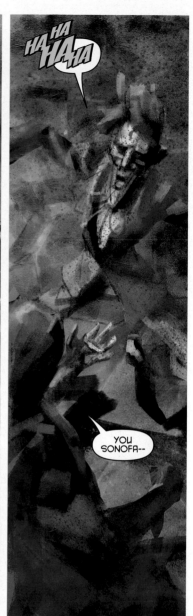

HA HA HA HA

YOU SONOFA--

I HAVE THE CHANCE TO RID THE WORLD OF YOU...

ALL YOU HAVE TO DO IS *DIE* ALONG WITH ME.

DO IT. I *DARE* YOU.

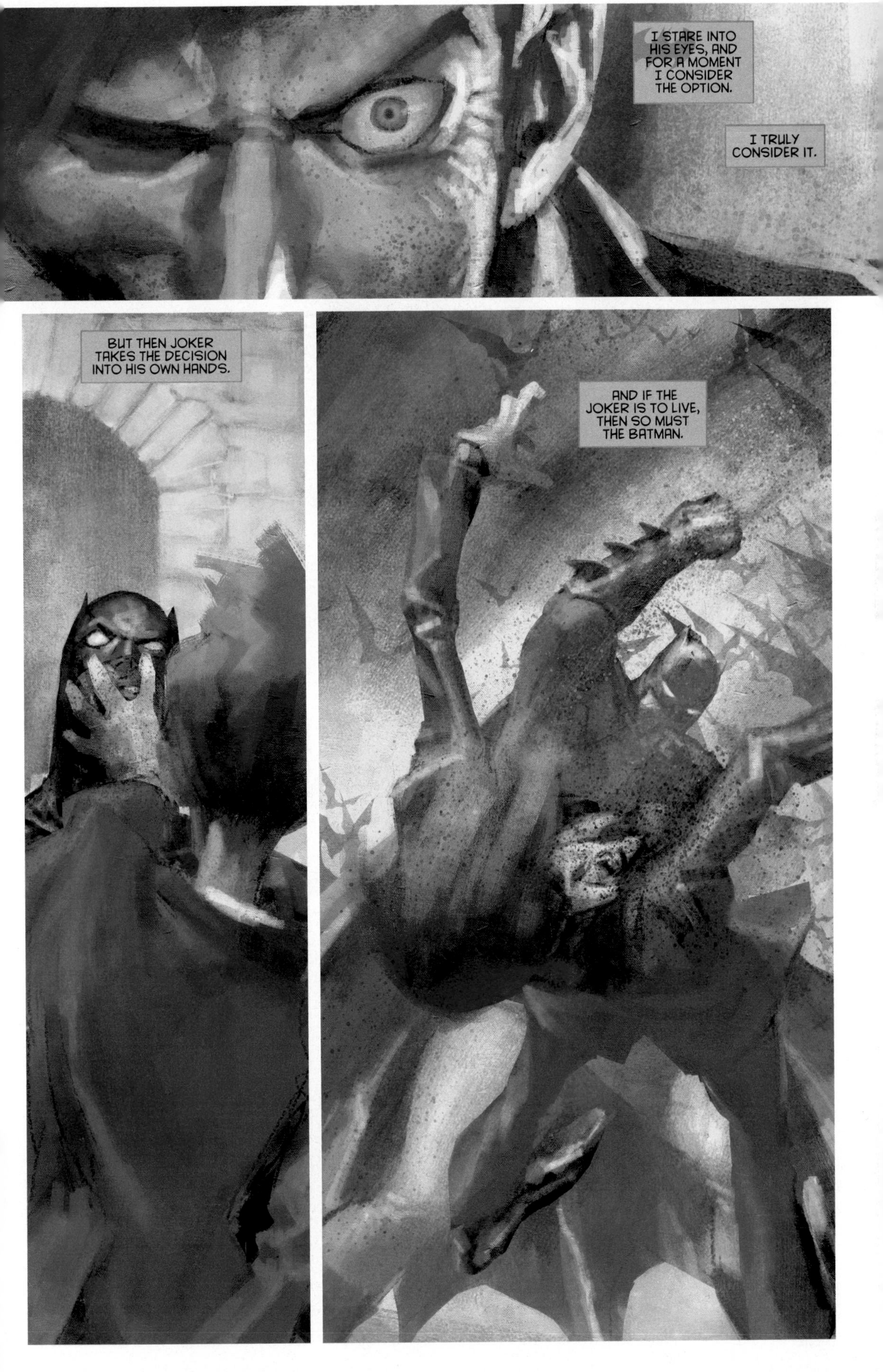
I STARE INTO HIS EYES, AND FOR A MOMENT I CONSIDER THE OPTION.
I TRULY CONSIDER IT.
BUT THEN JOKER TAKES THE DECISION INTO HIS OWN HANDS.
AND IF THE JOKER IS TO LIVE, THEN SO MUST THE BATMAN.

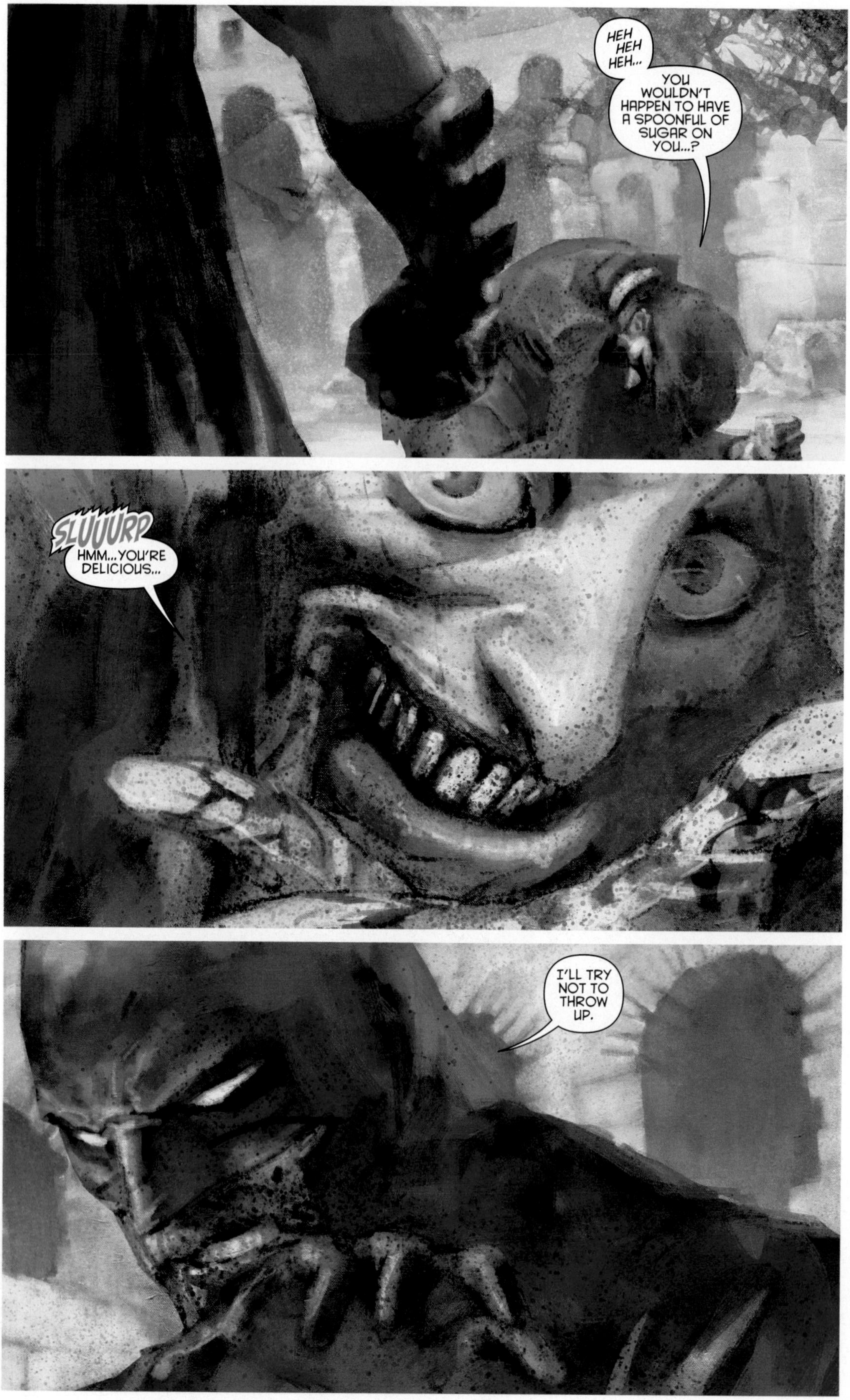
HEH HEH HEH...
YOU WOULDN'T HAPPEN TO HAVE A SPOONFUL OF SUGAR ON YOU...?
SLUUURP
HMM...YOU'RE DELICIOUS...
I'LL TRY NOT TO THROW UP.

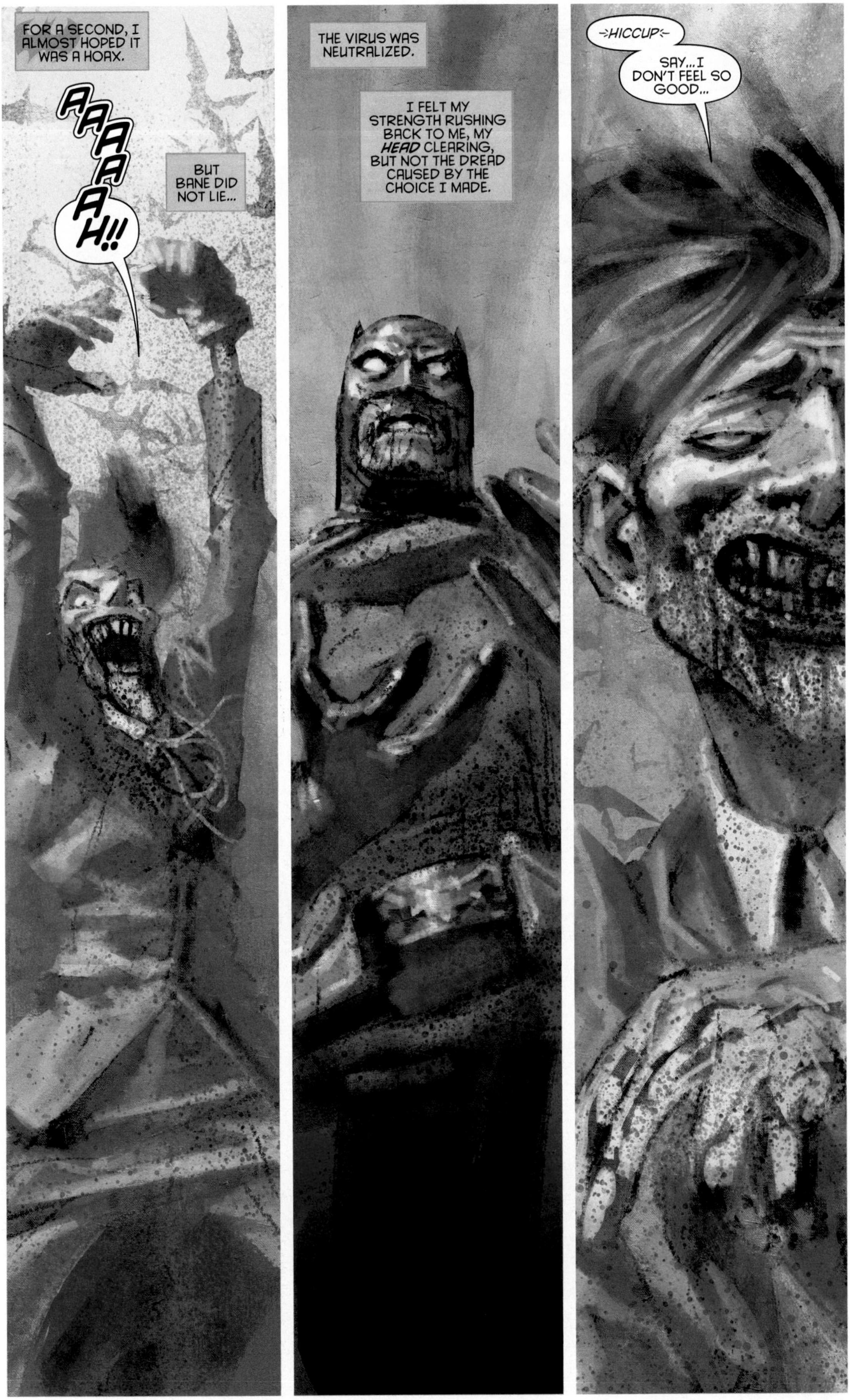
FOR A SECOND, I ALMOST HOPED IT WAS A HOAX.
AAAAAH!!
BUT BANE DID NOT LIE...
THE VIRUS WAS NEUTRALIZED.
I FELT MY STRENGTH RUSHING BACK TO ME, MY HEAD CLEARING, BUT NOT THE DREAD CAUSED BY THE CHOICE I MADE.
HICCUP
SAY...I DON'T FEEL SO GOOD...

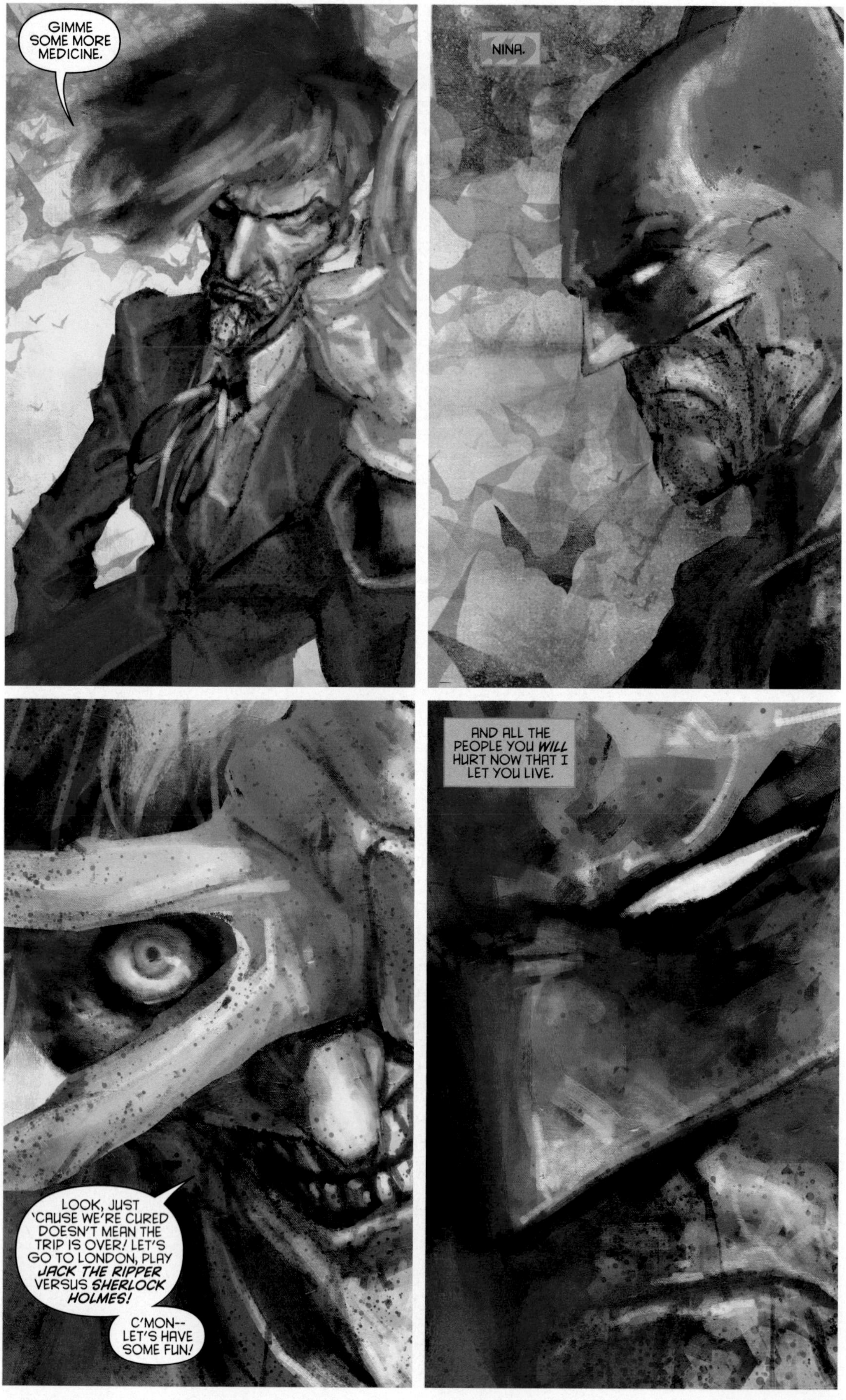
GIMME SOME MORE MEDICINE.
NINA.
LOOK, JUST 'CAUSE WE'RE CURED DOESN'T MEAN THE TRIP IS OVER! LET'S GO TO LONDON, PLAY JACK THE RIPPER VERSUS SHERLOCK HOLMES!
C'MON-- LET'S HAVE SOME FUN!
AND ALL THE PEOPLE YOU WILL HURT NOW THAT I LET YOU LIVE.

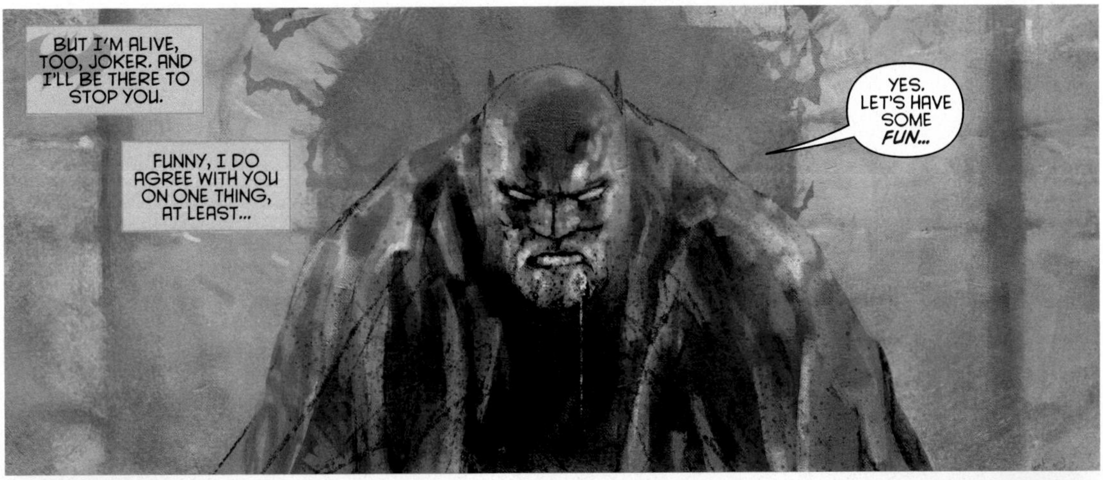
BUT I'M ALIVE, TOO, JOKER. AND I'LL BE THERE TO STOP YOU.
FUNNY, I DO AGREE WITH YOU ON ONE THING, AT LEAST...
YES. LET'S HAVE SOME *FUN*...

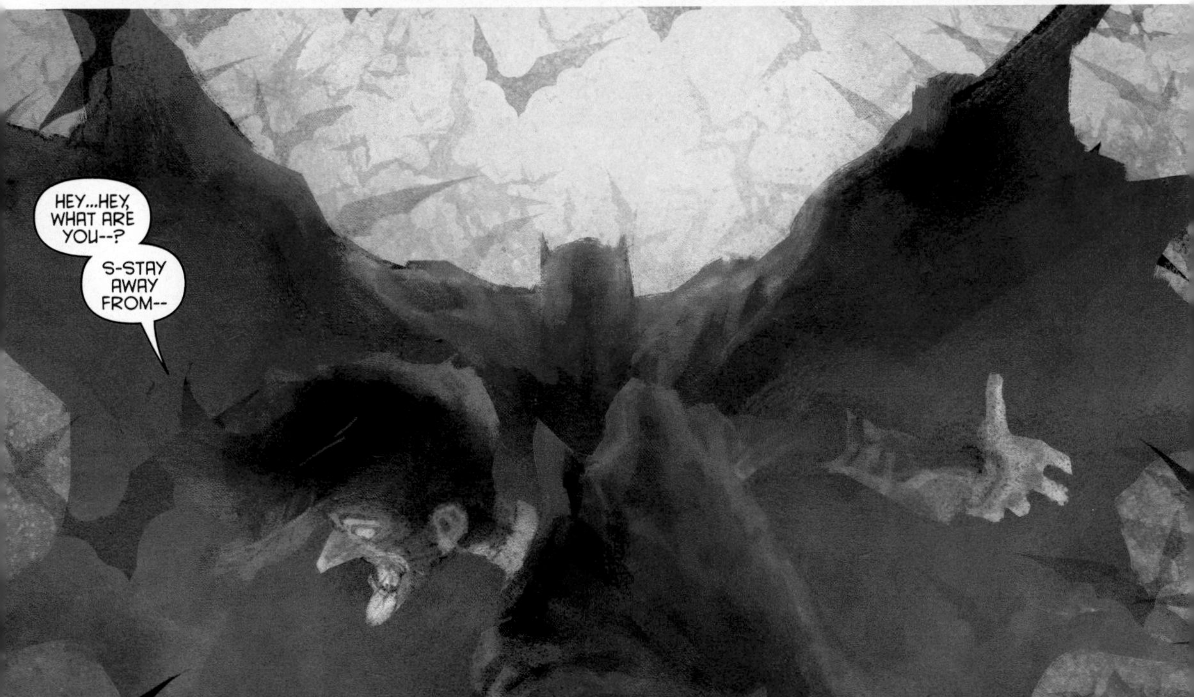
HEY...HEY, WHAT ARE YOU--?
S-STAY AWAY FROM--

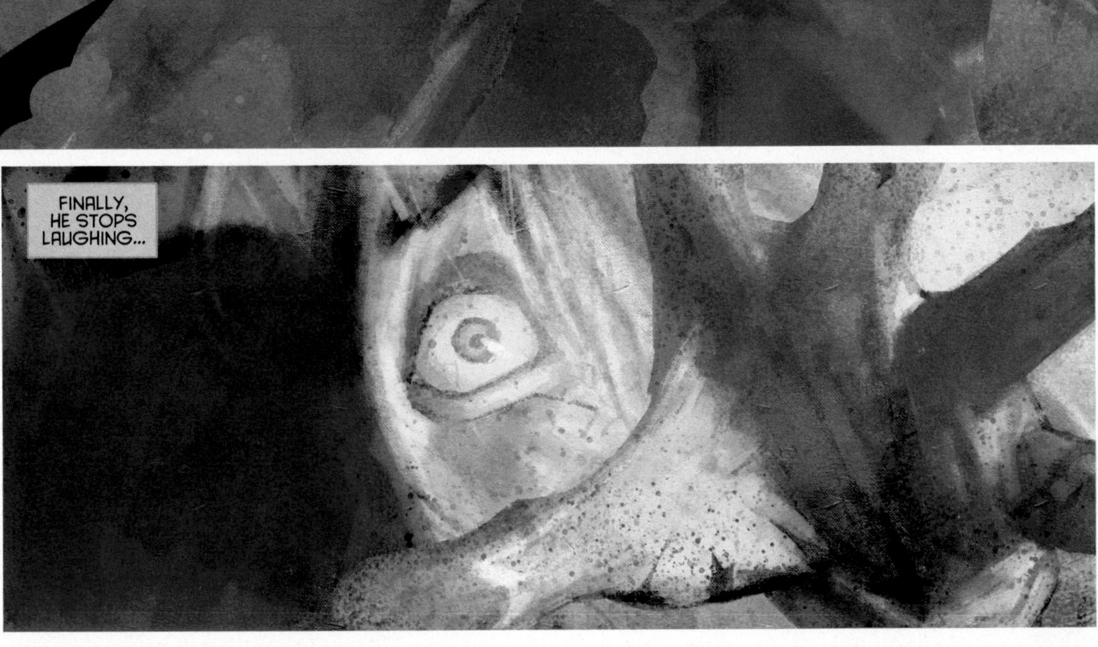
FINALLY, HE STOPS LAUGHING...

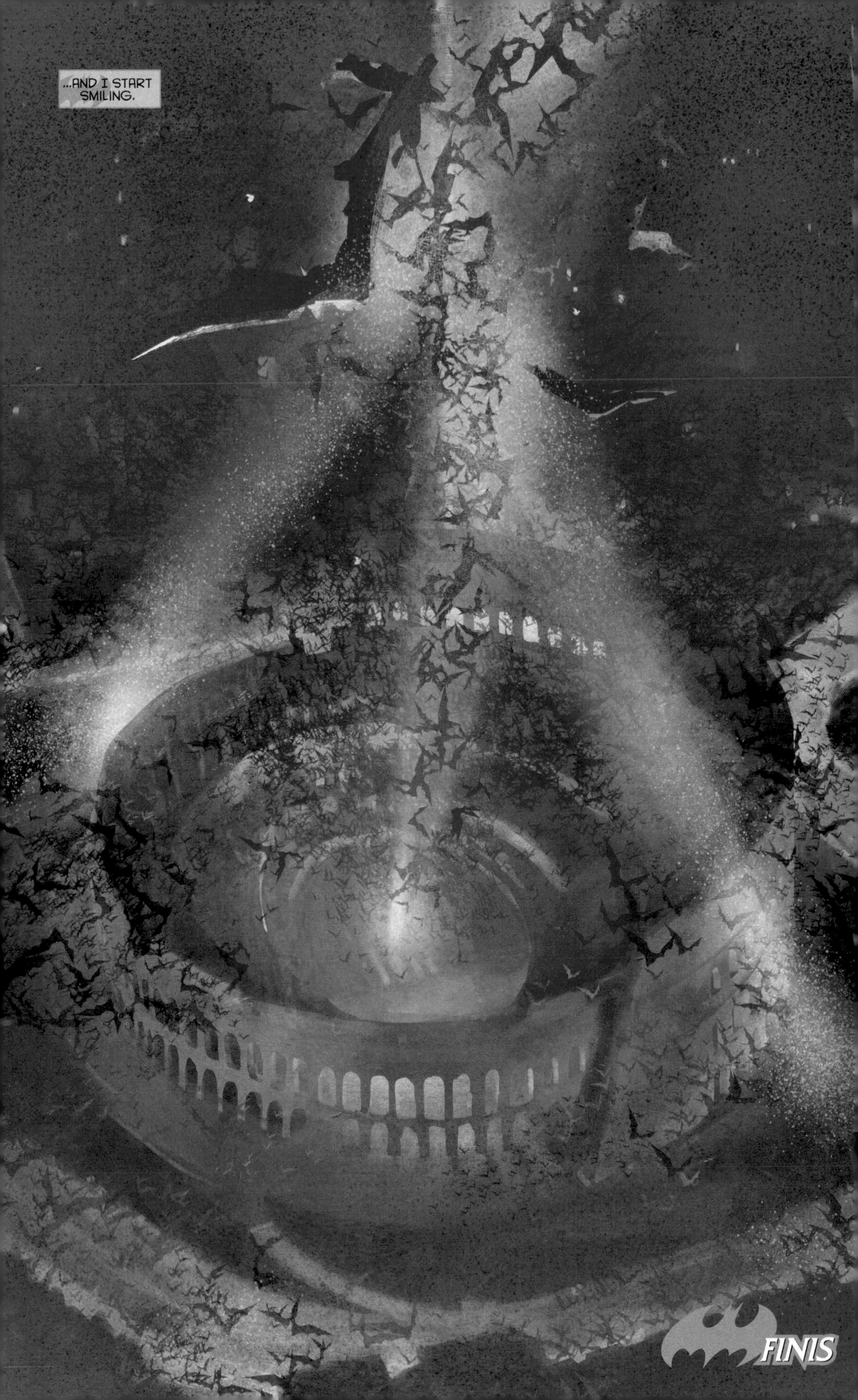
...AND I START SMILING.
FINIS

VARIANT COVER GALLERY

BATMAN: EUROPA #1 Variant by Lee Bermejo
BATMAN: EUROPA #2 Variant by Massimo Carnevale
BATMAN: EUROPA #3 Variant by Francesco Mattina
BATMAN: EUROPA #4 Variant by Jock
BATMAN: EUROPA #1 Sketch variant by Jim Lee
BATMAN: EUROPA #2 Sketch variant by Giuseppe Camuncoli
BATMAN: EUROPA #3 Sketch variant by Diego Latorre
BATMAN: EUROPA #4 Sketch variant by Gerald Parel

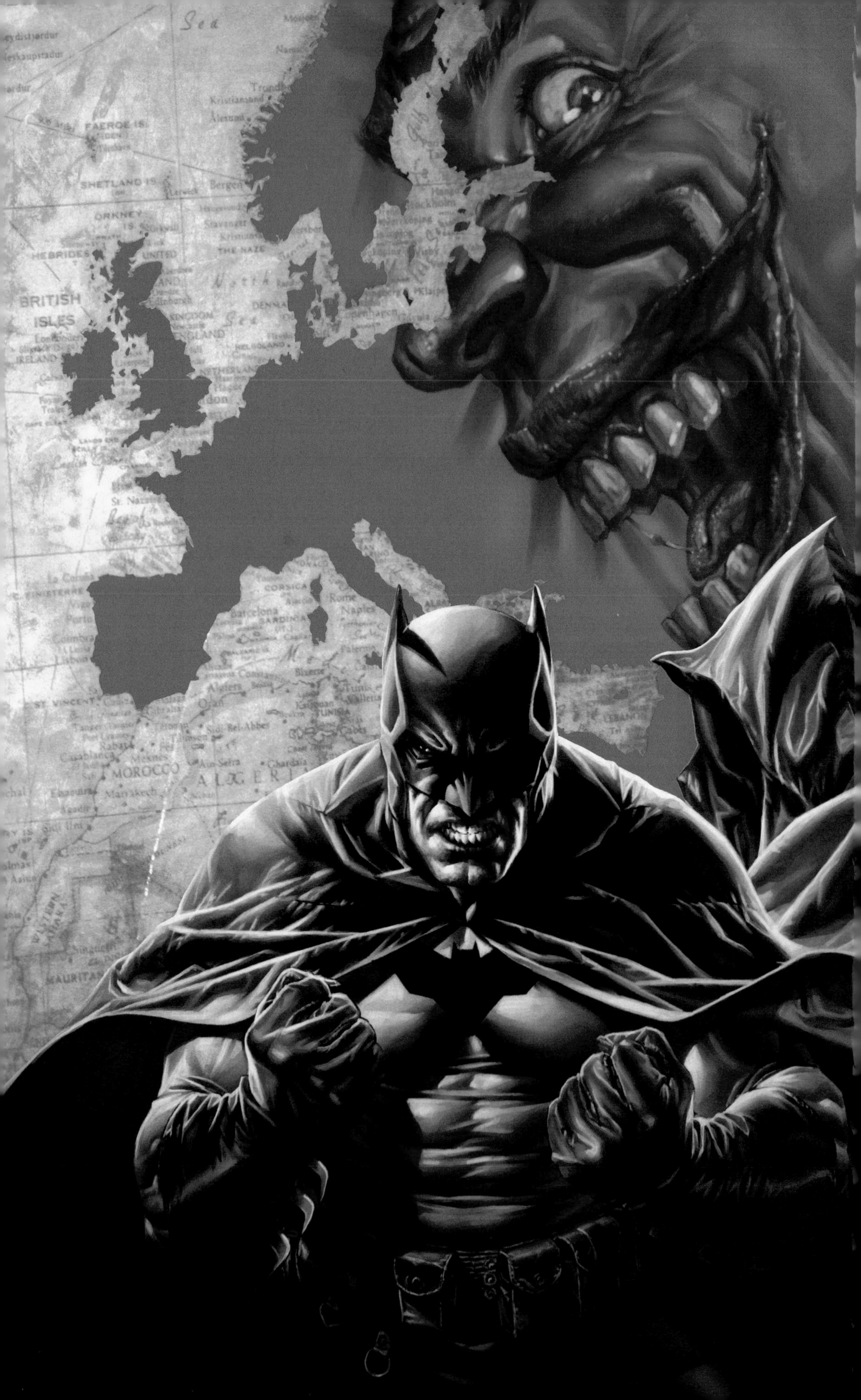
Sea
FAEROE IS.
SHETLAND IS.
Bergen
ORKNEY IS.
Stavanger
THE NAZE
HEBRIDES
BRITISH ISLES
Copenhagen
CORSICA
Barcelona
SARDINIA
Rome
Naples
Algiers
Oran
Tunis
TUNISIA
ST. VINCENT
Casablanca
Rabat
MOROCCO
Marrakech
Sidi-Bel-Abbes

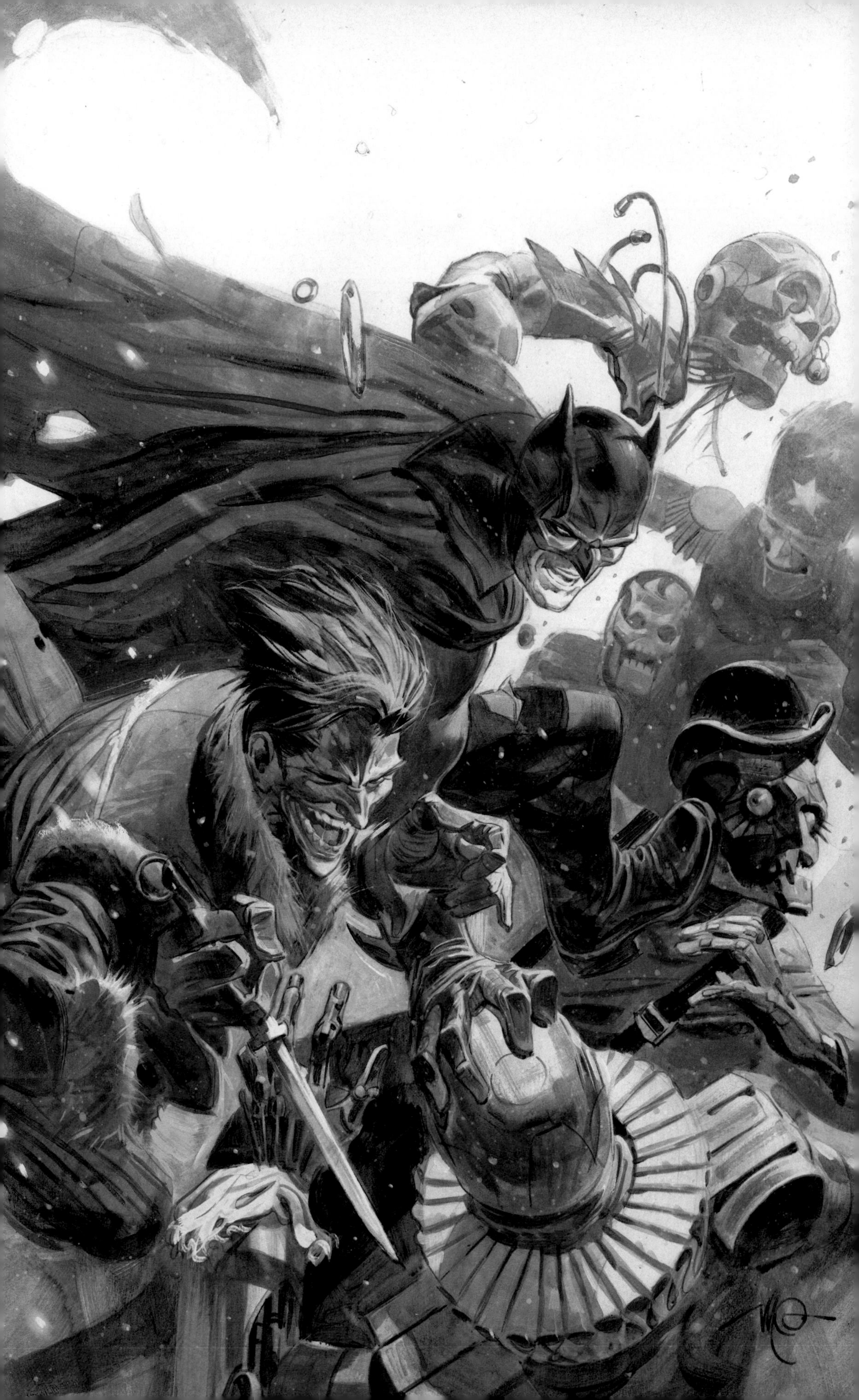

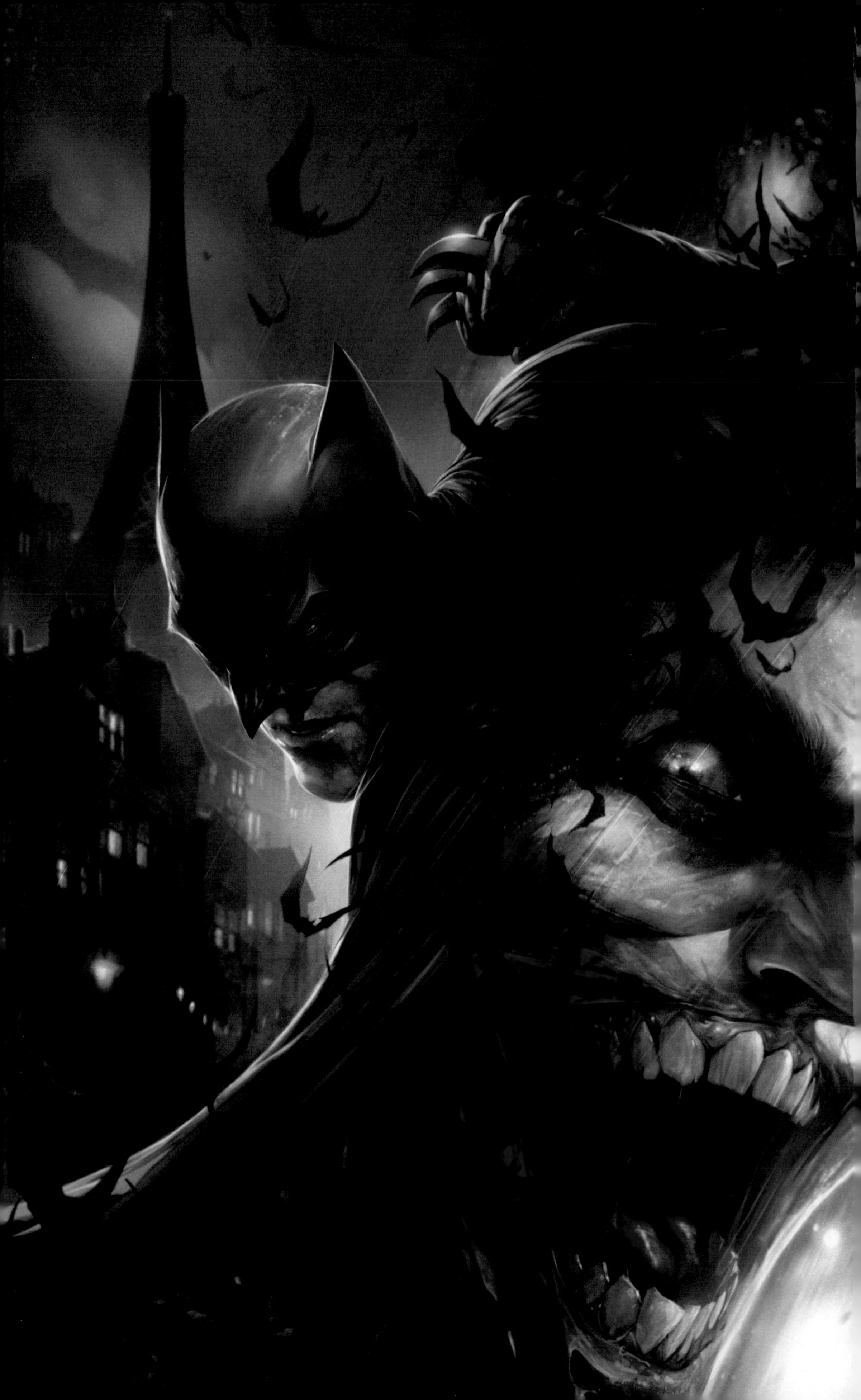

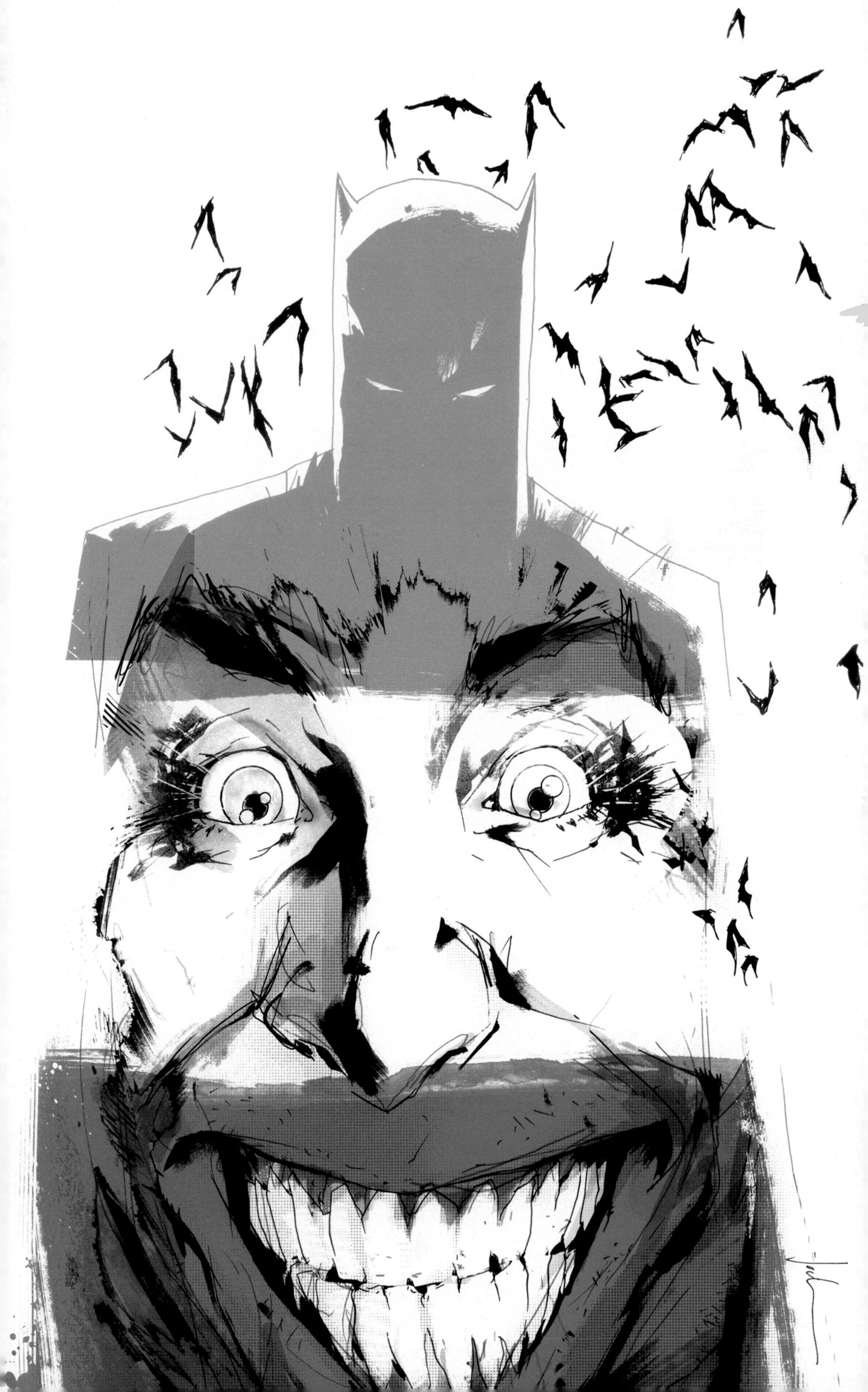

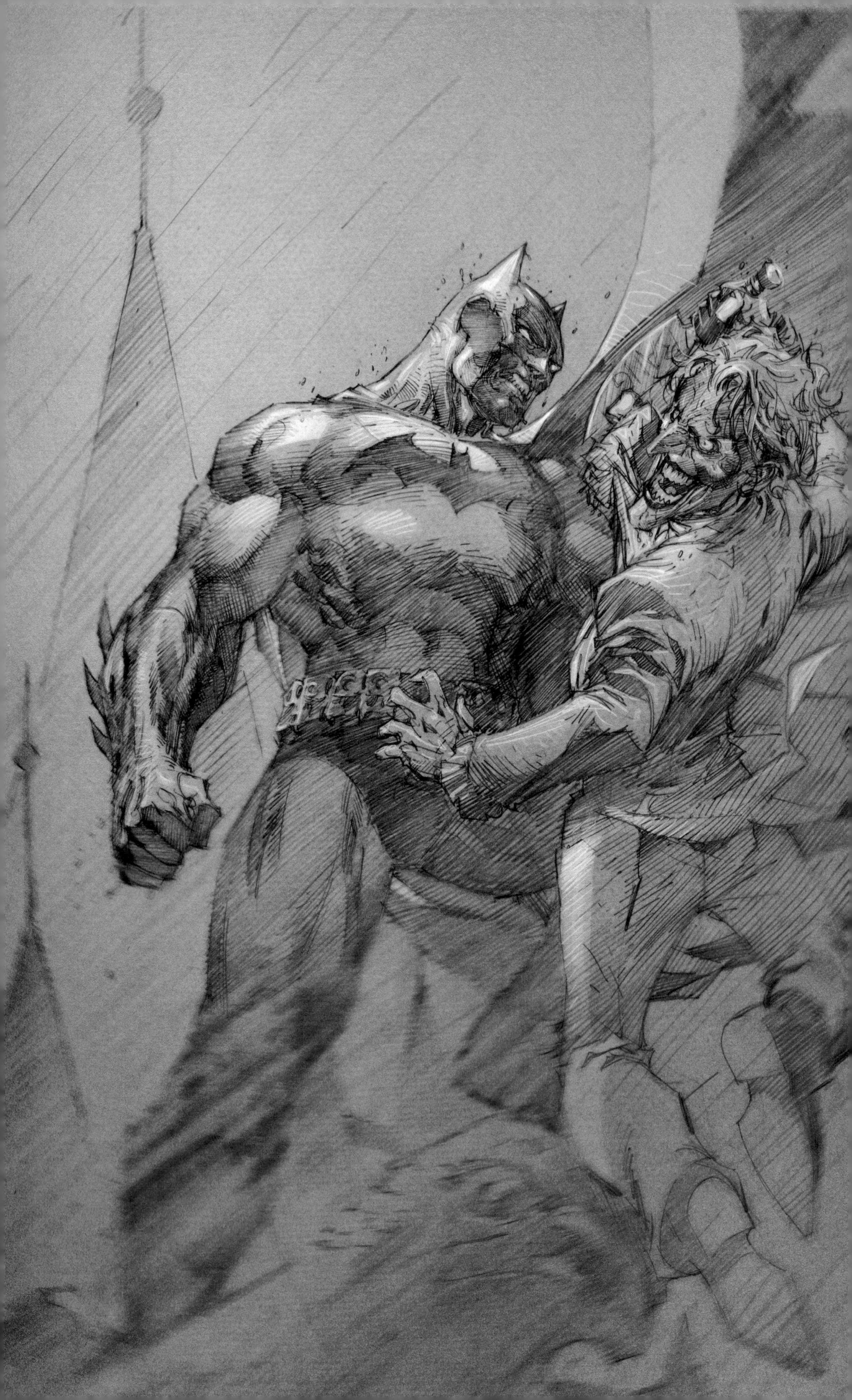

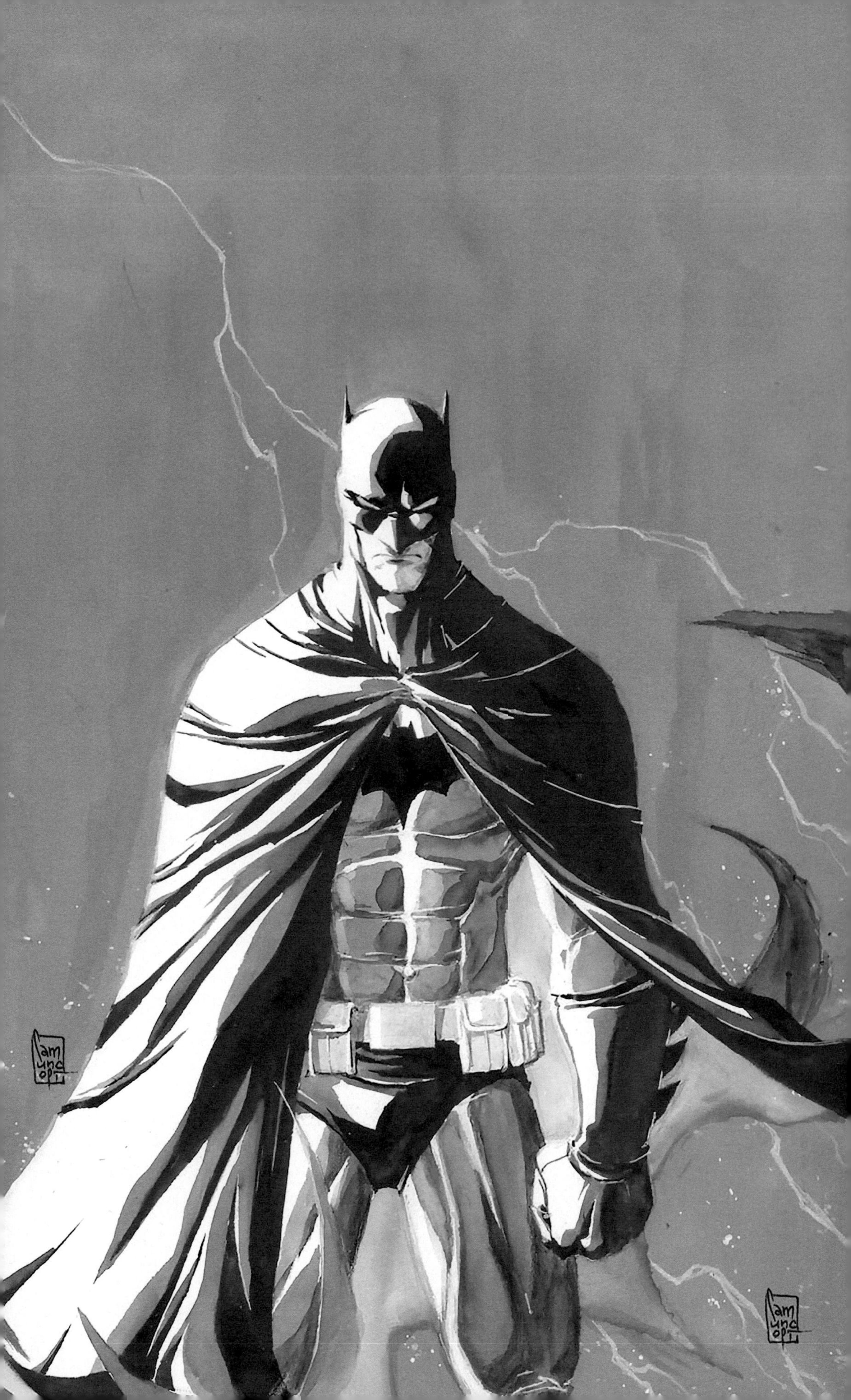

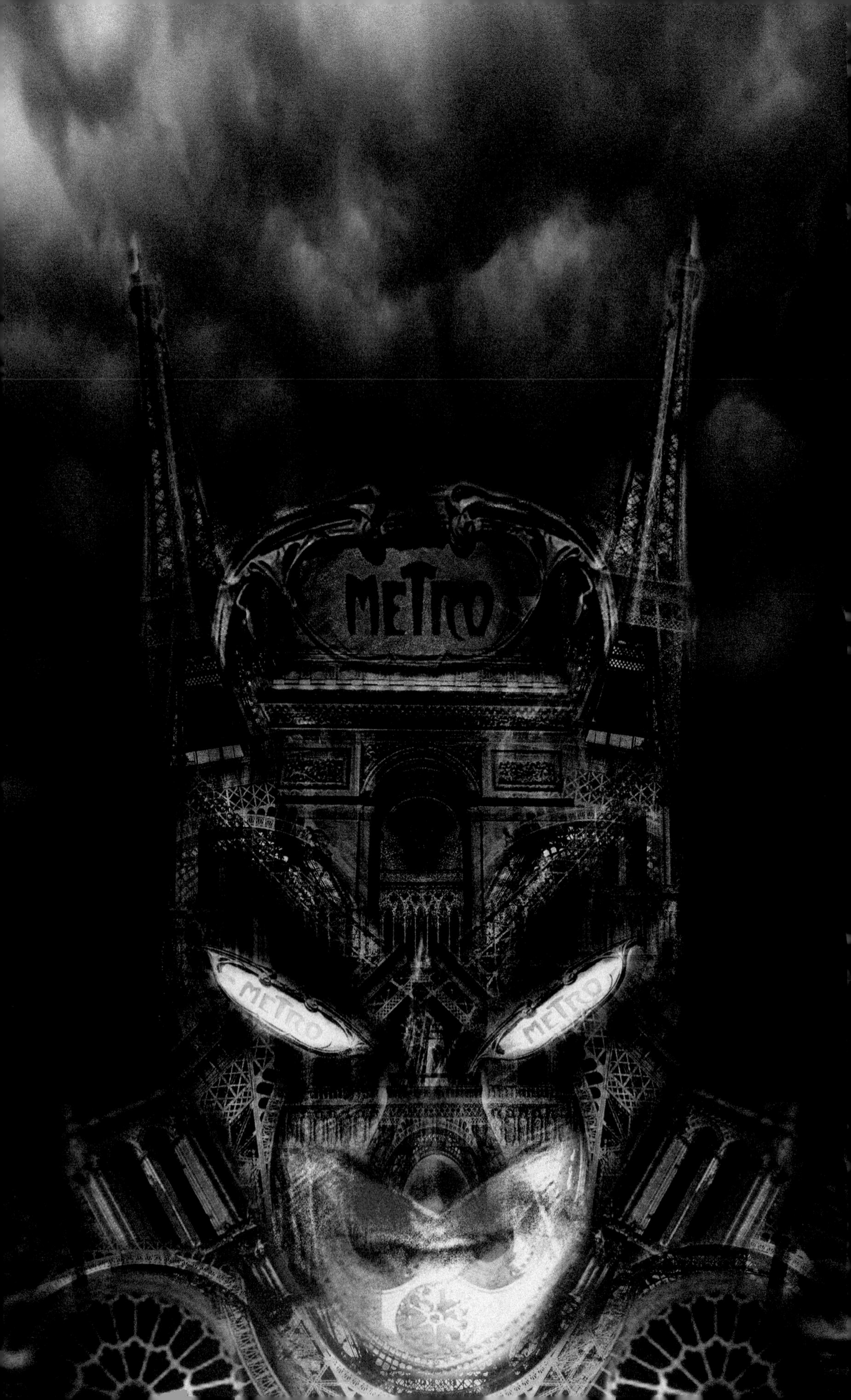
METRO
METRO
METRO

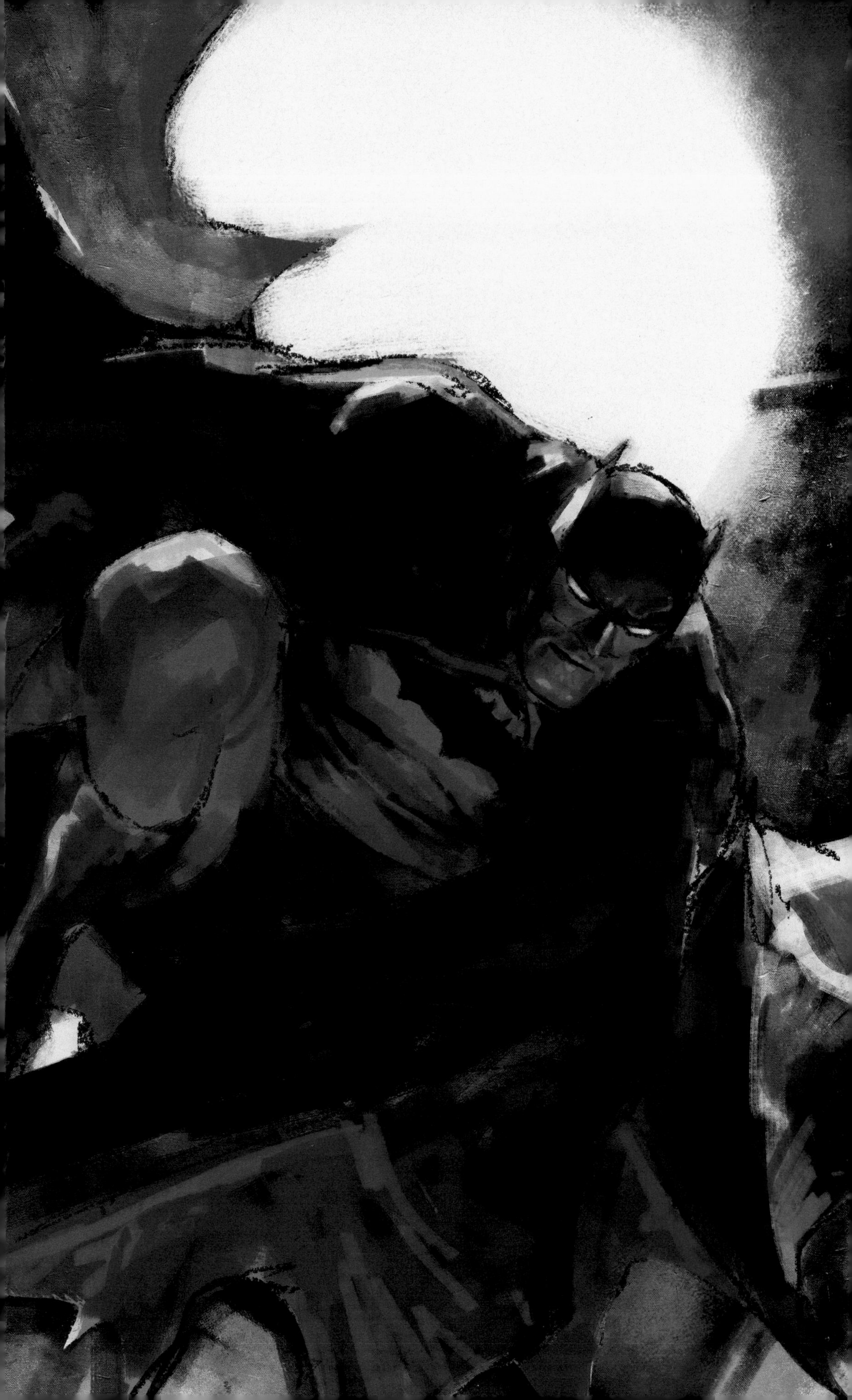

MATTEO CASALI hails from Italy, where he started writing comics, such as *Bonerest* and *Quebrado*, that took him around, well, Europa first—and then farther away. He has worked for various "old-world" publishers and is the only Italian writer to have worked for Image Comics, Marvel Comics and DC Comics, where he wrote stories for CATWOMAN, JUSTICE LEAGUE UNLIMITED and the graphic novel 99 DAYS, winner of the 2012 Spinetingler Award for best crime comic. He lives in Reggio Emilia, Italy, and teaches scriptwriting and storytelling classes at the International School of Comics, where he acts as creative co-director, along with his longtime friend and colleague Giuseppe Camuncoli.

BRIAN AZZARELLO has been writing comics professionally since the mid-1990s. He is the author of SPACEMAN, BATMAN: BROKEN CITY and the Harvey and Eisner Award-winning 100 BULLETS, all created in collaboration with artist Eduardo Risso. The *New York Times* best-selling author's other work for DC Comics includes the titles HELLBLAZER and LOVELESS (both with Marcelo Frusin), SUPERMAN: FOR TOMORROW (with Jim Lee), JOKER, LUTHOR and BEFORE WATCHMEN: RORSCHACH (with Lee Bermejo), BEFORE WATCHMEN: CO-MEDIAN (with J.G. Jones), SGT. ROCK: BETWEEN HELL AND A HARD PLACE (with Joe Kubert) and WONDER WOMAN (with Cliff Chiang). Azzarello lives in Chicago and twitters @brianazzarello only when he has something to say.

JIM LEE is a renowned comic book artist and the Co-Publisher of DC Entertainment. Prior to his current position, Lee served as DC's Editorial Director, where he oversaw WildStorm Studios and provided art for many of DC Comics' best-selling comic books and graphic novels, including ALL-STAR BATMAN AND ROBIN, THE BOY WONDER, BATMAN: HUSH and SUPERMAN: FOR TOMORROW. He has drawn JUSTICE LEAGUE and SUPERMAN UNCHAINED as part of DC Comics: The New 52. A veritable legend in the industry, he has received numerous accolades for his work, including the Harvey Special Award for New Talent in 1990, the Inkpot Award in 1992 and the Wizard Fan Award in 1996, 2002 and 2003.

Italian artist **GIUSEPPE CAMUNCOLI** first broke onto the American comics scene in 2001 with Vertigo's SWAMP THING. Since then, he has provided covers and interiors for Marvel and DC Comics, most notably on titles like HELLBLAZER, THE INTIMATES, *Daken: Dark Wolverine*, *Superior Spider-Man* and *The Amazing Spider-Man*. BATMAN: EUROPA is his first painted book. He lives in Reggio Emilia, Italy, with his wife, Jessica, and his daughter, Martina.

DIEGO LATORRE is a Spanish comic book artist, film director and designer. His American comic book work has been published by DC, Marvel and Dark Horse. Other clients include MTV, Diesel, Virgin, EA Games, Fox, Zero and Perspective Studios.

As a film director, he has directed the multi-award-winning short film *Blink*, as well a several music videos for top Spanish rock bands. His design work was exhibited several consecutive years at Milan Design Week. He lives on the Mediterranean coast with his son, Hugo.

French artist **GERALD PAREL** first became prominent in the United States for his work as a Marvel cover artist, lending iconic covers to such superhero titles as *Iron Man*, *Captain America*, and *S.H.I.E.L.D.* as well as literary comic adaptations *The Picture of Dorian Gray*, *The Three Musketeers* and *The Last of the Mohicans*, among others. His first American interior art was for the 2012 original graphic novel *Iron Man: Season One* (written by Howard Chaykin). BATMAN: EUROPA marks the artist's first work for DC Comics.